CHEATING
PARENTS

CHEATING PARENTS

Recovering from
Parental Infidelity

Dennis Ortman, PhD

NEW HORIZON PRESS
Far Hills, New Jersey

Requests for permission should be addressed to:
New Horizon Press
P. O. Box 669
Far Hills, NJ 07931

Dennis Ortman, PhD
Cheating Parents: Recovering from Parental Infidelity

Cover design: Wendy Bass
Interior design: Scribe Inc.

Library of Congress Control Number: 2013935929

ISBN 13: 978–0-88282–456–7

New Horizon Press

Manufactured in the U. S. A.

18   17   16   15   14   1   2   3   4   5

DEDICATION

To Nicole, Jackie, and David, who bring me untold joy.

AUTHOR'S NOTE

This book is based on the author's research, personal experiences, interviews and real life experiences. The names and details of the stories presented throughout the book have been changed to protect the confidentiality of my clients. The stories of several of my clients have also been stitched together to weave a single story. My thanks to those who have shared their lives with me.

For purposes of simplifying usage, the pronouns his/her and s/he are sometimes used interchangeably. The information contained herein is not meant to be a substitute for professional evaluation and therapy with mental health professionals.

CONTENTS

INTRODUCTION

Ryan sat on the top step, listening from the depths of his soul. He had never been so still, so focused, in his short eleven years of life. Awakening him from a sound, dreamless sleep, his parents' angry shouting and the crash of a broken dish had startled him but hearing his parents arguing grabbed his full attention. He lay awake in bed, afraid to move. Initially, fear gripped him as he was jolted from the comfort of sleep. Then, curiosity: "What's going on downstairs? What are Mom and Dad arguing about?" he wondered. The blood pulsed through his head to the rhythm of the familiar sound of their shouting. Ryan's mind raced with fearful thoughts: "Are they going to divorce? Is Daddy going to hurt Mommy? What will happen to me? Who will take care of me?"

Torn between fear and curiosity, Ryan argued with himself about whether to remain in the safety of his bed or get up and venture into the unknown. Finally, he decided he had to know. He crawled slowly out of bed and tiptoed to the landing at the top of the stairs. The light from downstairs seeped up into the darkness of the second floor. Ryan sat in shadows. He could not see his parents around the corner in the kitchen but he could hear the noise of their fighting. He could feel the intensity of their feelings, the rage that was spewing forth from both his parents. The fury he heard transfixed him to that spot, warning him to go no further.

So he simply listened, his mind in utter confusion. His racing thoughts and their fervent yelling prevented him from hearing exactly what they were saying. Perched on the top step with his elbows on his knees, head in his hands, he focused his attention and listened. First he discerned isolated words, swear words he was forbidden to speak and fragments like "another woman, betrayal." The words slowly took the shape of sentences in his confused mind. Then suddenly, the startling idea, *Dad was seeing another woman, and Mom could not stand it*. Ryan didn't know what that meant but he knew it was not right by the intensity of their arguing and what he had learned in Catholic school about marriage for life.

As Ryan sat there alone, lost in his perplexed thoughts, his mother bolted out of the kitchen to run upstairs, tears streaming down her cheeks. When she raised her head, her eyes met Ryan's. In that instant, he sensed she wanted to hide as badly as he did. He wished he were invisible, because he had witnessed what he sensed no child should ever have to see and hear. At some level, he felt the life he knew falling apart. He was being cast into a dark, scary future. His mother's expression instantly transformed from tearful rage to fear and sadness. She was exposed. Ryan felt as startled as she did for being an intruder in his parent's nightmare. Frozen with shame and embarrassment, his mother said softly, "Ryan, you need to get back to bed."

Imagine the impact of that bombshell on Ryan's fragile, preadolescent psyche. He returned to bed, his mind whirling with disturbing thoughts and his sense of safety lost forever. Perhaps his parents tried to explain their argument to him the next day, as they sorted out the confusion and madness of their own lives. Or maybe they pretended it never happened, to spare Ryan the pain and suffering, imagining that if they ignored it he would forget about it.

But he never will. His parents will continue to argue about the affair, but will be more discreet so Ryan will not be exposed to their bitter arguing. Nevertheless, he will feel the tension in the home. His parents may eventually work out their problem, deciding either to divorce or stay together. However, the explosion of that night and the events that followed will be etched permanently on Ryan's young, impressionable brain. He will live through the rubble of his parents' ruined marriage for the rest of his life. How will this childhood experience affect his future?

Working with individuals and couples for the past thirty-five years, I have observed the frequency of infidelity in marriages and its impact. Current research indicates that nearly 40 percent of men and 20 percent of women have had affairs while married.[1] Witnessing the pain and sorrow these couples experienced as a result of the betrayal and the long process of healing, I have come to believe that spouses who discover their partner's betrayal are deeply wounded and often experience symptoms similar to post-traumatic stress disorder. They experience the betrayal as a life-threatening event, a threat to destroy their marriage and their own mental well-being. Like those traumatized by war, they alternate between feeling numb and being overwhelmed by feelings of loss, rage and fear. They become anxious and hyper-vigilant, waiting for the next bombshell discovery. Their sleep is often disturbed by nightmares and their daytime tranquility interrupted by flashbacks. They live in terror as their familiar life and their images of their spouses and themselves crumble before their eyes, destroying any sense of security they found in the relationship. They no longer trust their spouses or themselves. And they are filled with a nearly all-consuming rage.

I described the traumatizing effects of infidelity and the process of healing in my book *Transcending Post-Infidelity Stress Disorder: The Six Stages of Healing,* using the acronym PISD (pronounced "pissed") to indicate the rage that all the betrayed experience.

Counseling with these distressed couples, I have been surprised to learn that most of them, though not all, had parents who were unfaithful. They seemed to carry a *cheating gene.* They were the victims of their parents' infidelity and often had only vague memories of it, if they remembered it at all, and little insight into the impact it had on their own marital life. I came to believe that, just as spouses are traumatized by the discovery of their partner's infidelity, the children who witness their parents' distress are similarly traumatized. Like their parents, they suffer a form of post-traumatic stress disorder (PTSD), the impact of which often becomes evident years later as they attempt to engage in intimate relationships. The time bomb of discovering their parent's infidelity often does not explode until years later, when confusion, fear, rage and infidelity emerge in their own relationships and when they become parents themselves.

The pain and sorrow that infidelity causes in relationships is highlighted in the popular press, news media and professional journals.

What is not so clearly seen are the other invisible casualties, the children who witness the chaos caused by their parents' unfaithful behavior and the troubled adults they often become. These children are the walking wounded who may appear to function normally for years. But sooner or later, cracks appear in the armor and they are flooded with overwhelming feelings, the origin of which escapes them. They get in relationships or find themselves always angry and argumentative with their partners. They become excessively attached, longing for closeness, losing themselves in their relationships. Or they become aloof and detached. They marry those who betray them or they become irresistibly drawn to others outside their committed relationships. When they become parents, they feel confused about what is normal in parenting and inadequate to respond to their children's needs.

For many years I have also worked with families caught in the web of addiction. I observed that growing up in an alcoholic family has a lasting effect on children as they grow into adulthood. Their views of themselves and relationships are inevitably shaped by the experience of the out-of-control drinking of their parents, along with the denial, hiding and open conflicts. These children grow up not allowing themselves to feel or express themselves openly, not talking about what really matters in their lives, and not trusting themselves or others. They have been described in literature and popular press as a group with identifiable characteristics called *adult children of alcoholic parents*.

I have begun to observe that children raised in homes in which one or both parents were unfaithful develop similar characteristics, not unlike those raised by alcoholic parents. Just as alcohol and its effects become the central focus when parents drink uncontrollably, the betrayal of the parent dominates the household when infidelity occurs. Parents become trapped in a web of deceit and mistrust. Fighting breaks out and the sense of safety is lost. Preoccupied with their own problems, they have little time or energy to pay proper attention to their children. The house becomes filled with shame, which the children absorb like sponges. And the shame follows these children into adulthood, infecting all their relationships, especially with their partners and their children. Furthermore, just as children of alcoholic parents are genetically predisposed to abuse alcohol, it appears that children of unfaithful parents are predestined to follow in their footsteps. Here are some characteristics I have observed in adult children of unfaithful parents:

- They are confused about what is normal behavior in relationships and parenting.
- They have difficulty creating and maintaining boundaries.
- They lack self-confidence in their ability to resolve conflicts in relationships and in the family.
- They either provoke confrontations or avoid them at all costs.
- They have difficulty trusting themselves and others.
- They are either over-controlled or under-controlled in expressing anger.
- They are confused about their sexuality and its appropriate expression.
- They are hyper-vigilant about being betrayed or lied to.
- They are extremely loyal or disloyal in relationships.
- They lie for no apparent reason.
- They feel anxious when not in control of a situation.
- They feel the need to be perfect and are fearful of being abandoned if they are not.
- They judge themselves harshly, holding unrealistic standards.
- They struggle to know and express clearly what they want.

SURVIVAL PATTERNS

As a psychologist, I spend my days listening to my clients tell stories about themselves, their lives and their relationships. Even though my clients express common concerns, their experiences and stories are unique, displaying an endless variety. I marvel at their ingenuity in finding ways to survive in the most adverse circumstances, in pursuing the loftiest goals and in making a mess of their lives through self-defeating behavior. Listening carefully, however, I can discern repeating patterns and themes.

Make no mistake about it. When parents are unfaithful, their children suffer. The effects may be hidden for many years, but they will eventually emerge as these young people engage in intimate relationships and parent their own children.

At the risk of oversimplifying, in this book I will describe some relationship patterns and parenting styles I have observed in adult children of unfaithful parents. Those traumatized cope with the pain by alternating between numbing themselves and reliving the trauma, flooded with memories and feelings of anger, anxiety and depression. Children raised in families torn apart by infidelity grow up to relive their childhood traumas by either identifying with the aggressor, becoming unfaithful themselves or identifying with the victim by marrying an unfaithful partner. Amazingly, despite their protests that they will never repeat what their parents did, as if they were genetically fated, adult children tend to become unfaithful or marry someone who cheats on them. A third group numbs themselves to their needs for intimacy, avoiding closeness and commitment in their relationships. They fear recreating the pain and confusion of their parents' marriage by becoming either cheaters or victims themselves.

The way adult children of unfaithful parents care for their own children has been deeply affected by their experience with their parents. Their parents were often overwhelmed trying to cope with the wreckage of their marriage and had little left for the children. The children often felt neglected, ashamed of their parents' behavior and confused about what is true and normal. To cope with the uncertainty and hurt feelings, these adult children often became controlling, overly-involved or disengaged parents. They lost a sense of balance in their parenting that mirrored the distorted care they received.

Under stress, like the animals from which we evolved, we instinctively respond in three ways: We fight, freeze or flee. Those who fight move against others in their relationships. This grouping of adult children identifies with their unfaithful parents. They tend to betray their partners by having affairs, becoming over-involved in work or developing addictions. In the first three chapters of the book, I will describe these personality types, what family experiences shaped them and a path to healing with an exercise. Those who freeze move toward others in their relationships, but become locked in their roles as victims, caretakers or perfectionists. They identify with their victimized parents. I will describe their relationship patterns, their origins in childhood and their healing paths in chapters four, five and six. Finally, those who flee move away from intimacy and commitment, losing themselves in their personal interests, fantasies and moods. Chapters seven, eight and nine describe the dynamics and recovery of these personality types. In each type, a symptom of PTSD, either reliving or blocking the trauma, becomes exaggerated.

PATTERNS IN INTIMATE RELATIONSHIPS

1) **The Betrayer Group**
2) **The Victim Group**
3) **The Avoidant Group**

The second portion of the book addresses the differing parenting styles I have observed in adult children of unfaithful parents. Some tend to fight for control over their children. Others cling to their children, becoming emotionally enmeshed with them. Still others disengage emotionally, fleeing intimacy. Chapters ten, eleven and twelve will address how these styles developed, with a path to healing and an exercise. The next two chapters will address the parenting challenges of the offending and offended parents and how to help their children through their crises. I conclude with suggestions on how to approach your children if your marriage is injured by unfaithfulness.

PATTERNS IN PARENTING STYLES

1) **The Controlling Style**
2) **The Enmeshed Style**
3) **The Disengaged Style**

Coincidentally, the nine typical relationship patterns I observed parallel the nine character types of the Enneagram, an ancient Middle Eastern guide to inner transformation updated by modern psychologists. In the Enneagram system, the personality is formed at an early age around a fault which is a compensation for the childhood experience of helplessness and loss. The faults, embraced with wisdom, become fertile ground for the growth of our unique strengths and virtues.[2]

I was a Catholic priest for fourteen years and have been a psychologist in private practice for twenty years. In my work I have attempted to integrate the wisdom of western psychology with spiritual traditions from both West and East. My spirituality gives me immeasurable hope when working with my clients. I believe in the possibility of transforming any unfavorable circumstance into a path to enlightenment and freedom. Working with couples traumatized by affairs, I have witnessed over and over that the infidelity can be a wake-up call in many troubled marriages. It can be a moment of crisis, an opportunity to work through long-buried problems and reach a higher level of intimacy and trust.

Such growth, however, can occur only through the power of forgiveness, a forgiveness that is authentic and does not hide from pain, anger and confusion. Furthermore, I learned that the path of healing for these adults who were traumatized as children was again through the power of forgiveness. Not only must they forgive their unfaithful spouses to recover, they must also forgive their unfaithful parents who provided such poor role models for them. Forgiveness entails the release of both anger toward them and the desire for revenge. It occurs over time, with a willingness to embrace painful feelings and understand themselves and their parents. In the end, forgiveness happens as the wounds heal, setting them free to love openly and fully.

My message is one of hope for those who feel lost. You can be healed through the power of forgiveness.

This book is written for those who have been unfaithful, have been betrayed or are considering affairs. It is also a healing guide for adult children whose parents had affairs. If you have been unfaithful, this book may help you understand the impact of your behavior on your children and seek ways of reconciling with them and facilitating their healing. Making amends will also help you in your recovery and in resolving your guilt.

For those who have been betrayed, you will become more aware of how your children also share your pain. Having compassion for their suffering, you will assist them in working through their trauma as you work through yours.

If you are considering embarking on an affair, I implore you to stop and think clearly about the consequences, especially for your children. Your urge to reach out to another outside the bounds of your marriage is a clear indication that something is awry in your marital relationship. Now is the time to address the problem before your desire to escape through an affair seems irresistible. Spare your children the trauma of your betrayal. Without a doubt, they will feel betrayed if you break your marital bond.

For adults who have come to realize the infidelity of your parents and its impact on your current relationship, this book can aid you in healing the deep wound of betrayal. You can be freed from the bonds of betrayal through the power of forgiveness.

Finally, if you are a concerned relative or a friend who is witnessing the destructiveness of a loved one's infidelity, I hope you will find the information in this book useful. It can help you understand more fully the damage inflicted on the children and give you knowledge with which to confront the guilty party.

Use this book in any way that you deem helpful. You may read it cover to cover to see what pattern seems to fit your life and hopefully gain some insight into yourself and ways you can heal and become a better parent. You may focus on a chapter that speaks to your life situation. Or you may choose any of the suggested exercises that open your mind and heart. Most of the exercises come from Eastern spiritual traditions that overlap with and deepen Western psychological practices. There are as many paths to healing as there are individuals who desire fuller lives.

Part 1
Those Who Identify with the Aggressor

Chapter 1

The Lustful Betrayer— Knowing No Limits

Pete, a middle-aged businessman, claimed he had never been happy in his marriage. He was raised in a poor Italian family and never went far in school. When he met his future wife, Jane, in high school, he was captivated by her beauty and intelligence. Her family was from the better side of the tracks, wealthy and sophisticated. Dating, he felt honored to have her as his girlfriend, believing that others envied him. After high school, Pete began working in the office of an electrical supply company as an errand boy. He was accustomed to hard work and ambitious to make something of himself. Jane went away to an Ivy League college where she earned a degree in liberal arts. For several years, they maintained a long-distance relationship and were together during Jane's vacations.

After Jane graduated from college, they decided to marry. Pete worked hard to put money away and advanced in the company. His superiors recognized his work ethic and natural leadership ability, despite his lack of education. Because both were Catholic, they refrained from having sex before marriage, although Pete constantly tried to coax Jane into it. She resisted his every advance, promising that saving herself for marriage would be worth it. They were married in a Catholic church in the wealthy suburb where Jane's parents resided. Local papers reported the ceremony as the social event of the season. Pete and Jane tied the knot in the presence of their family and friends, hopeful for a life of promise and bliss together.

The hope and promise evaporated quickly for Pete on their wedding night. Pete was anxious to consummate their marriage but Jane claimed she was too exhausted for sex and asked him to wait for the honeymoon. They flew to a resort in the Caribbean the next day. Jane remained aloof and passive, though willing, when he initiated sex during their honeymoon. Pete imagined it was just nervousness and inexperience that prevented Jane from enjoying sex, so he remained patient when they returned to the routine of their lives.

After the honeymoon, Pete went back to work and Jane occupied herself with putting their new home together. They fell into a routine of weekly sex in which Jim always felt an edge of dissatisfaction. He was always more interested in sex than she was. He complained and became increasingly irritable, occasionally erupting with temper outbursts. Jane was shocked at his anger, which she'd never experienced while dating. She saw Pete as a quiet man who worked hard. When he got angry, she withdrew in fear and became even more passive.

The distance increased in their relationship as Pete became more involved in work, and Jane focused on maintaining the home and pursuing her interests. Their infrequent sex nevertheless resulted in two pregnancies. Jane then occupied herself with caring for the two children, while Pete spent more and more time at work. He climbed the ladder at his company, becoming a hard-nosed manager who earned a substantial income. He was achieving the career success he had longed for.

Pete had always enjoyed the attention of women and he was feeling neglected at home. His secretary, an attractive younger woman, caught his attention. They became friends. She shared with Pete her marital problems and stress raising two young children with a deadbeat husband. They went out for a drink occasionally after work. Pete always made some excuse to Jane that he had to work late. He withdrew more and more into a secret life, fantasizing about a future with his young secretary. Eventually, they began regular meetings for sex. Pete justified it because his wife could not fulfill his natural desires. He saw her as a frigid woman. "I'm just a normal man with natural needs," he told himself. Pete never considered divorce because of his Catholic upbringing and position in the community as a successful businessman. Furthermore, he did not want to break up the family.

For several years he maintained a double life, keeping the façade of a happy family man while indulging his sexual and emotional needs with his mistress. He became an expert at subterfuge, keeping his wife in the dark about his other life.

Then the inevitable occurred. His wife found a motel receipt and confronted him, threatening divorce. At that point, to preserve the marriage and his image, Pete agreed to come to therapy. I met with them as a couple and with each of them separately.

I explored Pete's family background with him. He was the oldest of three children in a traditional Italian family. His parents grew up in Italy and were married there. They moved to the United States to escape the poverty of their village. Pete's father was a quiet, hardworking man who labored long hours at a construction company. During the winters he had his own home improvement business. Pete remembered his father being absent most of the time. His mother was a simple, uneducated woman who kept herself busy doting on the children and caring for the home. His parents showed little affection for each other and never seemed to talk. His father was a domineering, strong-willed man in his silence, and his mother followed his directions without complaint or questioning. They just seemed disengaged from each other.

Pete enjoyed his freedom in his father's absence. He feared his strong-willed father and manipulated his weak mother. Outwardly, he conformed to his parent's requests, but secretly he did what he pleased. He rode his bike to school, but often skipped classes on the sunny, warm days to go fishing. His parents were fervent Catholics. As a teen he told them he preferred to go to Mass alone. He often skipped church to play baseball with his friends. His friends nicknamed him "Sneaky Pete."

When I asked Pete about his parents' marriage, he observed, "It was just your traditional, old country Italian marriage." I inquired about the possibility of either having been unfaithful and Pete mentioned that his father spent much time with his female cousin, saying, "They connected because they were from the same town." Further probing led Pete to admit, "I heard some rumors that she was his mistress, but I didn't think anything about it. In the old country, the men often had mistresses and it was no big deal. The women took care of the home, while the men took care of themselves." He added, "I guess

I became more like my father than I thought. My father crossed the line and I did the same thing."

Pete decided, "I want to be honest with myself, perhaps for the first time in my life. I have never been happy in my marriage, and I can no longer tolerate living a double life." He told Jane he was filing for divorce.

CHILDHOOD CONNECTION:
IDENTIFYING WITH THE AGGRESSOR

For better or worse, the relationship of your parents becomes the model for your own relationships. What you grow up observing as a child becomes your norm, until you are older and can compare your childhood family experience with others. Then you may question your upbringing and its impact on your own life. Unless you develop a discerning attitude, you will repeat what you observed in your parents. You naturally gravitate toward what is familiar, finding comfort in the known and avoiding insecurity in the unknown. Even if you judge your upbringing as deficient, you have no positive role models on which to base a different life for yourself, unless you were fortunate enough to find some surrogate parental mentors.

If your parents' marriage was troubled and you came to admit that, you undoubtedly told yourself, "That will never happen to me." You will make every conscious effort to be different from your parents. But genetics always seem to take over and you may catch yourself behaving in ways you detested in your parents. Biology appears to be destiny and you pray you do not have the cheating gene.

Furthermore, as you focus closely on your past family life, you may discover a subconscious urge to repeat what you grew up with in order to create a different result. You unconsciously repeat your parents' marriage in order to repair it and gain mastery over a painful past. In psychological jargon, it is called "repetition compulsion." You are compelled to repeat a painful past to make it different.

As the saying goes, "Imitation is the highest form of flattery." Children naturally imitate their parents as a way to stay bonded with them. When your parent was unfaithful, he or she betrayed not only his or her partner, but also you and the whole family. The decision to venture outside the marriage caused a severe disruption in family life. Peace and stability in the family were shattered. Furthermore, your secure relationship with your parents was strained beyond the breaking point. Even though you were not fully aware of the reason for the disruption, you instinctively knew that something your parents did caused it. At some level, you blamed your parents, developed mistrust of them and were angry with them. In turn, their preoccupation with the betrayal caused them to be emotionally unavailable to you and the other children. Their absence and your reaction strained your bond of closeness with them. The fear of losing them was intolerable to you as a child. One way of compensating for the strained relationship was to become like them. You identified with them to keep them close—to maintain the bond—when you feared losing it.

When you repeat your parents' relationship, you may be drawn to identify with either your mother or your father. The tendency is to identify with the parent of the same sex, but that does not always happen. In the case of parental infidelity, there is a powerful tendency to identify with either the betrayer or the victim, thereby becoming unfaithful in your own marriage or marrying someone who cheats on you. If you identify with the betrayer, you gain a sense of his power and freedom, which is really an illusion. It is called "identifying with the aggressor." The person who has the affair seems to have the upper hand over the other who is victimized. Relatively speaking, the betrayer is more powerful, the victim more vulnerable.

Are there signs that you may be drawn to the betrayer role? Remember that having an affair is a conscious choice. No one is irresistibly drawn to be unfaithful with another. The more you know yourself, the more information you have to make a conscious decision about what behavior is in your best interest. Look within yourself honestly and ask the following questions.

AM I A BETRAYER?

- Do I have a strong desire for power and control, for doing what I want?
- Do I feel dissatisfied in my marriage?
- Do I sweep problems under the rug and not address them?
- Do I crave the attention of women and/or men?
- Does my self-esteem depend on how others react to me?
- Do I like to flirt?

- Am I easily bored and looking for excitement?
- Am I preoccupied with sex?
- Do I believe that I cannot be happy without a satisfying sex life?
- Do I feel neglected by my spouse?
- Do I feel smothered in my marriage?
- Do I have difficulty communicating with my spouse?
- Do I lack a strong sense of commitment to my marriage?
- Do I lie easily to myself and others?
- Can I justify cheating to myself?
- Am I seriously considering divorce?

Your honest answers to these questions may alert you to character components that make you vulnerable to betray your partner.

PATH OF HEALING: GIVING UP THE SHAME AND GUILT

The path of healing leads to an honest acceptance of yourself and to forgiveness of your unfaithful parent for not providing you with an adequate role model for your own relationships. How do you arrive at self-acceptance and forgiveness? For those who have been unfaithful to their spouses, they must face the shame and guilt they feel.

As much as you may rationalize it, when you are unfaithful to your spouse, you are filled with guilt, shame and self-loathing. Guilt has a bad reputation in our Puritan society because its excesses receive so much press. However, pangs of guilt serve a purpose in alerting us that we are not living up to our standards. They indicate a refusal to accept the limits of our own moral standards. Sometimes those standards may be unrealistic and we live with a constant sense of failure. However, most often, we can discern and measure ourselves against reasonable standards. In the case of infidelity, we disregard the boundaries of marriage in becoming emotionally and/or sexually involved with someone other than our spouses. Self-will and lust run rampant of moral restraint. The uncomfortable sense of remorse for violating our standards of behavior leads us to change and make restitution for the behavior, and the guilt disappears. Lingering guilt expressed in beating ourselves up serves no useful purpose and may be motivated by some hidden urge for self-punishment.

Guilt arises from the experience of missing the mark, making a mistake, not living up to personal standards or ignoring moral limits. Shame emerges from a deep sense of personal deficiency. It proclaims, "I am a mistake." It attacks our sense of self-worth and leads to self-loathing. While guilt touches the surface of our behavior, shame grips our inner cores and destroys our feelings of personal worth. If we think of ourselves as worthless, we then begin mistreating ourselves and allowing others to abuse us. We treat ourselves as junk and invite others to do the same. Of course, this occurs mostly on an unconscious level. So there is an urgency for us as betrayers to either face our guilt and shame honestly or suffer the consequences of a miserable life.

One of the best mechanisms I know that helps resolve shame and guilt is to utilize the twelve-step program of Alcoholics Anonymous. The steps are used to heal a broad range of compulsive behaviors: drug addiction, eating disorders, gambling, sexual addiction, excessive shopping, compulsive emotions and codependent behavior. The steps embody both psychological and spiritual wisdom in addressing the character defects that underlie the compulsive behavior and allowing natural goodness to shine through. There is often a compulsive character to the unfaithful behavior of betrayers whose origin is in childhood. They see their behavior as giving in to an irresistible natural urge, something automatic and thoughtless. Most often, those who cheat on their spouses do not see clearly the connection between their behavior and that of their unfaithful parents or the devastating effect on their partners. Self-awareness and a firm resolution to change promote recovery.

1. ACKNOWLEDGE THE PAIN.

The process of recovery begins with the recognition of your own suffering and the misery you are causing your partner with your behavior. All personal change and growth arises from suffering and embracing it fully, not running away from it. If you pretend you are not hurting yourself and your partner, you will continue to be stuck repeating the hurtful behavior. The experience of this suffering launches you into a search for some escape. The wisdom of the ages, both psychological and spiritual, teaches that accepting reality with honesty and sincerity is the only path to happiness. So you must desire with your heart and soul to be radically honest with yourself. Only honesty will move you forward.

Such radical honesty can be difficult for anyone because of our tendency to live out our fantasies of how we think life should be. But for you who grew up in a home where your parent was unfaithful, your childhood model was one of deceit. Affairs are sustained by lying. In fact, the greatest harm of an infidelity is not the individual acts, but the cover-up that undermines any sense of trust in the relationship. The basic trust that is the foundation of a marital relationship is destroyed by the deceit. The spouse comes to mistrust anything that his or her unfaithful partner says or does. If your parent was unfaithful, you grew up infected by the deceit. You were caught in the web. You learned, without fully realizing it, that you could lie to yourself and others with impunity. You lacked models of truthfulness.

2. MAKE A MORAL INVENTORY.

If you desire to be honest with yourself, then you must undertake a moral inventory. This is also called an examination of conscience in religious circles. To undertake such an inventory, you must stop, look and listen to the stirrings in your heart. You must also step back and become an observer of your own behavior: what you have done and what you are doing now with your life. What do you see going on within you? You may discover that being introspective is a new experience that can be unsettling, because you are so used to keeping busy and active without thinking seriously about what you are doing. But take courage and continue the inner examination. Eventually, you will realize that you are better than the cheating behavior that has caused so much distress for you and your family. When you examine yourself, be totally honest and see both your strengths and your weaknesses. That is genuine humility, seeing yourself as you really are, not just being preoccupied with your own fault-finding.

3. CONFESS YOUR FAULTS.

The next step is to confess what you learn about yourself to another. Shame and guilt want to hide in darkness, but exposing them to the light causes them to evaporate, like the mist that all feelings are. It is really pride and an inflated self-image that motivate you to hide yourself from others and even yourself. Talking about your failings and strengths with another can be liberating because you surrender the

burden of secrecy you carried so long in hiding your affair. The acceptance of another can also help free you from your own harsh judgments about yourself and your behavior. Of course, there is always
the danger of self-deception, especially since infidelity had become
a way of life for you. Requesting honest feedback from someone you
trust can help you to be honest with yourself.

Be careful about choosing the person to whom you confess. The
person must be trustworthy to keep your confidence. It might be a therapist, trusted friend, priest or minister. That person should not be your
spouse whom you betrayed, because the honest and detailed revelations
may well be overwhelming. Over time you will find effective ways of con-
fessing to your partner that will be beneficial in rebuilding trust.

4. MAKE AMENDS.

The next step involves making amends to all the people you harmed with
your behavior. Catholics call it doing penance. Making amends needs to
be done carefully so as not to create more harm. You are entitled to privacy and do not have to announce your indiscretion to the world. People
do not have a right to know your business or your failings. Thinking
seriously about the people you have harmed by your wayward behavior
makes the consequences of your self-indulgence more real. You become
more aware of how your self-centered behavior caused others severe
harm. Such awareness can increase your sense of healthy remorse and
determination never to be unfaithful again. It can accelerate the process
of overcoming your self-obsession, becoming genuinely concerned about
the well-being of others. In making amends, you think about how you
can restore the balance in relationships that have been upset by your
behavior. You ask yourself, "How can I make up for what I have done?
How can I be more loving and truthful?" Reversing the downward trend
of your life, you can replace dishonesty with truthfulness, the stealing
of time and energy with loving attention and the hiding with openness.

5. MAKE A NEW START.

The final step flows naturally from the preceding ones. You make a firm
decision never to be unfaithful again. You are resolved to make a new start
in your life. Once you have honestly looked at yourself and the hurt you
have caused others and yourself, you will naturally be determined to avoid

that behavior. You realize that you as a person are better than that behavior. You will feel relief in not having to hide yourself and lead a double life. Your spouse may take some time to trust you again and may be suspicious that you will revert to your old ways. But be patient with him or her and acknowledge to yourself that you deserve his or her suspicion as a consequence of your behavior. Your resolution to be honest and loving will eventually move your spouse's heart, if you are meant to remain married.

Through this process of facing your guilt and shame, you will come to greater self-awareness and self-acceptance. By acting in truth instead of deceit, in love instead of selfishness, you will come to forgive yourself. You will give up your self-loathing and desire to punish yourself.

PATH TO HEALING: GIVING UP GUILT

1) **Acknowledge the pain you caused.**
2) **Make a moral inventory.**
3) **Confess your wrongdoing.**
4) **Make amends.**
5) **Resolve to make a new start.**

As you become more aware of your unhappiness as an unfaithful spouse, think about your parent who betrayed the family. Think back on your memories and try focusing, not on your hurt, but on the suffering of your unfaithful parent. His or her infidelity arose from a sense of emptiness and pain, just as yours did. As you get in touch with your own suffering, feel the suffering of your betraying parent. Feel compassion for your parent as you begin to have compassion for yourself. Replace the anger and resentment, which only harms you, with love and tenderness. It will likely be difficult to feel genuine compassion for the parent who harmed you and the family, but begin with the intention to forgive. Be patient with yourself if resentment persists. Healing takes time and a willingness to forgive.

EXERCISE: METTA

Forgiveness begins with you. You will likely discover that fully accepting yourself because of your transgressions is no simple matter and requires time, patience, perseverance and effort. Others may mistakenly misjudge you, imagining that you do not take your betrayal seriously enough and are not sufficiently guilty. They expect you to live in "apology mode" for an indefinite length of time. However, if you embark sincerely on a path of healing, you will face squarely the obstacle of forgiving yourself.

Make no mistake about it. Unless you can learn to be compassionate and forgiving of yourself, you will not be able to be compassionate and forgiving of others, especially your cheating parent.

A traditional Eastern practice to develop compassion is called *metta*, or loving-kindness. This deceptively simple and powerful practice has been used for over twenty-five hundred years to cultivate loving feelings as an antidote to fear, hate and guilt. The practice is reinforced by modern psychology, which teaches that the way we think about ourselves profoundly affects our attitudes and behavior. Metta invites us to shower ourselves and others with kindness and compassion.[3]

For this exercise, sit comfortably in a quiet place. Try to shut out all distractions, especially your racing thoughts, and focus on the rhythm of your breath. Also relax your body, being aware of any tension you feel. Imagine breathing relaxation into the tense muscles you discover. As distracting thoughts arise—as they inevitably do—gently let them pass.

With a relaxed mind and body, imagine yourself in your pain. It may be helpful to hold in your hand a picture of yourself when you were a child. Transport yourself back to your childhood in your memory and relive the experience. See yourself as a child caught in the maelstrom of your parents' unhappy marriage. Allow yourself to sense the innocence and helplessness that marked who you were as a child. Don't rush it. Let the memories and feelings emerge. Feel some compassion for yourself as the child victimized by your parents' troubles.

When you are ready, imagine yourself as an adult feeling the pain and turmoil of your unhappy marriage and your guilt and shame in seeking an escape through the affair. Again, feel some compassion for yourself, as difficult as it may be. Then select some phrases that express wishes for you in the present moment. For example, you may say to yourself, "May I be happy. May I be free from suffering. May I be at peace with myself. May I forgive myself for the wrongs I have done. May I be loving and truthful with my spouse." Repeat three or four of these phrases for a period of time, allowing the words to penetrate your soul. Say the words slowly and thoughtfully in time with your breathing. Simply relax and repeat these phrases for at least ten minutes, longer if you are inclined. Throughout the day, if you are feeling tense, stop to repeat the phrases to bring a sense of serenity.

This exercise can also be used with other significant people in your life. At this point in your recovery you are probably most aware of the pain you caused your partner by your infidelity. You are aware of how much you betrayed his or her trust and that you must rebuild the relationship. It is your responsibility to take the initiative in the rebuilding process. As a starting point, you can begin by extending loving-kindness in thought and intention to your partner, developing compassion for that person in his or her suffering. Only love will overcome your sense of shame and guilt.

Begin this exercise again by quieting your mind, body and heart. Sit still in a quiet place. You may hold a picture of your spouse in your hands. Imagine the pain he or she is experiencing in this moment. Recall when he or she first discovered your cheating, the shock, hurt and rage. Allow your heart to reach out to your beloved. Then select phrases that express your heartfelt wishes for this person. "May she be happy. May he be free from the suffering I have caused. May she have joy in life. May he be at peace." Slowly repeat these words, feeling your love pouring out to your partner, creating a bond of love. Repeat these words for a period of time, allowing your guilt to dissolve in a sea of love.

Undoubtedly, feelings of being betrayed by your unfaithful parents may emerge as you face your own infidelity. Although you are responsible for your behavior and no one else is to blame, you were influenced by your parents. In your own recovery, you will experience your need to forgive them and to release your anger toward them.

The metta exercise is a good way to kick-start that recovery. Again, hold a picture of your parents, preferably from your childhood. Imagine what their life was like when you were a child, what distress they may have been suffering. As a child you did not understand their problems, but as an adult who has walked in their footsteps, you have more insight. From a relaxed place, follow your breath until you feel still in your mind, body and heart. Now reach out to your parents with wishes for their well-being. "May they be happy. May they find peace. May they be free from suffering. May they enjoy good health." The phrases need not be elaborate, just simple wishes from the heart. Slowly repeat these words, sensing the love and peace radiating from you to them. Throughout the day you can pause and repeat these phrases, renewing your intention to extend compassion to yourself, your partner and your parents.

Chapter 2

The Excitement-Seeking/Addicted— Holding On for Dear Life

As a child, Ken loved to talk. He was a chatterbox with the gift of gab. He could talk his way into and out of any situation. He spent his free time wandering about the neighborhood, talking with anyone he met. Since Ken was such a talker, his parents predicted he would be a salesman.

Ken grew up to fulfill his parents' expectations. He became a successful sales representative for a large company. Ken also loved adventure, which was satisfied by his job. He got to travel around the world, often to exotic places like Saudi Arabia, India and Vietnam. Ken enjoyed the thrill of the chase in putting together complicated business deals and trying to sell to difficult clients. He planned his strategy well, pursued his goals with energy and celebrated his victories with abandon. His job always kept him on the move and Ken preferred it that way. He was easily bored and could not sit still. When he tried to stop and relax, his mind raced with plans and projects he wanted to accomplish and a nervous restlessness overtook his body.

Ken could not keep himself busy enough, even when he was not working. He watched sports incessantly, baseball in spring and summer, football in fall and hockey and basketball in winter. At home, he always had projects going. When he was not home or on the job, he worked out at the gym, "just to keep my sanity," he claimed.

Everyone was surprised when Ken dated and married Alice, a quiet, withdrawn, mousey woman who seemed to be his opposite in every way. While Ken ran around pursuing his interests, Alice stayed at home cooking, cleaning and relaxing with a book. They appeared to be the odd couple, but were content with each other nonetheless. After a long courtship, they married and settled into a routine, Alice as the anchor at home, and Ken on the go with restless energy.

Despite appearances of normality, Ken had a secret life. As a teen he developed the habit of masturbating daily to relax and help him sleep, because he was always so wound up. He discovered his father's cache of adult magazines and videos, indulging himself to fulfill his fantasies. He complained that sex had become routine and boring in his marriage. Often he could not maintain an erection and felt discouraged. From magazines and videos, Ken graduated to Internet pornography. His wife often retired early to bed, leaving Ken alone and restless. The only way he believed he could relax after a grueling day of chasing sales deals was with his computer. He scanned pornography sites, finding images that matched his fantasies of being desired by beautiful, buxom women. He adopted pornography as his preferred sleep aid.

Being a member of a strict Protestant church, Ken felt a nagging guilt for his secret habit. However, he justified it to himself by thinking, "That's the only way I know how to relax." The thought passed through his mind that he was being unfaithful to his wife, but he quickly dismissed it, thinking, "I'm really not having sex with anyone, just myself." He also began drinking more in the evenings to relax and wondered if it was becoming a problem. As time passed, Ken spent more time late into the evenings with his habit, feeling exhausted the next day at work. One late night, his wife awakened to notice his absence. Looking around the house, she found him hovering over the computer screen, indulging his fantasy. Outraged, she confronted him about how long it had been going on. She threatened divorce unless he got help.

The shame, guilt and fear of losing his marriage brought Ken to therapy. He admitted feeling relief that his secret was in the open, and now he had the motivation to address the problem. He always took pride in being a resourceful problem-solver, but he could not beat what he came to acknowledge as a sexual addiction. During treatment, Ken became aware of a deep feeling of inner emptiness which he filled up with exciting experiences. He never intended to hurt anyone with his behavior, but realized the harm he was causing himself and his family. He was determined to stop.

Ken had always had happy memories of his childhood. "It was normal, just like everyone else's," he insisted. Both his parents worked and provided well for him and his younger sister. They lacked for nothing, and everyone seemed to get along. After some time in therapy with gentle probing, some unhappy memories and a different picture of his childhood emerged. Ken felt alone and without much guidance growing up. His parents were unaffectionate and preoccupied with their own business. Ken remembered his mother was often lonely and bored, because his father worked long hours. She began to drink heavily to escape her boredom and went out to bars where she met men for one-night stands. His parents often argued about her going out, each blaming the other for their unhappiness. Ken could not stand the fighting and constant tension. To cope, he distracted himself outside the home in the pursuit of his adventures. "I just kept myself busy so I wouldn't think about what was going on at home. I went to parties every weekend," he explained. Keeping busy became a way of life for him. Sex became his tranquilizer.

"I'm sick and tired of all the hiding and games," he admitted. Facing his shame, he walked into a Sex Addicts' Anonymous meeting and began the journey toward recovery.

CHILDHOOD CONNECTION: LIVING WITH HIGH DRAMA

When a betrayal occurs in a family, powerful emotions are aroused. The home atmosphere is one of intense excitement, which is contagious. The offended parent becomes enraged, depressed and worried. The unfaithful parent becomes guilt-ridden and defensive. Emotions are often buried, simmering beneath the surface of a calm façade and erupting periodically like a fireworks display. The atmosphere around the home is alternatively chilly and heated, but always hostile. No one can anticipate when an outburst will occur or what crazy behavior will follow. The children watch the drama as participants fully engaged in the unfolding tragedy.

As your parents were caught up in their drama, they probably lost themselves in their struggle. Surviving the betrayal, with all the uncertainty it created, consumed an enormous amount of energy.

Their lives were falling apart and they had to figure out how to keep it all together. Unfortunately for you as a child, you received the leftovers of their time, energy and attention. Your parents were in a fight for the survival of their emotional well-being, their broken marriage and the disrupted family. They were in a life-or-death struggle, having to decide the future of their marriage and the family. In the midst of this all-consuming struggle, you felt the pain of their emotional absence and longed for the security of the "good old days."

As a child, you were a helpless participant in the drama that your parents created. You did not choose the stage or write the script. Yet you were forced to assume a role just to survive. That role was determined both by your temperament and the circumstances. If you were so disposed, you may have been caught up in their excitement, thus becoming an excitement junkie. Just to survive the chaos, you embraced it, got used to it and thought of it as normal. In fact, you may have come to enjoy the stimulation, which made you feel alive. The ordinary life most people live came to seem dull and boring. You internalized the drama and came to love the stage with all its demands for performance. Without knowing it, you developed an aversion to ordinary daily routines.

Excitement-seeking and emotional deprivation created fertile ground for developing an addiction later in life. In fact, one or both of your parents may have become addicted to sex, drugs, alcohol, eating or shopping to cope with the chaos and confusion of their lives, providing you with a negative role model. We know that there is a strong genetic component to addictions, which you inherited if either of your parents had an addiction. Consequently, you were prone to develop your own addiction as a way of filling the void of your emotionally-deprived childhood. Chasing the high with alcohol, drugs, gambling, sex or another compulsive behavior provided the burst of stimulation you were accustomed to growing up.

One of the characteristics of addictions is that they tend to come in clusters. People rarely have one addiction, but tend to be addicted to several different substances and engage in a variety of compulsive behaviors. Without knowing it, you return to the familiar drama of your childhood in pursuing the addictive behaviors, creating a chaos you know all too well. But now you are the author of the tragedy you are living.

The intense, unresolved conflicts and fighting in your parents' marriage made a deep impression on you. You developed a fear of emotional closeness with another person. You learned that you could not depend on anyone else to be there for you. Your drug of choice provides a substitute intimacy in which you imagine you are in control. Your drug is always there for you, giving you the emotional high you need whenever you want. It allows you to escape painful reality when you feel the need. It gives you an intense high that humdrum daily life cannot match. You develop a love affair with your drug of choice, whether it is a chemical or a behavior. Over time, you develop the unshakable belief that you need your drug to be happy.

When you have a love affair with your drug of choice, whatever it happens to be, you withdraw from your intimate relationship. You may not intend to hurt your partner, but the harm is real, both to yourself and your loved one. As the addiction deepens, your life becomes more centered on the pursuit of your drug, leaving your partner on the outside. Your spouse feels the pain of your absence, as much as you try to hide it. And you become increasingly possessed by a sense of shame and guilt. Without knowing it, in excitement-seeking and addictive behavior you distance yourself in your intimate relationship and identify with your unfaithful parent.

What are some of the signs you are prone to seeking excitement and addictive behavior?

AM I ADDICTED TO BEING ADDICTED?

- Am I easily bored?
- Do I crave excitement or seek adventure?
- Do people see me as a charming person?
- Am I dissatisfied with the old, thus constantly seeking the new?
- Am I restless or do I have difficulty sitting still?
- Is my mind always busy planning and preparing for the future?
- Do I have the sense that I can never have enough?
- Do I have an excess of energy?
- Am I a glutton for new experiences?
- Do I like to stay emotionally high?
- Do I like to keep a lot of options open and not settle on one thing?
- Do I tend to avoid conflict in relationships?

- Do I always have backup plans for whatever I am doing?
- Do I have difficulty relaxing?
- Do I have difficulty enjoying the simple pleasures in life?

PATH OF HEALING: LIVING IN THE REAL WORLD

We live in a society that encourages us to seek happiness in all the wrong places. One of the most confusing messages it preaches regards addiction. While condemning those who abuse drugs, modern society promotes values that lead to addictive behavior. As a recipe for happiness, it encourages an "I want it all and I want it now" way of living. We're told to "live the dream." But the wholehearted pursuit of that fantasy turns into a nightmare.

Dissect for a moment that statement: "I want it all and I want it now." It is about "I," focusing on self-fulfillment above all else, even a loving concern for others, which can only result in isolation and loneliness. It also encourages the uninhibited pursuit of whatever you "want." What is the "it" of those desires? Physical comfort and ease. You seek pleasure and avoid pain, without consideration for meaning and higher values. The statement promotes the single-minded, self-centered pursuit of "all." No half measures here. "Accept no limits" can only lead to disappointment and frustration when you have inevitable collisions with reality. Regarding time, it is "now," with no delays, no waiting and instantaneous results. How is this promise of happiness to be fulfilled in the real world? It can't be. However, addictive behaviors, which provide a quick fix, satisfy the fantasy.

Addictions are more widespread than you may imagine. Anything you do that you know is harmful, yet cannot stop yourself from doing, possesses an addictive quality. You feel powerless over the behavior. Chemical dependency on alcohol or other drugs falls under this category. Changes in brain chemistry stimulate almost irresistible urges to use the substance. Compulsive behaviors, such as sexual acting out, gambling, shopping and overeating are also experienced as uncontrollable. The strength of habit makes the behavior persistent beyond any useful purpose. Finally, mood states such as anger, worry and sadness and their accompanying negative, self-defeating thinking can be intoxicating. Temperament and emotional programming from childhood govern many of our mood states.

When I meet with people who are addicted, they are inevitably overwhelmed by feelings of shame, guilt and despair. They also feel helpless to control themselves. They may hate themselves for what they are doing but feel powerless to stop it. They have reached the end of their rope, disillusioned by the promised happiness of their addictive behavior. These feelings may not be immediately evident, but they are just below the surface and soon emerge in treatment. I offer them hope that recovery is always possible—no matter how severe the problem—and that facing the addiction can be a path to new life, enlightenment and a freedom never imagined. Addressing addiction requires several steps:

1) ACKNOWLEDGE YOUR SUFFERING.

Recovery begins with honest recognition of the suffering it is causing you and those you care about. Addiction is so powerful that no one gives it up until they believe that the trouble it brings outweighs the benefits. The benefits of the addiction, with its good feelings, pain relief and relaxation, are so enchanting that it is extremely difficult to give up its pleasures. Nothing can replace the intense pleasure of being high. Unfortunately, it often takes a catastrophe for the addicted person to wake up to the trouble it is causing. He may have to be arrested for drunk driving, be divorced by his spouse, lose his job or experience a financial crisis. It may take years for the trouble to accumulate enough to get the addicted person's attention. The accumulated losses to his well-being may be devastating.

2) RECOGNIZE THE EMPTINESS OF YOUR URGES.

Second, recognize your urges and the patterns of their rise and fall. The urges are really "have to" thoughts about using your drug, engaging in your compulsion or indulging your obsession. Physical discomfort may accompany the idea that it is urgent to act in a particular way. However, the urges come and go and, as you become more acquainted with yourself, you will learn their inner and outer triggers. They often signal underlying distress. Observe carefully when and where the urges arise and grow in intensity. What is the physical sensation? What is your mood at the time? What were you thinking about? Observing your urges carefully, you can learn much about yourself and your vulnerabilities. For example, when you are angry or anxious, you may want to comfort yourself with alcohol, food or pornography. Notice the situations that provoke rage reactions or worry in you. Awareness of your urges and their patterns can be a beneficial avenue of self-awareness, a way of learning about your vulnerabilities. When you learn about your sensitivities and inclinations to escape through your addictive behavior, you can begin to develop alternative ways of responding.

You may mistakenly think that urges express deep physical needs that must be satisfied for you to survive. You think you will die, or something terrible will happen to you, if you do not give in to the urge. That urge may be so powerful that it seems to be a life-or-death matter for you. In reality, your addiction is mainly in your mind. I refer to addictive thoughts as "thought bubbles" to express their emptiness. These thoughts gain power over you to the extent that you give them importance. You cannot control the rise and fall of these urges. However, you have control over how much weight you give them.

3) ACCEPT, DON'T ACT ON THE URGES.

Third, accept the urges for what they are, mere thoughts, and do not act on them. You do not have to fight them or try to control them. Just let them be. It may seem that they are so intense and so long-lasting that they will not pass. They always do, if you are patient enough with yourself to ride the wave. Most of all, resist the temptation to act on the urges. You cannot control their coming and going. It is futile to try. The effort to stop them will only lead to frustration and a sense of defeat. Whether you believe it or not, while you have no control over the urges, you do have control over your behavior. As enslaved as you feel, you are still free to choose how to act.

4) KNOW YOUR OWN MIND.

Fourth, become acquainted with both your addictive and rational minds. I see addiction as primarily a disease of the mind. The word "addiction" comes from the same root word as "dictator." Distorted thoughts rule the mind. If you discover you have an addiction to a chemical, a behavior or a mood, recovery proceeds by becoming acquainted with your addictive way of thinking and awakening your rational mind. You may hear echoes of your own addictive thinking in the following statements:

"I can stop using my drug (or doing the compulsive behavior or indulging my mood) any time I want." When you are trapped in an addiction, hanging on for dear life, you are usually the last person to acknowledge your problem. Those who know you and love you realize long before you do that you are in trouble and need help. You rationalize your behavior, deny any problem and blame others for being the cause of your misery. You may even try to prove to others and yourself that you can control it with brief periods of abstinence (during Lent, for example).

The truth is that in trying so desperately to control your mood with your drug of choice, you have lost control of yourself. It is not the drug but your desire for it that possesses you. Your greed for the pleasure the drug or compulsive behavior offers rules you. You are attached to the familiarity of the mood state. The primary symptom of any addiction is loss of control over your desires. You continue the behavior despite all the problems it causes you and those you love.

"I can't stop using my drug (or doing the compulsive behavior or indulging my mood)." Once you acknowledge your addiction, you may feel helpless and think you have no control over your behavior. The truth is you may not care to stop, for good reason. You experience great benefits from getting high. The benefits for you are so great that you overlook the problems the addiction is causing. So why stop? You will only stop when you look realistically at what your addiction is doing to you and your loved ones. Your rational mind possesses more power than you imagine. Listen to it and act on it.

"I can't stand the pain, and my drug gives me relief." Many use drugs or repetitive behaviors to self-medicate pain they believe is intolerable. Again, you only imagine your lack of strength to endure pain and have a false belief that only your drug can provide you with adequate relief. Listening to your rational mind will give you another story. First of all, pain and suffering are an inevitable part of life. Second, pain serves a useful purpose. It alerts you to a problem. Imagine what our lives would be like if we never experienced physical pain. You may immediately think that would be paradise. But think again. If you injured yourself, like putting your hand on a hot stove, and never felt the pain, you would continue the harmful behavior. Eventually, you would suffer irreparable damage. Pain, both physical and emotional,

alerts you to danger and serves a survival purpose. Your rational mind tells you to pay attention to what is causing you pain and do something about it. Instead of covering up the pain, it makes more sense to understand what is causing it and then take action to find lasting relief. Finally, you realize that drugs are not the only way to cope with pain. Addressing the cause of the pain is much more effective. In fact, the more you rely on your drug of choice, the less you develop your own internal resources to solve problems and cope with life's inevitable difficulties.

"I can't fight the urges to use my drug, to indulge my compulsive behavior or moods. They're too strong and irresistible." The addictive mind is ruled by the word "can't." You believe you are powerless to resist urges, which are just passing thoughts. You imagine you will suffer extreme discomfort or even die if you do not give in to your urges. The reality is that the urges are just thoughts that come and go. You cannot control your thoughts and feelings because they just flow from some deep, hidden source. However, it is you who decides what importance to give those thoughts and feelings. And you do have control over your behavior. Recovery involves becoming more aware of these urgent thoughts, noticing how they arise and disappear, realizing what triggers them and learning to let them pass without acting on them.

"I'm impatient and always need a quick fix." The more you turn to your drug of choice or preferred compulsive behavior to cope with the trials and tribulations of life, the weaker you become. As your tolerance for suffering decreases, time takes on a different meaning. You want everything and you want it now. You want immediate gratification in whatever you do and begin losing the capacity to delay pleasure for future gain. In the fantasy life you are creating for yourself, you hope to achieve whatever you want quickly, easily and with little effort. You expect that you can have complete control over your life and your experience. You can make a painful world disappear magically by indulging in your addiction.

"Nothing compares to the high I get from my drug." That's true. Drugs activate deep pleasure centers in the brain, making their use seem irresistible. The more you indulge in your addictive behavior, the more self-centered you become in focusing on the pursuit of your own pleasure to the neglect of your responsibilities and care for others. You become more childlike in the pursuit of pleasure and fun. You always

want more and are never satisfied with what you have in the moment. But eventually, your drug provides you with brief moments of excitement that are never enough and long periods of pain. And you begin to lose the capacity to enjoy the simple pleasures in life like a walk in the park, because nothing can compare with the rush of the high.

"I am worthless, and no one will love me." All addictions arise from suffering, an attempt to cope with the harsh realities of life. The addicted come to think of themselves as losers in life and use their drug, behavior or mood of choice to comfort themselves. Their sense of worthlessness and loneliness reinforces their tendency to find relief and happiness in addictive behavior. However, your low opinion of yourself, often disguised behind an arrogant façade, is really an invention of your mind used in the service of your self-defeating activities. It is just another thought and not a fact. The truth is that you think less of yourself as a result of indulging in your addictive behavior. You do not like how it controls you, leads to embarrassing, harmful actions and violates your moral standards. The more you lose yourself in the addiction, the more you distance yourself from others and push them away. Your addiction causes a sense of worthlessness and loneliness.

ASSUMPTIONS OF THE ADDICTIVE MIND

1) **Life should be easy.**
2) **Seek pleasure and avoid pain at all costs.**
3) **You can have it all and have it now.**
4) **You cannot count on anyone else to meet your needs.**
5) **You are worthless and alone.**
6) **Rely solely on yourself.**
7) **Only your drug can bring you happiness.**

5) JOIN A SUPPORT GROUP.

Finally, seek the fellowship of others who are suffering like you. Addictions are too powerful to face alone. The path to healing involves a clear awareness of your distorted beliefs and thinking and a commitment to change your behavior. You will also need the support and guidance of others who are well acquainted with the addictive mind, such as the twelve-step fellowships, which address the full range of addictions. These groups provide a mirror for you to see yourself and your thinking realistically. Alcoholics Anonymous, which offers expert practical advice, teaches an acronym to guide recovery. The acronym is SOBER, which stands for "Son of a B****, everything is real." Recovery involves surrendering the magical thinking and choosing to live in the real world, which provides satisfaction that lasts a lifetime.

PATH TO HEALING THROUGH ADDICTIONS

1) **Acknowledge your suffering.**
2) **Recognize urges as passing thoughts.**
3) **Don't act on the urges.**
4) **Investigate your addictive and rational minds.**
5) **Join a support group.**

Facing your excitement-seeking and addictive behavior with compassion may open your heart to understanding your parent's compulsion to be unfaithful. Recognizing your own emptiness may help you appreciate the emptiness that drove your parent. Eventually, your understanding will open the door to forgiveness.

EXERCISE: FOLLOWING YOUR BREATH AND THOUGHTS

We live in a culture that is dominated by noise, greed and speed. "I want it all and I want it now" is our mantra. Such expectations provide a basis for the urge to seek excitement at all costs, even to the loss of ourselves. In turn, the endless pursuit of stimulation leads to addictive behaviors. The prevalence of various addictions testifies to the powerful influence of our driven culture and the need for an alternative.

I offer guidance in the midst of the turmoil: learn to sit down, shut up and pay attention. As a regular practice I encourage exercises which are called "following your breath" and "mental noting."

First of all, sit down. You may think you are so busy with so many projects that you have no time to sit down. If you are honest with yourself, you may discover that you are really too restless to stop your constant activities. Stopping makes you feel uncomfortable. Your mind races, unpleasant thoughts and feelings arise and you feel like jumping out of your skin. I encourage you to resist the impulse to keep running and sit still for a few moments each day. Just sit there with nothing to do. Find a comfortable, quiet place. Sit in a chair with your back straight and your feet firmly planted on the floor. Feel yourself settling into the chair and becoming still in your body. Close your eyes to remove any distractions and breathe deeply. Feel your body unwinding as you breathe consciously and deeply from the pit of your stomach.

Next, while sitting there doing nothing, shut up. It is hard enough to quiet your body; now allow your mind to quiet. Be aware of all the internal chatter that Eastern meditators refer to as the "wild monkey mind." Just notice all the frenetic activity of your mind, the chaos of disorganized thinking. For a few moments, try not to run away with your thoughts in a million directions. Instead, feel like you are stepping back to observe the colorful parade of thoughts, feelings and sensations that seem to arise from nowhere and disappear like mist in sunlight. Notice how the thoughts, feelings and sensations come and go as if they had a mind of their own. Just observe their passing and do not hang onto them. Instead of chasing after your thoughts, focus on your breath, on the slow rhythm of inhaling and exhaling. Your breathing, which keeps you alive, is so automatic that you usually do not even notice it. Now pay close attention to your breath. As thoughts, feelings and sensations arise to distract you, gently let them pass and return your attention to your breathing. You may be surprised how difficult it is to focus on one thing, like your breath, but persevere. As you relax while breathing, calmness will slowly fill your mind and body. It will not happen immediately, but with practice the calmness will deepen.

Once you are still and quiet for several minutes, you can begin to pay closer attention to what arises within your consciousness. Shift from focusing on your breath, which helped to calm you, to noticing the activity of your mind as an observer. Sit back and watch. What do you see? You likely notice subtle thoughts, feelings and sensations that arise from deep within you, from some unknown source. You may be amazed at the variety and confusion of your mental activity. You may also notice how you spontaneously try to organize and make sense of the thoughts, feelings and sensations. You formulate stories in your head. You may begin to recognize patterns in the stories, which you take as firm beliefs about your reality. The stories may clash and contradict each other. Just notice them without analyzing anything, because your analyzing is just another series of thoughts about your thoughts.

This daily exercise in following your breath and mental noting is a way of becoming acquainted with yourself. Perform this practice for twenty minutes each day and see how relaxed you can become and what you learn about yourself. I suspect you will discover that you are infinitely more than just your thoughts and feelings about yourself and your world.

Chapter 3

The Disengaged Workaholic— Being an Actor in a Play

Marcy grew up Daddy's little girl. Her father never hid his desire that he had wanted his first-born to be a boy. His disappointment at Marcy's birth was evident to those who knew him but hidden from those outside the family circle. As Marcy grew up and displayed extraordinary intelligence and talent, he grew attached to his daughter, developing the ambition to nurture her talents. Marcy loved her father and wanted to please him more than anything. She became his constant companion on weekends as he did chores around the house and ran errands. She listened attentively to his words of advice and guidance and complied with all his wishes.

Marcy's mother was a fun-loving, sociable woman who spent a good deal of time at parties. She was not around the house much. So Marcy gravitated to her father as if he were a single parent. Her father owned a small factory that produced auto parts. His energy and ingenuity made that small enterprise into a thriving business. He had the ambition that one day Marcy would run the business and he carefully prepared her for the job. Occasionally, he took her to work with him to show her off and introduce her to his business. The employees doted on her, remarking how much she looked and acted like her father.

In school, encouraged by her parents, Marcy worked hard and achieved good grades. Her father would not accept anything less than an A for any class and Marcy's name regularly occupied the top of the honor roll. Her skills were not limited to the classroom. Marcy was an accomplished tennis player, winning several tournaments in high school. Her proud parents attended every big match, bragging about their intelligent, athletic daughter. With her exuberant personality, Marcy had many friends and was a member of the "popular" group at school. In recognition of her overall ability and popularity, she was elected senior class president and graduated as valedictorian.

Marcy went away to college at a prestigious university to pursue a degree in business and marketing. Her father's plan for her was unfolding just as he wanted. Marcy threw herself into her studies with enthusiasm, willingly following her father's dreams. She graduated, as expected, at the top of her class. Her father had her work in his company's office, preparing her to take over the role of vice president of the growing business.

While in college, Marcy fell in love with John, a fun-loving guy much like her mother. John took Marcy to parties and taught her to laugh and have fun. He was a carefree student who did just enough to get by. Marcy didn't care, because she believed she had enough ambition for both of them. After college, John worked for a large corporation selling mortgages, while Marcy began working in her father's business. A year later, when both were established in their careers, they were married in a lavish ceremony that dominated the society page.

While dating, Marcy had made it clear to John that she intended to be a career person and he agreed. True to her word, Marcy threw herself into her work at the factory and advanced to the position of vice president. As her father neared retirement, he passed more and more of the responsibilities and control of the company to Marcy. She thrived on work and seeing the fruit of her labors in expanding the business beyond what her father had ever achieved. Her father beamed with pride at her accomplishments. John also enjoyed the fruits of Marcy's labors, especially the lavish lifestyle it afforded them. He did not take his work nearly as seriously as Marcy did. He did what he needed to do to get by, particularly enjoying golf outings with clients. John became an avid golfer, spending most of his free time at the country club they had joined. When their two daughters were born, Marcy took a brief maternity leave and then hired a nanny to care for their children. Keeping the business growing and maintaining their lifestyle were her main priorities.

Being so preoccupied with work, Marcy did not recognize the growing distance in her relationship with John. When he complained about her absence, she responded, "You certainly enjoy the lifestyle I'm providing." He grew quiet, immersing himself even more in his hobbies and social life at the club. Marcy became married to her job and John felt like an outsider. Eventually, the loneliness became too much for him. John began a secret affair with the hostess at the club. John thought he was discrete, but soon became careless in leaving a hotel receipt in his pants pocket. When Marcy discovered it, all hell broke loose and they began therapy to put the pieces back together.

John and Marcy both admitted that they had lost the connection they enjoyed in college. John still admired Marcy's energy and drive but felt neglected emotionally. Marcy could no longer laugh and have fun with John, because she resented and secretly envied his casual and carefree life. Exploring her childhood in depth, Marcy realized how much she had lived her father's dream for her and neglected to consider what she wanted for herself. She remembered him bringing her to a bar on many occasions where he met with an attractive woman he identified as a good friend. Her father cautioned, "But don't tell your mother about her, because she would not understand. This is our little secret, just between you and me."

Marcy kept that secret for years. She felt a sense of loyalty to her father, who had given her so much. However, she was also angry with him for making her an accomplice in the betrayal of her mother. Guilt gnawed away at her. To relieve the guilt and shame, she worked hard to prove her own worth, pushing herself relentlessly. She became addicted to striving for the success her father desired for her, losing a sense of intimacy with herself and others.

One day, disillusioned and exhausted with her chase after success at work, she told John, "Let's take a long vacation. Work can survive without me. I love you and want to rebuild our life together."

CHILDHOOD CONNECTION: LIVING IN A HOUSE OF LIES

When parents are unfaithful, their children dwell in a house of lies. The most harmful aspect of the affair is not the sexual encounter itself but the web of deceit to hide it, in total disregard for the truth and the partner's feelings. Affairs live in the dark, avoiding the light of exposure. The unfaithful partner lives a double life. What is visible to the family and the public is the pretense of a committed relationship. What is hidden is a secret life of passion with another. When the betrayal comes to light, as it inevitably does, the lies are revealed. The house collapses under the weight of the deceit.

Your parents played a confusing game of hide and seek with the truth, with each other, with themselves and with you. Your unfaithful parent hid the affair, but his or her guilt led to carelessness in order to be found out. Your parent pretended to be a good and faithful person, but knew deep inside that he or she was living a lie. Your offended parent, perhaps picking up clues of the infidelity, wanted to know, yet did not want to know. Acknowledging the truth would have been too overwhelming and would have required decisive action. The offended parent pretended to the world and to him or herself that everything was okay. Your parents likely kept secrets and lied to you about the affair, just to protect you from the overwhelming truth of the betrayal. As a child, you watched this game being played out, not understanding the rules and wondering what was true and real. You were left confused, not knowing whom or what to trust.

Remember what it was like for you as a child when you placed all of your trust in your parents. You counted on them to guide and protect you. You looked up to them as role models. Little did you know what was simmering beneath the façade of normality they created. And you believed them that everything was okay, even though you witnessed some arguing and felt the tension in the home. That was all normal to you. After all, what you grow up with you come to believe is normal. Isn't everyone's home just like mine?

When the bombshell of your parent's affair is dropped, your faith in them, yourself and your perception of the world is shattered. Your sense of security in knowing what is true and real is lost. Your mother is not the kind, loving, faithful person you imagined her to be. When you see your father depressed and outraged, you wonder if he is really the strong person you thought you could always count on. Your parents taught you to be honest and truthful and now their marriage is exposed as a big lie. You imagined your home as a safe and secure place and your parents always reassured you that it was. Now you don't know if you can trust anything they say. You doubt your faith in what you thought was true.

Your parents' cover-up planted seeds of deceit and mistrust in you that would flower in adulthood. To survive the trauma of betrayal, the insecurity of not knowing what is true and real, you look for a safe haven. Not trusting that the world of intimate relationships can offer security, you create a sense of safety in competent activity. Your parents may have told you that you were talented in some way, perhaps intelligent, hard-working or creative. So you put your energy into developing that talent and work hard at it. Feeling insecure and unsure of yourself deep down, you begin to feel good about yourself through a sense of accomplishment. People recognize your abilities and praise you for what you accomplish. You feel proud, somehow making up for the travesty of your parents' failed marriage.

As much as you gain by immersing yourself in your chosen field of activity, something important is lost. In performing so well, you become an actor who so identifies with his role that he forgets who he really is. You lose yourself in the image you are creating. Furthermore, you become married to your work, have an affair with your job and abandon your partner. Without knowing it, you learn to identify with the deceitful betrayer by hiding your true self.

What are some signs of a tendency to hide your true self, instead finding your sense of self-worth and identity in your work?

Am I an Emotional Actor?

- Am I overly sensitive about what others think of me?
- Do I have a strong need for recognition and approval?
- Do I like to perform before an audience?
- Am I driven by a sense of achievement?
- Does my self-esteem rise and fall according to how others see me?
- Do I thrive on competition and fear failure more than anything?
- Am I extremely conscious of my image?
- Am I willing to lie to make myself look good?
- Is it important for me to create a favorable impression?

- Do I tend to lose myself in my work?
- Do I believe that love comes from what I produce, rather than from who I am?
- Do I tend to focus on the positive and overlook the negative?
- Do I often set aside my feelings to get the job done?
- Am I uncertain about what I really feel in many situations?
- Am I a vain person?

PATH OF HEALING: BE TRANSPARENT TO YOURSELF

When people come to me for therapy, they are suffering and look to me as an expert in pain relief. Often, they ask me, "What can I do so I don't feel so bad?" Or they may ask more specific questions: "What should I do about my marriage—stay or leave?" They look to me for the answer. They have exhausted themselves trying to work out the problem with their own resources and hope that I can provide the solution. I may be their last hope.

My response initially causes them dismay, "Who do you think knows best what you need to do? Who is the expert on you?"

"I know I should be the expert and know what I need," they say.

I encourage them, "Perhaps we can discover what keeps you from recognizing what is best for you." Busy people especially do not want to waste time. They want quick answers and a clear plan of action to solve their problems. They often squirm in their chairs when I suggest, "I want you to just pause and pay attention to yourself. And we'll talk about it in our sessions."

My clients, after many years of pain and frustration because they feel so stuck in their dilemmas, want me to cure them by providing some magical solution quickly. However, I do not see myself as the expert answer man, but as a man of many questions, like Socrates. I invite them to explore a fascinating world that they have ignored most of their lives: the inner workings of their minds. By looking outside themselves rather than inside, they have become stuck. Their distance from themselves has become the source of much of their suffering, although they may not be consciously aware of it. So I ask questions that will help them to become acquainted with themselves and explore their own unacknowledged wisdom. Truth, goodness and beauty lie within them, close to their hearts, if they will only come to recognize them.

My clients, especially the hard-working ones, want to know how they can change themselves, get rid of the behaviors, thoughts and feelings they do not like. They want direction and a recipe for change. I tell them, "You have it all wrong, backward, inside out." I explain that they want to manipulate themselves by working from the outside in, changing their behaviors in order to change their hearts. Instead, the process of change and growth is an inside-out job which involves acknowledging and releasing the natural power and goodness within them. Change comes through self-awareness and self-acceptance at a deep level. It involves surrendering to the unrecognized power within yourself.

I tell my clients my view of therapy: "I do not see therapy as some self-improvement project, a way to create a better version of yourself. Instead, I view it as a way to come to know and accept yourself as you are, not as you wish yourself to be. Together we explore what keeps you from knowing and accepting yourself as good enough."

Most of my clients see themselves as somehow defective and hopelessly entangled in problems. They feel helpless and hopeless, lacking resources to work out their problems. They feel imprisoned by the circumstances of their lives, unable to escape. I present an alternative vision, that they are a wondrous mystery to be explored and relished, not a problem to be solved. I invite them to undertake a journey of exploration with me to a little-known and fascinating land with untold riches. I invite them to travel beneath the surface to the center of their lives from which all their hopes, desires and values arise. They hold the keys to their freedom but don't know it.

Like Socrates, the Greek philosopher, I ask questions to make my clients look within, to appreciate their own truth, beauty and goodness. The truth about themselves will set them free, if they will only make the effort to uncover it. Through my questions and our thoughtful explorations together, I try to impress upon them that they are not who they think they are. They are much more. In searching for the answers to these questions, I ask them to become observers of themselves and their inner worlds. In the process, I hope they gain a sense of their own transcendence, their freedom to just be themselves and escape the tyranny of the many roles they play.

1) WHAT IS YOUR TRUTH?

My questions focus on three areas that overlap in reality. First, I ask the "truth" questions. When clients sit in my office for a session, they sometimes tell me, "Nothing is going on, just the same old thing."

Astonished, I respond, "How can that be? You may see nothing different around you but how can nothing be going on in your mind?" I ask them to talk about whatever comes to mind. If you observe your own mind closely, you immediately notice a flood of thoughts, feelings and sensations. The movement is continuous, overflowing and unstoppable. It comes from some hidden source that you experience deep inside.

Sometimes clients dismiss their own thoughts and feelings quickly, exclaiming, for example, "I wanted her to hug me. But that's just silly, childish." They interrupt the natural flow of their thoughts with critical judgments.

I ask my clients to be objective observers of what is going on in their minds. I invite them to be endlessly curious about what they discover and refrain from judging. Together we examine the flow of consciousness and try to understand what it is telling us. If you observe closely what emerges from your mind, the isolated thoughts will reveal patterns and repetitions. They will echo what you have heard from others and from your past. I say to my clients, "Isn't that an interesting thought, an interesting way to look at things? How did you come to think that way?" If you stop and reflect on the various thoughts, beliefs and assumptions you have about your life, you will notice that most are not original. They come from someone else who influenced your life, likely your parents or some authority figure. Without questioning it, you came to accept on faith what was passed on to you. You never measured it against the bar of your own experience.

Look at the parade of thoughts and realize that they are relative, not absolute truths. Those thoughts may even be a distortion of reality, not corresponding to your present day experience as an adult. They are ways of thinking you inherited from childhood. If you discover a thought or belief that disturbs you, ask yourself, "Does that make sense to me now?" Ask further, "What do I believe about myself now?" Perhaps you never consulted with yourself or took your opinions seriously. If you don't take your opinions seriously, no one else will. It may be liberating to realize that you have your own truth and are entitled to your own opinions.

2) WHERE DO YOU FIND BEAUTY?

Second, I ask about beauty. What inspires you with a sense of wonder and awe? A moment when time stood still for me was in St. Peter's Basilica while I was gazing at the Pietà, Michelangelo's sculpture of Mary holding a lifeless Jesus. I was transported beyond myself—inspired—and filled with an uplifting, divine spirit. At that moment, transfixed by the beauty before me, I felt a sense of communion with something greater than myself and a deep tranquility. All was well and would be well, beyond the chaos and confusion of my life. Most of us do not stop long enough to contemplate the beauty around us: a radiant sunset, a bee pollinating a flower, a look of love. When we do, we do not recognize it as a reflection of the beauty within us and every human being who walks the earth.

Most of my clients suffer from low self-esteem. They lack awareness of their own dignity. Instead, they are caught up with problems that overwhelm them and behaviors that cause shame. They see only their faults and feel pressure to prove themselves adequate. They do not stop to consider their innate beauty. Do you consider yourself a beautiful person, someone who inspires others? I am talking about both an outer and inner beauty that you desire to display to others. Have you ever asked yourself what you consider your most beautiful quality? Do you see the beauty of everyone around you, or are you preoccupied with their flaws? Do you only see your own flaws? We project onto others what we do not accept in ourselves. If you do not see your own native beauty, you will never really see it in others or in the world around you. Can you view your life as a magnificent, unfinished tapestry that the world is waiting to see? Can you see the fine strands of suffering, successes and failures as essential to the unique beauty of the design?

3) WHAT IS THE GOOD YOU SEEK?

Finally, I ask about goodness. What is the good you are aiming to create with your life? When my clients tell me that they are no-good losers, I remark, "What an interesting way to view yourself." I follow up with two questions: "How did you come to think of yourself that way? What purpose would it serve for you to think that way?" These questions usually stop them in their tracks. We explore together the payoff in thinking of themselves as no good and useless. If you think you are a loser with nothing to give, you do not expend the energy to do anything of value. You withdraw into self-pity and ignore any sense of responsibility to make yourself and the world a better place. Low self-esteem arises from and reinforces a self-centered preoccupation. Instead, if you appreciate your own goodness, you spontaneously seek ways of sharing it.

If you stop to observe that flow of consciousness, you will immediately notice many desires, wishes and strivings. A close examination of them, again, reveals a pattern whose origin can be discerned with some analysis. You discover an emotional program, an unconscious agenda, that guides your life. It is likely you inherited that program from your parents, based on choices for or against how they lived. When you feel the inevitable conflicts in your life while pursuing your goals, you are probably not living out of your own freely chosen value system. Your inherited values clash with what you really want in life. Those moments of painful conflict are invitations to explore what is the good that directs your life. Ask yourself, as I ask my clients, "What are your deepest desires? What do you want in your life? What makes you feel alive? What kind of person do you want to be? Where do you want to go in your life?" When looking at your values more closely, I believe you will discover you want something more than the conventional mindless pursuit of pleasure and avoidance of pain. You search for something that gives your life enduring meaning. What would you want your obituary to read?

QUESTIONS FOR SELF-AWARENESS

1) Who am I?
2) What do I believe about myself?
3) What within me reflects the beauty of the universe?
4) What are my deepest desires?
5) What makes me feel fully alive?

Taking seriously your own opinions and desires, become aware of how much your parents' agenda guided your life. You played roles assigned by them, not created by yourself. As you gain freedom from their dreams for you, you will liberate yourself from the anger toward them that has imprisoned you.

EXERCISE: SELF-QUESTIONING

Instead of being an actor in a play scripted by your unhappy, unfaithful parents, you can begin to direct your own life according to your own truth. In the process of finding yourself, you can develop a sense of compassion for your parents who lost their way, becoming dishonest with themselves and each other. Continuing your efforts at self-awareness, reflect deeply on some questions that may further help you wake up to yourself, to be fully present to yourself.

Ask yourself, *What is going on in my life right now?* Be aware of all the circumstances of your life that may be influencing your thoughts, feelings and reactions. Be aware, too, of your reactions to the events going on around you and the stories you are telling yourself about them. Are you seeing yourself as a helpless victim at the mercy of what is happening around you? Or do you see yourself as the master of your fate, navigating through the various challenges of your life circumstances? Awareness of the influence of the conditions of your life helps you to respond consciously, rather than react mindlessly.

"Can I see my life conditions as my path to healing and wholeness?" As much as you would like to write your life script, having it turn out according to your plan, the unexpected always occurs. You did not choose your parents or a childhood marred by their infidelity. Nevertheless, your past and the present conditions help shape your life. But not entirely. You are still the author of your life, working with the material given to you. Do you see the inevitable problems you face as opportunities to awaken and exercise your freedom? While you cannot control many of the circumstances of your life, you can control your attitude toward them.

"What are my most cherished beliefs about myself and my world?" Not only the circumstances, but how you think about your life shapes the way you live it. You react automatically to events according to your emotional programming, unless you develop self-awareness. Be aware of the automatic thoughts, beliefs and assumptions that arise as you encounter difficulties. We all have beliefs that guide us through the

chaos of our experience. Life is too overwhelming without these inner guides. Being aware of our beliefs gives us the opportunity to evaluate them and not make them absolute. Some beliefs may not match the reality of our life experience and need to be discarded or altered.

"What am I experiencing now?" We create a false sense of security with our beliefs about life, living out of our heads instead of out of our current experience, which is always new. Our belief system is a scaffolding that both supports us and separates us from our everyday experience. If you have suffered the trauma of your parents' infidelity, you have likely constructed walls of beliefs, routines and roles to protect yourself from being overwhelmed by the pain. Healing will come only from allowing yourself to feel and work through the pain, and not skirting around it. Pay close attention to all that you are experiencing in the present moment, recognizing and setting aside the scaffolding of your thoughts about yourself. Listen especially to the sensations of your body that hold much of the pain you seek to avoid. Your body often knows more than your mind and can give you useful information in making decisions about your life.

Can I accept my present experience wholeheartedly? We usually relate to our lives with a divided mind, with an eye on our beliefs, expectations and wishes for how we would like it to be and an eye on our ongoing experience of the moment. The divided mind inevitably leads to conflict, confusion, indecision and pain. With a fuller awareness of your circumstances, reactions and beliefs, you can avoid the human compulsion to cling to pleasures and get rid of pain. You can avoid the tendency to judge yourself and your experience as defective and flee from it into the fantasy world of your wishes. Accepting your current experience, which is always new, wholeheartedly is the only path to healing and living a full life.

Part 2

Those Who Identify with the Victim

Chapter 4

The Vigilant Victim— Shrinking from Life

M arlene, a dark-haired beauty, came to therapy obsessing that Robert, her husband of eight years, was having an affair. The year before, while on vacation, she noticed that he paid a lot of attention to her longtime girlfriend. She confronted him angrily and he denied it vehemently. Not reassured, she could not get it out of her mind that something was going on between her husband and her best friend. She could not sleep at night, because thoughts of being betrayed whirled through her head. She had frequent nightmares of Robert in the arms of her friend. Her suspicions never left. She constantly checked his phone records and whereabouts, monitoring his schedule like a hawk. Marlene even hired a detective to follow her husband, but he reported nothing out of the ordinary. Therapy was her last resort. She lamented, "I just know my husband is having an affair, but can't prove it—yet. I'm going out of my mind." Despite being so tormented and convinced of his infidelity, Marlene did not want a divorce, protesting, "Then the other woman would win."

When Marlene met Robert, their attraction was instantaneous. Marlene had endured a bitter divorce and was frightened to date until a friend introduced her to Robert. He was a calm, down-to-earth, stable man who worked hard, unlike her wild, irresponsible, abusive first husband. She saw Robert as her "knight in shining white armor" who would rescue her from all the pain of her failed relationships. She admired his strength, calm demeanor and ambitious pursuit of his goals, qualities she saw lacking in herself. Marlene, a high-strung woman, reacted intensely to any disappointments and rarely followed through with projects or jobs. She had worked as a waitress at several different restaurants and in child care. But some dispute always ended her employment, because, she claimed, "You can't trust anyone." Her one lifelong passion, however, was rescuing animals that had been mistreated by their owners. She claimed, "I can see myself in those poor creatures." In contrast to Marlene's flaky work ethic, Robert persevered at whatever was important to him and he earned a good living.

After dating only a few months, Marlene and Robert moved in together. The romance continued and they soon married. Marlene was happier than she had ever been. She felt loved and secure. Robert worked long, hard hours at his job as a sales manager, but knowing Marlene's sensitivity, he called her often. Marlene admired his work ethic, but the long hours began to bother her more and more. She felt lonely and insisted he take more and more time off from his job to be with her. He declined, saying, "Honey, we have so many bills and I want the best for us." Her pouting led to arguing. The arguing led to Robert withdrawing more. His withdrawing led to Marlene feeling more lonely and neglected. And the seeds of suspicion were planted: *I wonder if he loves someone else.*

Marlene began having nightmares that featured Robert transformed into her ex-husband. Robert's absence provoked flashbacks of her ex-husband being with another woman. She was flooded with dread, worry and anger. Before they were married, Marlene hardly knew her first husband, Bradley. The families had arranged for them to meet and eventually marry. Marlene, who had little dating experience, just followed her parents' program for her. Little did she know the nightmare she had entered by marrying Bradley. He expected to be the master of the house and for Marlene to be his slave. He was part owner of a family clothing store and came and went as he pleased, expecting Marlene to stay home. She felt like a prisoner. When she protested, Bradley beat her. As the beatings and threats continued, Marlene withdrew into her own miserable world of depression. She heard through the grapevine that Bradley was seeing other women and felt humiliated. When she dared confront him, he beat her. Finally, Bradley decided, after five brutal years of marriage, to leave Marlene for another woman. Marlene felt relieved, yet also lost and terrified about her future. Until she met Robert.

Marlene had never been allowed to live on her own, as was her culture's custom. After the divorce, which heaped more humiliation on her, she moved back home with her mother. Her parents had separated many years before but never divorced. Living with her mother, with whom she had never gotten along, only caused her to relive painful childhood memories. Her father was seldom at home when Marlene and her sister were growing up. He owned a business and loved to gamble. Her mother, who was a beauty, loved to shop and keep herself beautiful. She refused to stay home alone. Instead, she went out with her girlfriends and met men at bars and clubs.

Marlene recalls feeling unwanted by her parents, who were preoccupied with their own pursuits. "They were just too busy," she said. However, Marlene wanted desperately to be loved by both of them. "If you cannot trust your parents to love you, who can you trust to love you?" she asked herself.

Marlene also felt disgusted and stimulated when her mother brought men home and they walked around the house in various stages of undress. The sight of naked men assaulted her and her reactions confused her. Marlene also felt her father's humiliation, but still kept her mother's secrets. She felt torn by an impossible dilemma. Whose side would she take? Would she betray her mother by telling her father, risking her mother's wrath? Or would she keep the secret and betray herself? The seeds of mistrust, guilt and confusion were planted in Marlene's subconscious with the firm belief, "Everyone in life is dishonest, leads double lives and cannot be trusted." Without knowing it, Marlene entered relationships with the expectation of being rejected. And it had become a self-fulfilling prophecy.

Now Marlene decided to take a different path. In therapy she began to focus more on what she wanted in her own life. To her astonishment, the more she began doing things for herself, the less her suspicions of Robert occupied her. "Deep down, I believe he is a faithful person," she affirmed.

CHILDHOOD CONNECTION:
IDENTIFYING WITH THE VICTIM

If either of your parents was unfaithful, one was the betrayer while the other was the victim. That distinction is clear. As I brought up earlier, you carry your parents' genes, not always certain whose genetic heir you are. "Am I more like my mother or my father?" you wonder. There is also an unconscious compulsion to repeat what was traumatic for you as a way of gaining mastery over a painful past. If a parent was unfaithful, your immediate reaction is predictable. You feel anger at the betrayer for hurting your innocent parent, and sympathy for the one who was victimized. Yet your feelings are not quite so simple. Secretly, you may admire the betrayer who boldly sought her own pleasure, disregarding the rules. You envy her freedom. At the same time, you resent the weakness and blindness of your offended parent who ignored or tolerated the abusive behavior.

What may be confusing to you is why you would ever want to follow in the footsteps of the parent who was betrayed. You saw how vulnerable and hurt your parent was and may have wanted to protect him. You witnessed how he coped with the trauma of the affair, becoming anxious, depressed and enraged. You felt his pain. Just to keep from falling apart, he may have turned to you for support, complaining of his misery. You wanted to help in any way you could. You enjoyed being your parent's caretaker, but may also have felt inadequate and overwhelmed by the role.

Your anger distanced you from your betraying parent, while your sympathy drew you closer to your wounded parent. Your attention focused on his suffering and you wanted to help. His vulnerability and powerlessness elicited strong feelings of compassion in you and, without knowing it, you slowly identified with him in his pain. His pain became yours. As you grew into adulthood, you felt an innate closeness to him in his woundedness and slowly transformed into his likeness. In relationships, you sensed your weakness and helplessness, seeking someone strong and self-confident, someone to lean on. You looked to your partner rather than yourself for a sense of security. You began to cling to him or her. At the same time, aware of your vulnerability, you knew the danger of relying on another person who could betray you. Anxiety and wariness crept into your relationship. You watched carefully for any signs of danger, developing a vivid imagination about possible betrayal. Mistrust and vigilance, driven by fear, shaped the way you related to your partner.

In your sympathy for your wounded parent, you also sensed the benefit of playing the victim role. It's hard to imagine a payoff for bearing so much pain, but there is. A victim shares all the glory of being a martyr, someone who sacrifices him or herself for a noble cause. The victim can claim innocence in being faithful to the marriage, while the betrayer is the obviously guilty party. The wounded partner can righteously blame the unfaithful one for all the troubles in the marriage and avoid taking responsibility for any problems that led to the affair. She can indulge her anger in attacking her partner for the hurt he caused her and the family, enjoying watching him squirm with guilt. She persecutes her partner subtly, in the guise of being a victim. Her family and friends offer her sympathy for all that she endured, share her anger at being betrayed and praise her courage in going on with her life. For a moment, she feels powerful in being a victim, lording it over her betraying partner.

If you enter a marriage with deep insecurity, you may set yourself up to be victimized. Your insecurity makes you cling to your partner, becoming overly dependent on that person. Your anxiety about losing the all-important relationship may drive you to monitor and question your partner's every behavior. Eventually, she will resent the intrusion and protest, "Don't you trust me?" Over time, with enough persistence, your suspicions and accusations may drive your partner to rationalize, "If I'm being accused of something I didn't do and being punished for it, I might as well do it."

What are some signs that you may have a tendency to embrace the victim's role? Here are some questions to ask yourself.

AM I SETTING MYSELF UP TO BE THE VICTIM?

- Do I live with a sense of dread that something terrible will happen to me?
- Am I frightened by the unknown, rather than fascinated by it?
- Am I usually suspicious of the motives of others?
- Do I have extreme reactions to those in authority, either submitting to them or rebelling against them?

- Do I look for someone strong to rely on because I feel so weak and vulnerable?
- Do I have difficulty completing projects or being successful at work?
- Do I identify with the underdog?
- Am I frightened of direct expressions of anger?
- Do I always scan the environment for threats?
- Am I a person especially sensitive to danger?
- Am I regularly overwhelmed with feelings of helplessness?
- Are skepticism and doubt prevalent attitudes of mine?
- Do I see life as basically unfair?
- Do I often give in to feelings of self-pity?
- Am I preoccupied with finding safety and security, because they are so elusive?
- Do I have a pessimistic view of the world, expecting the worst for myself and my family?

PATH TO HEALING: BEFRIENDING YOUR FEAR

When you are in the grip of fear, all you want to do is escape it. Your body is tense, your heart is racing and your stomach is in knots. Your mind is whirling with disturbing thoughts and you cannot relax or sleep. You cannot sit still and you feel like jumping out of your skin. Your desire to escape the discomfort is natural. When clients come to me, begging me to rid them of their fear and anxiety, I empathize with their suffering and tell them, "Let's walk through it together and see what we discover." Although I don't tell them in the beginning, eventually I invite them to make friends with their fear instead of viewing it as an enemy.

What are anxiety and fear? They are natural human reactions when we sense danger. They are warning signals that there is some threat on the horizon and we must prepare for it. Anxiety and fear, as signals of danger, serve a survival purpose to help us defend against threats to our well-being. Animals react instinctively to threats by fighting against them, fleeing from them or freezing to become invisible. We humans, who are really animals with developed brains, react in a similar fashion in the face of threats. However, because of our intelligence, we perceive not only present dangers, but possible future threats. Because of our developed memories, we remember past hurts and foresee their repetition in the future. We know that we will face the ultimate threat to our existence someday and try to delay the inevitable as long as possible. We know we are destined to die and live with a fearful sense of mortality. Our intelligence enables us to project into the future and anticipate threats and the consequences of our behaviors to protect ourselves. We can make reasonable plans to avoid the danger and adapt to changing circumstances. Our "what if" thinking can protect us in the face of an uncertain future.

Fear and anxiety naturally make us shrink from life to protect ourselves. We tell ourselves, "I just want to feel safe, to feel in control in my own world." We withdraw to survive. However, protective walls of fear can easily become a prison if we don't develop the capacity to look beyond them. In the grip of fear, we feel out of control in the face of the perceived danger and seek safety.

One path of safety is to worry constantly, to ruminate about the coming catastrophe. We imagine, "If I think hard enough about it, I can prepare myself and be protected." We imagine the worst so we will never be caught off guard or disappointed. In the face of an unknown future, we already have certainty about the worst that can happen. After all, pessimists are never disappointed except by happy events.

We also tell ourselves, "If I worry about it, I can keep it from happening." The worrying mind imagines that somehow, magically, thinking about dangers will cause them not to happen. Like a child, we believe in the power of our fantasies.

However, the belief that worry protects us is an illusion. Indulging in worry may sap our energy to make realistic plans to protect ourselves. It substitutes thinking about the negative for constructive action. Our fear builds an imaginary protective barrier of worry and obsessive thinking about dangers to ward them off. When we hide behind that wall of fear and worry, something is lost. We lose a sense of joy in life and do not live the present moment fully.

Worry can become a drug that seems to give temporary relief from the struggles of life. It can become a deeply ingrained habit of thinking that is preoccupied with the future and worst-case scenarios. The worry keeps us stimulated. Clara, one of my clients, admitted to me, "If I didn't worry, I wouldn't know who I was. I would feel lost." The worry gives them a sense of security, as false as it is, like a drug. They can take a worry pill whenever they feel distressed. But the worry addiction comes at a price. The cost is a constricted life with little joy and freedom.

Make friends with your fears and become well acquainted with them. Fighting them as the enemy will only lead to defeat. Your fears come from within you, from nowhere else. So you are only fighting yourself, making your inner life a painful battlefield. You cannot win the battle against yourself. The alternative strategy I suggest is to embrace your fear lovingly and discover its hidden message for you. There is a wisdom in your fearful reactions that is waiting to be discovered. I recommend a five-step process to befriend and learn from your fear.

1) RECOGNIZE YOUR FEAR AND GIVE IT A NAME.

First, recognize honestly when you are frightened. You may try to suppress your fears, pretending you are strong and courageous. However, true strength and courage is not the absence of fear but living fully in the presence of fear and not allowing it to dominate your life. You may try to delude yourself into thinking that if you deny your fear you gain power over it. Instead, the opposite is true. When feelings are suppressed they grow in intensity, gain a hidden power over your life and express themselves indirectly. The indirect expression of a repressed feeling is a psychological symptom that often brings people into treatment, because it is so painful. The repressed returns with a vengeance.

2) ACCEPT THAT YOU ARE AFRAID.

Second, accept your fear for what it is. Anxiety and fear are facts of life because our existence is conditional. We live constantly under the threat of death, of nonexistence. Fear seeps in naturally as the faces of various threats reveal themselves, motivating us to take action to protect ourselves. It is important to recognize that fear is about the future, about what might happen. The fearful mind, sensitive to danger, engages in "what if" thinking rather than "what is" thinking. If you stop and think about it, the future does not exist and neither does the past. Only the present moment is reality. Many of my clients tell me their greatest fear is of the unknown. I remind them, "The future is always unknown because it does not yet exist. You only imagine you know what will happen." It follows that fear exists only in the imagination about what might happen in the future. It tends to imagine terrible things and worst-case scenarios. Fear actually arises from a preoccupation with the known, with current pleasures that we fear losing. So what you fear is not a fact, but a thought about what might happen. Your fears, like any thought or feeling, pass and have no more reality than you give them. Your thoughts come and go, but you decide what importance to grant them.

3) EXPLORE THE MEANING OF YOUR FEAR.

Third, investigate your fears. Take your fears seriously because they have important messages to give you. You may want to dismiss your fears as overreactions to some situation. But ignore them at your own peril. If you bury your head in the sand, you may not see real threats to your well-being on the horizon and allow yourself to be hurt. Take a close look at what is frightening to you in the moment. Your brain is on high alert. Step back and assess the danger. If you see a realistic threat, take action to protect yourself. For example, if your partner is engaging in behavior that compromises his commitment to your relationship, take some constructive action to address it. Confront him about it and express your fears. If the behavior persists and you come to believe that he is unfaithful, protect yourself by getting out of the relationship. If, after investigating your fear, you see that it exaggerates the threat, try to put it in perspective and let it go. You may not be able to eliminate the fear by looking closely at it, but you can learn to turn down its volume. Your specific fear of the moment may just be mental noise. There is an acronym for unrealistic fear, F.E.A.R.: False Evidence Appearing Real. Do not give your fear more weight than it deserves.

4) LEARN FROM YOUR FEAR.

Next, learn the wisdom of your fear. Fear serves a purpose in alerting you to danger. Observe closely the pattern of your fears or what tends to provoke anxiety in you. Undoubtedly, you will notice that you are not frightened by everything. If you were, you would be paralyzed and could not live. Certain events provoke anxiety in you. For example, you may be afraid of being abandoned, being humiliated, being inadequate, being powerless, etc. Exploring the pattern of your fears can be an avenue to self-awareness of your sensitivities. It is important to know your unique sensitivities so you can take steps to protect yourself as needed. Real dangers exist in life; knowing what threatens you as a person enables you to create zones of safety in your life. Remember that you are not your thoughts and feelings but infinitely more. Your fears alert you to areas of your life that call for self-care.

5) SHARE WITH ANOTHER.

Finally, share what you learn with another. Fear wants to lurk in the darkness where it feeds on you like a cancer and slowly strangles the life out of you. When you expose it to the light of awareness, you begin to see its emptiness. When you take the further step of sharing your fears with someone you trust and listening to their reactions, you see more clearly how you imagined and exaggerated dangers. Sometimes just saying your fears out loud reveals their silliness. In the mirror of feedback from another, you gain a new perspective to sort out the real threats that deserve your attention from the imagined ones that you can dismiss.

Facing your fears becomes a foundation for you to develop the virtues of humility and courage. You don't have to maintain the pretense of always being strong and oblivious to danger. You are only human. In acknowledging your weakness, you become strong. Actually, your strength only becomes evident when you face adversity and all your anxious reactions to it. Courage is not the absence of fear. Being fearless in the face of real danger is crazy and reckless. Rather, genuine courage acknowledges fear and refuses to be ruled by it. It sees fear for what it is and undertakes the required action despite the fear.

PATH TO HEALING: STEPS TO BEFRIENDING FEAR

1) **Recognize honestly when you are frightened.**
2) **Accept your fear for what it is.**
3) **Investigate your fear.**
4) **Learn the wisdom of your fear.**
5) **Share your fear with another.**

Developing courage in the face of fear can help you face the pain of growing up with an unfaithful parent. Accepting the pain courageously will enable you to heal and give up your protective anger toward your parents.

EXERCISE: THE BODY SCAN

Your anxious mind tends to dwell on the future and imagine terrible things happening. You are inclined to become addicted to worry, obsessing about possible danger. The more you worry, the more you live in your head and separate from your body and your current experience. Living in your mind, you disengage from life, which can only be lived in the present moment. You keep yourself busy thinking, not living.

A traditional Eastern practice that cultivates mindfulness of the body is the "body scan." Reflect for a few moments on the nature of your body. You are not alive without it; you live through your body. Through your body, you are rooted to the earth and to the natural world. The physical components of your body unite you with the material world. Your individual cells, which are composed of atoms and molecules, the building blocks of matter, are in continuous exchange with the world. Virtually all the cells of our body participate in an ongoing process of decay and rejuvenation until death.

You act through your body. In particular, your emotions provide an essential link between your mind and your body. Your thoughts generate feelings which come to expression through your body. And your various feelings provoke thoughts that lead to actions.

Through this body scan exercise you can enter into the wonder of your body and fully engage in the present moment. The body cannot live in the future; only the mind can. The body is rooted in the present moment, which is the only reality. Focusing on the sensations of the body can help you break your addiction to worry and ruminating. It can also facilitate being present in your immediate experience. Here is the simple procedure for the body scan:

First, lie down on your back in a comfortable position. Find a place that is quiet where you will not be disturbed. Begin to relax as you lie on the floor and feel the solidity of the floor or carpet meeting your body.

Next, while entering more deeply into relaxation, focus on the rising and falling of your breath. Sense the movement of your abdomen and feel the air flowing through your lungs and out of your mouth. As you focus on your breath, give up dwelling on any thoughts that arise. Do not try to stop the thoughts, but gently acknowledge them and let them go.

Feeling more relaxed following your breath, shift your attention to different areas of your body. Begin with the top of your head and work your way down to the tips of your toes. Pause to notice any places where you feel tension or constriction. The body holds the pain the mind forgets. Observe closely the physical sensation you experience and the quality and intensity of the sensation. For example, the stomach holds much of the tension you experience. What movements, pressures or irritations do you notice? Do you feel cramped, tight or free flowing? Do you feel a churning sensation? Do you sense the release of gastric juices? Also be aware of your reactions to these sensations. Do you feel disturbed by them or relaxed? Stop and pay particular attention to those areas that feel most intensely constricted.

Next, as you bring the light of awareness to the various parts of your body, imagine breathing into that area. Bring the dynamic power of your breath, which represents life, into the different areas of your body. As you continue your body scan, stop at the areas of most tension and breathe deeply into the tension. Allow yourself to feel relaxation enter into the constricted area. Then breathe out with calmness and peace. Breathe into the tension and breathe out peace. Continue this process for at least twenty minutes, allowing enough time for you to enter deeply into relaxation and awareness.

Finally, bring your awareness to your body as a whole. Sense the unity of your body that expresses who you are as a person enlivened by the spirit. You are one with your body and you are one with the universe. After being engaged in this exercise, you should feel refreshed and not as captivated by your anxious mind.

Slowly arise and continue your day, remembering the experience of being in your body. Practice this exercise daily as an antidote to worry.

Chapter 5

The Angry Perfectionist—
Standing Against Reality

Roger came to therapy despondent. His wife had just left him and he felt entirely responsible. "I brought this on myself," he lamented. "It was my temper. I could not control it." After ten years of marriage, his wife walked out, saying she had had enough.

Roger had been battling the anger demon since he was a child who threw temper tantrums when he did not get his way. He tried to be perfect in everything he did, tending to become frustrated with himself. While easily angered by others, proclaiming, "I don't tolerate fools," he was mostly the victim of his own wrath. Whenever he made a mistake he considered foolish, he berated himself mercilessly. Roger realized that he inherited his high standards and quick temper from his parents. His father was a career Army officer who ran his home like a military camp. He gave marching orders to his three children. Roger, the oldest, was expected to be the best. His father constantly challenged him to do better in school, not tolerating any B grades. He also pushed him to excel in sports and Roger became a fierce competitor on the basketball court. However, Roger was bullied in school because he was short. His father taught him to fight for himself. Nevertheless, whenever Roger did not live up to his father's standards, he received a beating. Roger came to believe he could never please his father, yet pushed himself to try, while believing the effort would make him the best. His mother went along with his father's harsh regime, strictly enforcing the rules and dispensing discipline.

After graduating from high school, Roger joined the Marines, thinking to himself, *If you can't beat them, you can join them.* For a brief moment, his father seemed proud of him: "My son, the Marine." Roger adapted well to the harsh regimen of boot camp, because it reminded him of his home. He was proud to be a Marine, among the bravest, the best and most dedicated to the noble ideal of defending freedom and his country. Roger did not realize at the time how little freedom he really enjoyed. He merely sacrificed himself for his standards of perfection, rationalizing, "If you do not advance, you will retreat. No one can rest on his laurels." Nevertheless, Roger thrived on the order, routine and discipline of the military. He quickly advanced in the service. Within a few years, he became a drill sergeant and achieved the reputation of being the best at "making men out of boys." He pushed those under his command mercilessly, like his father had, to make them ready for combat.

While in the service, Roger began dating Joan, a caring and nurturing woman. Her gentleness offset Roger's harsh demandingness. Roger was drawn to her kind, loving nature. She had a way of calming his emotional storms by talking with him rationally and affectionately. After dating for a year and keeping a lid on his anger, they were married. Roger felt some peace for the first time in his life. But soon the stress and strain of daily life together caused Roger to release his pent-up frustrations with Joan. He was especially sensitive to criticism, reacting defensively whenever he sensed Joan was not pleased with him. Her efforts to be helpful often felt like criticism to Roger, and he became increasingly guarded and brittle. Whenever he felt he was being treated unfairly by her, he counterattacked with a verbal barrage. As a drill sergeant, Roger learned how to project his voice and speak with a harsh intensity. He also had the colorful vocabulary of a Marine, which caused the more delicate to wilt. Determined not to be physically violent like his parents, Roger restrained himself to yelling and verbal eruptions. He admitted that he was not in control of his rages. He felt stimulated and powerful when angry, but drained and regretful afterward. "I guess anger is my drug," Roger conceded. An honest man, Roger also admitted that he felt an underlying sense of powerlessness that his rages hid. He lived with the constant fear of failing, an inheritance from his childhood. He believed that if he were not perfect, he would be attacked.

Taking a closer look at his childhood while in therapy, Roger realized that he grew up on a battlefield and saw relationships as power struggles. His parents fought constantly about everything. His father ruled the family with an iron hand and his mother alternately complied with and defied his orders. Deep down, she was as stubborn as he. Tension never left the household, even when his father went away for special assignments. In his father's absence, his mother enforced her own rules and occasionally erupted in anger. Roger never knew what his parents were so angry about. They were like two scorpions trapped in a bottle, constantly going after each other, but never leaving. He wondered what kept his parents together. It appeared that anger was the glue of their relationship and the bond between the parents and children as the kids grew into adulthood.

Then one day his mother suddenly left. Roger was twenty years old at the time. Apparently, his mother had been preparing for her departure in secret, saving money and moving things out of the house. She left a note announcing the end of the marriage and moved in with another woman who became her lifelong partner. Roger was in shock. Later, he learned about his mother's many secret affairs with other women and understood what the fighting was about between his parents.

Roger never told anyone about his mother being a lesbian and secretly wondered about his own sexuality. "How could Dad have kept this from us, and how could I be so clueless?" he asked himself accusingly. Roger was enraged at his mother for abandoning the family. A deep sense of betrayal and confusion set in that nurtured his lifelong resentment.

Roger gradually became determined not to let his anger control him and immersed himself in therapy. "This is the first time I have taken an honest look at myself." He saw a psychiatrist for medication, which gave him a calmness he had never realized was possible.

CHILDHOOD CONNECTION: LIVING IN A WAR ZONE

In a marriage torn apart by infidelity, family life becomes a war zone. The offended partner is enraged, pissed (hence the acronym PISD for post-infidelity stress disorder) and the betrayer often becomes angrily defensive. A hostile atmosphere dominates the household and as a child you become a helpless victim of the fighting. You live in the rubble of your parents' ruined relationship and witness the battles. Sometimes the anger is hot and expressed in verbal explosions, loud arguing and name-calling. It may even erupt in violent behavior which is terrifying to you and leaves an indelible mark. You may think that the blazing anger, expressed in fire and heat, harms you most. Yet the cold anger, the anger which goes underground and creates a hostile atmosphere, can do even more damage.

As a child, you absorb the rage like a sponge and wonder what has caused it. You naturally think with your child's mind that you are the center of the universe and the cause of everything. Therefore, you reason that somehow you caused your parent's anger. "What did I do wrong?" you ask yourself. The fires of self-blame are stoked, fires which continue well into adulthood.

When your parents are so filled with anger, they seek targets for their pent-up frustration and rage. They may fight with each other, either overtly or covertly, and you witness their mutual destruction. Regrettably, you and the other children may become the targets of their overflowing anger. Your parents likely do not know how to cope with all their overwhelming feelings, especially their anger, and seek ways of relieving it. They imagine that by expressing it openly they will find relief. Instead, their frustration mounts, becoming expressed in a near-constant irritable mood. You pick up their mood, wondering if they are angry with you and what you did to deserve it. And worse, your parents may displace their pent-up rage onto you, treating you like they treat each other. They may assault you verbally, pick on you and even punish you excessively. You may become the victim of physical abuse. Inexcusably, they may even become violent with you. You may become a verbally and physically abused child, living out the ramifications of that for the rest of your life.

Furthermore, when your parents are so consumed by their problems and their anger about them, there is little energy left for them to be responsible, nurturing parents. Preoccupied with their own needs, they lack attention for the children, who are often left on their own. Many clients have told me that their parents were so troubled that they had to raise themselves. In fact, many had to take parenting roles with their younger siblings. They suffered a lost childhood, growing up to be little adults as children. Anger has a way of becoming all-consuming, burning up the angry person like a raging fire. What is left for the children? Nothing but ashes.

Your parents' anger is contagious and infects you like a plague. The rage runs rampant through the family, and no one escapes its reach. You become angry with the parent who betrayed the family, causing all the hurt and turmoil you experience. Even though you may have some sympathy for the betrayed parent, you may also experience anger toward him or her for allowing, ignoring or not protecting the family from the infidelity. Your anger may frighten you and you may not know how to express it. Being so angry with the parents you depend on for survival scares you and threatens the emotional bond you need with them. Furthermore, your rage provokes guilt. "Parents deserve honor, respect and obedience," you learned. Your aggressive feelings toward them contradict long-established societal values.

Reflect on what you are learning about intimate relationships. For better or worse, your parents' marriage is your model, always at least as a shadow in the background of your own relationships. You begin to form the image of marriage as a battleground, a constant, relentless power struggle in which there are no winners. There is no peace or resolution of conflict. You also identify with your parents: either with the aggressor, the unfaithful parent who exhibited hostility in having an affair, or with the rage of the offended parent. Witnessing their anger, you are both fascinated and frightened by its power. You may become an overtly angry person, unable to control your temper. You experience that anger like a drug, which makes you feel powerful for a moment but results in feelings of guilt and despair in the wake of destroyed relationships. The harm to yourself and your loved ones soon becomes evident, filling you with shame and guilt. Or you may become so frightened by your anger that you bury it, expressing it indirectly in passive-aggressive behavior, a depressed mood or health problems. Anger is like a poison which eats away at your body and mind.

Being either under-controlled or over-controlled in your anger has devastating effects on your relationships. Your loved ones pick up on your simmering rage. It cannot be disguised. The anger keeps them at a distance, afraid of you. They fear some outburst, either verbally in sarcastic, critical remarks or physically in abusive behavior. The anger, even if suppressed, will motivate your partner to flee in fear for his or her safety. It may even drive him or her into the arms of another, completing the circle of repeating your parents' unhappy, unfaithful marriage.

Here are some signs you may be susceptible to an anger sickness.

AM I ALWAYS ANGRY?

- Do I dwell on past hurts?
- Do I tend to hold a grudge?
- Do I have high standards which I refuse to compromise?
- Am I easily impatient with myself and others?
- Do I judge myself and others harshly?
- Am I a perfectionist?
- Do I take myself too seriously?
- Am I sensitive to criticism?
- Am I easily offended by the words and actions of others?
- Do I have a temper?
- Do I become resentful when I do not get what I want?
- Do I think my way is the only right way?
- Am I demanding of myself and others?
- Do I compare myself with others and think I am superior?
- Do I become upset when my routine is disturbed?

PATH OF HEALING: TAMING YOUR ANGER

Angry people believe they are possessed by a demon and want me, as their therapist, to exorcise it: "I hate my anger. Help me get rid of it." They feel helpless in the clutches of the anger. They expect that I can perform some miracle to rid them of that hated feeling. Anger is their enemy and they are bound to defeat it. Their strategy is to engage the enemy in battle to overcome it. They hate the feeling and fight it with all their strength. In the process, they use the weapons of the enemy, hatred and rage expressed in self-criticism, expecting to outwit him. They seek to beat anger with anger. Instead, they deepen the enemy's hold on them, increasing their sense of helplessness and frustration.

I offer them a different approach, a proven strategy combining both ancient spiritual traditions and modern psychology. I invite them to love their enemy, to embrace their anger with love, which assures them that the only path to freedom is through acceptance and love. Almost without fail, the reaction of my clients is stunned disbelief. "How can I love something I hate so much in myself? How can I love something that has caused me and those I love so much harm?" they ask. I respond, "You hate your anger because you do not understand it and do not see its beauty." So I encourage them to get to know their anger intimately: what causes it, how it arises and how it expresses itself. And as they make friends with their anger, I assure them that it will become their ally. Their head-scratching reaction does not deter me and I ask them to change their relationship with their feelings and not the feelings themselves.

I proceed to teach them to be astute observers of themselves and to stand back from all their reactions while noticing how they rise and fall. I explain that all of our thoughts, feelings and sensations are like waterfalls, streams of consciousness that flow without stopping. As much as we believe to the contrary, these thoughts, feelings and sensations are not us, but only come from us. Consequently, we can stand back and observe. We have three choices regarding the stream of consciousness. We can try to stop it, as many want to do. But that does not work. You can check that out with your own experience. The pressure builds and the dammed up feelings burst through, overwhelming you. Or they seep around the imaginary dams you build and are expressed indirectly. The thoughts, feelings and sensations cannot be stopped effectively.

A second approach, again pursued by many, is to jump into the stream and indulge in the thoughts, feelings and sensations. This group identifies with the feelings as natural and lets themselves go with the flow. But eventually, they drown in the feelings and lose themselves.

The third approach, which I strongly advocate, is to observe the flow of thoughts, feelings and sensations and try to understand them. We can bring the light of awareness to that ongoing stream of consciousness.

Another image I use to explain the nature of feelings is that of the clouds. Thoughts, feelings and sensations are like clouds that are really mists of water that constantly float by. Sometimes it seems like storm clouds arise and never leave for an extended period of time. But all clouds eventually pass. What remains is blue sky. I tell my clients, "You are the blue sky that is clear and lasts; the clouds come and go."

1) RECOGNIZE AND EMBRACE YOUR ANGER.

"What about anger? How can I ever love my anger?" you may ask. Consider what life would be like for you in the real world, not the fantasy world you would like to live in, if you did not ever get angry. People would push you around and you would not stand up for yourself. You would remain passive in all circumstances and not fight back. You would not have the energy or motivation to overcome the obstacles you inevitably face in life. You would become a victim in a hostile, competitive world.

I believe Charles Darwin's theory of natural selection was right. Only the fittest survive in this competitive world. What is true of the plants and animals is also true of us. In short, anger helps us to survive in a tough and brutal world. It arises from sensitivity to being wronged or threatened and leads to a desire to retaliate to protect ourselves. Anger serves a survival purpose, stimulating us to have an active response to a perceived threat. It gives us the energy to protect and assert ourselves.

You may not like to admit you are angry, because anger had such a bad reputation when you were growing up. It may have been associated with violent behavior, stubbornness, verbal abuse and temper outbursts. However, it is important to recognize that how anger is expressed is very different from the feeling of anger. Anger is the energy to assert and fight for yourself and can be expressed in either a constructive or destructive manner. The first step in healing is to recognize and embrace your anger for the neutral feeling that it is. Become familiar with your personal signs of anger, such as feelings of tension in your body, clenched teeth, withdrawing into silence and thoughts of retaliation. Be aware of the subtle emotional and mental tugs that signify the initial arising of an irritation that can grow into full-scale fury.

2) EXPLORE THE MEANING OF YOUR ANGER.

Admitting to yourself that you are angry is the first step; the second is to explore its meaning. Anger is a secondary emotion, a reaction to something we perceive as threatening to what we value, often our self-esteem. You react with anger according to the meaning you give to an event. If you feel attacked in some way, you automatically want to counter-attack in anger. Think of anger as a howling baby that needs to be nursed. When you are angry, it indicates that something is not right for you. You are in pain. Your angry reaction, like tears, may be the only way that you can express your discomfort. Ask yourself, "What am I really angry about?" Often you are feeling insecure and offended by what someone says or does. You feel diminished and must strike back to restore the balance of power. You may also feel frightened that something important to you is being threatened and you have to defend yourself. Furthermore, you may maintain an unrealistic image of perfection for yourself and feel violated when you are criticized or make a mistake. Beneath anger lies hurt feelings, sadness or fear. Unless you understand the feelings that underlie the angry reaction, you will always feel powerless in its grip. Exploring precisely what you are angry about reveals your tender spots that need to be protected and nurtured, like a crying baby.

A common cause of anger is disappointment. Resentment arises from unfulfilled expectations. The world and others do not behave the way we think they should. Your anger may reveal a rift within your own psyche. You have many expectations and ideas of how the world should be for yourself and others. You react instinctively with anger when your expectations are not fulfilled. Without knowing it, you may be living in your own mental world of "should" and not in the world as it is. You are living under "the tyranny of the should," your ideas of how you wish life would be. Pay close attention to your expectations of yourself and others. How realistic are your expectations? Do you allow yourself and others the freedom to be themselves? Ask yourself if it is fair to impose your expectations and your wishes on yourself and others.

Anger also springs from hurt feelings. When you have been offended by someone, you want to retaliate and make the other person feel the hurt you feel. "They deserve it," you rationalize. If the person is someone you care deeply about, their offense leads you to believe that they do not care about you. Expressing your anger to them can have an added purpose. It is a test to see if they will tolerate your anger displays and still show love. Your anger tends to push them away. If they stay, you feel assured that they still care. But that is a dangerous game that can destroy relationships.

3) DECIDE HOW TO ACT.

After recognizing the source of your reaction, you can decide how best to respond. You do not always have to fight fire with fire. You can stop to think about responding in a way that furthers your best interest. Approach your anger with wisdom, figuring out the best way to use the energy of the anger, which gives you strength and endurance to assert yourself and fight when needed. You can make a controlled response to any perceived threat to your well-being or self-esteem. You can channel the energy of the anger to overcome obstacles and achieve your own goals, rather than dissipate its energy in an ineffective response like yelling and screaming. Your anger is a power that can be used for positive purposes.

Remember that your anger is the outer armor that protects the soft, vulnerable insides. If you stay in an angry state you will be protected for a while. But the anger will seep inside like a poison and destroy you. As twelve-step programs teach so insightfully, "Nurturing anger is like consuming rat poison, expecting the rat to die." Your anger can eventually kill you, causing numerous medical problems like cancer, high blood pressure and heart disease.[4] It can also kill you emotionally because it will push people away and isolate you.

PATH TO HEALING: STEPS TO TAMING YOUR ANGER

1) **Recognize and do not shun your anger.**
2) **Explore the cause and meaning of your angry reaction.**
3) **Decide how best to respond to your anger.**

In your struggles with anger, you have probably identified with your parents in their excessive anger over being betrayed. You can use your self-understanding to learn about your parents and their struggles. Beneath their anger and destructive behavior, they felt profoundly wounded by the betrayal. Become sensitive to their pain, and not preoccupied with their hurtful behavior. Let the compassion you begin to feel for yourself overflow to them.

EXERCISE: REMAINING LIKE A LOG

You may feel like a prisoner of your anger and hate, unable to escape its domination. With anger, more than any other emotion, there is a powerful, seemingly irresistible impulse to act. Once the anger has gained momentum, like an avalanche, nothing can stop it. The secret in working with anger is to learn to be slow to react and quick to stop and pay attention to your thoughts and feelings as they arise. It is important to nip the reaction in the bud and learn its wisdom. You are angry for a reason, but often the real underlying reason eludes you because you are caught up in your passionate reaction in the moment. When you stop, look and listen to your rising anger, you gain valuable information about your sensitivities and need for protection.

An ancient Eastern exercise from the classic text *The Way of the Bodhisattva* provides helpful advice for those who feel helpless in the grip of anger:

> When the urge arises in the mind
> To feelings of desire or wrathful hate,
> Do not act! Be silent, do not speak!
> And like a log of wood be sure to stay.[5]

The sage's advice is to remain still like a log when anger arises and not react. Remaining like a log means following the middle path between ignoring the feeling, pretending you are not angry, and indulging it by acting it out. The middle path is one of self-awareness. If you deny your anger, it will build up and take control of your life in unconscious ways. Resentment will grow like a cancer and eventually erupt either inwardly in health problems or outwardly in destructive, hostile actions. Remaining like a log keeps you in contact with the energy of your anger through the power of mindful awareness. It brings the greater power of the mind into your emotions.

To remain still like a log makes a commitment to being aware of, not reacting to, your feelings. Our culture invites us to be spontaneous and to go with the flow. But more often, what is praised as spontaneous and natural is really impulsive and self-centered. You need to become committed to pausing before acting. In that pregnant pause you bring the wisdom of your mind to the energy of your emotions. Learning to pause requires exercise and dedicated effort, like body

building. We train the mind like we train the body—with perseverance and effort.

Be attentive to the first stirrings of anger. It arises as a subtle
annoyance, an irritation or a sense of frustration. A thought or memory of some hurtful event may tug at your emotions. A comment or
behavior of someone you encounter or a situation is distasteful to
you and triggers an angry reaction. You perceive something as being
threatening or wrongful. Acknowledge the irritation. Do not hide the
feeling from yourself.

Next, be aware of the spontaneous thoughts that accompany
the irritation. Develop an attitude of curiosity about all the thoughts
that arise and avoid judging yourself. Do not tell yourself, *That's silly;
that shouldn't bother me; I'm just too sensitive.* All of your feelings are
important and provide valuable information for your well-being. The
spontaneous thoughts give clues to the message of the feelings. They
reveal sensitivities that need to be taken seriously. Ignore your sensitivities at your own peril. Carefully notice the thoughts of hurt, fear
and revenge.

If you ignore the subtle frustration and the accompanying
thoughts, the anger can quickly snowball into an avalanche that will
overwhelm you. Next, pay attention to the patterns of your thoughts.
You will notice that you tell yourself stories to explain the reactions of
yourself and others. You may notice familiar patterns of thinking that
emerge: *You can't disrespect me; I deserve better than that; you shouldn't
behave that way toward me.* We all tell ourselves stories about how we
think our lives should be and react with fear, hurt and outrage when
reality does not match our expectations. Be aware of your expectations regarding yourself and others that become clear in the stories
you tell yourself. At this point, you can stand back and analyze what is
really going on. What is the real threat, the real wrong, the real hurt?

Finally, having gathered all this information about yourself and
your reaction in the moment, you can decide how to act in a way that
is most beneficial to you, the other person and the situation. You can
decide whether to be silent, to speak up or to take action. The anger
energizes you to act, but you must decide how to use the energy in a
constructive way. Aware of the destructive potential of your anger,
you restrain yourself in order to channel that energy. Often, our
anger reveals that some boundary has been violated and we need to
set limits to protect ourselves. How do you need to protect yourself

and fight for your well-being in this moment? What response would be in your best interest?

Anger is one of our most powerful emotions. Its energy can be used for constructive or destructive purposes, so it needs to be handled with care. You may find that working with your anger is too dangerous to do alone. Do not hesitate to consult a counselor, trusted partner or friend in learning to work with this dynamic emotion.

Embracing your anger by remaining still demonstrates to yourself that you are not helpless in the face of intense, seemingly overwhelming emotion. It reminds you that you are not your thoughts and feelings, although they come from you and reveal something about you. You, as a person, with your wise mind, can transcend your stormy reactions to life.

Chapter 6

The Proud Caretaker—
Feeling Superior in Love

Susan, an attractive young nurse, came to therapy complaining of "burnout." "I'm so exhausted, I don't think I can go on anymore," she complained. She could not sleep and always felt tired. Headaches, neck and back pains plagued her. She felt depressed and wanted only to sleep when she was not at work. "That's not me," she lamented.

Susan had been working in a hospital emergency room for the past seven years since graduating from nursing school at the top of her class. She loved the excitement of treating patients in crisis and comforting distressed family members. She took pride in knowing exactly what needed to be done in any critical situation and worked harder than any of her coworkers. Her supervisors also recognized her ability and promoted her to a supervisory position in the emergency room.

Susan loved her job and she worked long hours, accepting any extra shifts offered. She said she needed the money, because her husband had a seasonal job. Mark worked construction during the summer when jobs were available and plowed snow in the winter. He had a lot of free time which he used to indulge his hobbies of hunting, fishing and snow-mobiling. Susan and Mark had a daughter and Mark became the "stay-at-home Dad" when he was not working or it did not interfere with his hobbies. Susan was the rock on which the family rested securely.

Mark and Susan met in high school. She was attracted to him because he was so fun-loving and carefree. He knew how to make her laugh. Susan was a bookworm and Mark had a way of getting her out of her shell to participate in his adventures and have fun. They went to parties, dances and the prom. Because she was so beautiful, many boys had asked her out. She had briefly dated guys she recognized as "bad boys," because they were exciting. But the relationships never lasted. It was different with Mark. He knew how to joke with her and help her not take herself so seriously.

When Susan and Mark were married, they appeared to be a perfect match. Mark's carefree attitude balanced Susan's conscientious seriousness. Susan finished nursing school and pursued her lifelong passion to help others and make a difference in the world. Mark worked at a leisurely pace and kept their social life alive by dragging Susan to parties. All went well until their daughter, Jennifer, was born. Mark's activities proceeded as if they were still a newly-married couple, while Susan assumed all the responsibility for child care and keeping the house organized. The arguments began and Mark displayed a side of his personality she had never seen before, his temper. After she begged him for help around their home, he exploded in anger and left the house. She noticed he began drinking more and smoking marijuana. Frequently, arguments ended with him going to a bar. Susan was feeling overwhelmed and Mark hardly noticed. Her distress reached a boiling point when she discovered one night that he was indulging in pornography. Despite his denials, a search of his computer history revealed that he had become a regular user almost every night for a long time. That helped explain his loss of sexual interest in her.

Susan had always taken pride in her ability to handle her own problems and everyone else's. She saw herself as a strong, independent person who wanted to help others. It was only her desperation and her fear of having a breakdown that brought her to therapy. Initially, she had trouble talking about herself, focusing instead on all the trouble her husband and others were causing her. But slowly she began to look inward, noticing how difficult it was to know herself and what she wanted. She was only aware of her unhappiness, which she assumed that others caused.

Recalling her childhood, Susan related that all she wanted to do was please her father, who was a demanding, critical man. She never knew exactly what her father wanted, or what would make him happy.

He seemed so depressed, and Susan wanted to rescue him from his misery. He drank to sedate himself, falling asleep each night after a few drinks. Her mother, an equally gloomy person, often withdrew to the bedroom as a refuge. Many times, Susan entered a room and found her crying for reasons she did not know. Immediately, she went to hug her mother, offering comfort, which was hungrily accepted. But her mother never gave a clue to the cause of her sadness.

Susan was the oldest of five children. From as early as she could remember, her parents expected her to care for the younger children, bathing, changing and feeding them, while her parents withdrew into their own worlds. She became an expert caregiver, taking pride in her dedication and efficiency and never considering the emotional price she was paying

When she turned twenty, a light went on. Her mother told her that she was born out of wedlock and the man she thought to be her father was not. The news stunned her. But it also explained why her father was so distant, demanding and critical of her. She was not his child and he considered her an embarrassing intrusion in the family. Susan sensed her exclusion and worked hard at caring for the younger children to gain acceptance and approval. In that unusual moment of candor, her mother also revealed that the father Susan grew up with had many affairs which her mother kept secret from everyone. Susan then understood her mother's depression and tears and felt sympathy for her. Her desire to be a caretaker was forged with the pain of her parents' infidelity.

Susan still loved Mark, but knew something had to change. She could not change him, but realized she could change herself. She joined Al-Anon, a group for friends and family of problem drinkers that offers support and understanding. "When I understand myself and am strong enough, I will decide what to do about my marriage," she told herself. Her assertiveness caught Mark's attention and he joined Alcoholics Anonymous.

CHILDHOOD CONNECTION:
WHO CARES ABOUT ME?

When one of your parents is unfaithful, both are absorbed in finding a way to survive the wreckage of their marriage. Your offended parent often suffers from symptoms similar to post-traumatic stress disorder, as has been mentioned previously. She feels overwhelmed with anxiety, depression and rage, hanging on for dear life just to survive. The betrayer expends enormous energy leading a double life, torn between a sense of responsibility for his family and his passionate desires, constructing a web of lies. Little time, energy or attention are left for the children, who often feel abandoned. The children may even imagine that something is wrong with them, causing their parents to withdraw.

How does a child cope with the parenting void? At some level the child senses the parents are not around much and are not active parents, although the child likely does not understand what personal struggles consumed the mother and father. The betrayed parent may have turned to the son or daughter for support and assistance in caring for the other children. The child felt deeply the insecurity created by the parents' absence, unconsciously looking for the child's own way to survive. Like all children who see themselves as the center of the universe and the cause of all that happens, the child may have blamed him or herself for the unhappiness. Seeds of guilt were planted as well as the desire to rescue unhappy parents and siblings.

If you tended to be a responsible child, as the oldest often is, you coped with the anxiety of your home by trying to be as helpful as you could be. You kept yourself busy and distracted by taking care of your younger siblings and being "mommy's little helper." Your parents perhaps showed some appreciation and began to expect more and more of you. And you expected more and more of yourself. Soon you became like a responsibility magnet, taking on whatever task needed to be done. Others noticed how much you were doing and said admiringly, "Look what a good little girl she is." The adulation, which filled the void of neglect and self-blame, propelled you to work harder. The payoff for all your work was the admiration of others and a hollow sense of self-satisfaction that could not really fill the emptiness of your longing to be loved and cared for yourself.

As you grew older, you became even more expert at caring for others and taking on heavy responsibilities, which brought more praise and recognition. Your sense of responsibility also led to many achievements, which bolstered a self-esteem more fragile than anyone around you imagined. Without knowing it, you may have become addicted to the caretaking role, pushing yourself to work hard for the brief pleasures of others' approval and moments of accomplishment. Yet you were little aware of the cost to you personally, until you were overcome with exhaustion and the disillusionment of being so neglected. You lost a sense of who you were as a person.

When you chose a mate in life, your temperament guided your choice. As a caretaker, needing to be needed to survive, you chose a person who needed to be cared for. You chose a partner who depended on you, an immature person who later could resent you for acting like his mother. Without knowing it, you identified with your victimized parent and grew to feel drained by your needy partner. The pressure of unhappiness may build so much in such a relationship that either you or your partner may want to escape into an affair.

What are some signs that you may be drawn to the caretaking role as a way to manage your anxiety? Consider these questions.

Am I a Caretaker?

- Am I the first to volunteer for tasks and take on responsibilities?
- Do I take pride in my ability to get things done right?
- Do I like to be in control in any situation?
- Do I work hard to gain others' approval?
- Am I especially sensitive to being rejected?
- Am I perceptive of others' needs, but oblivious to my own?
- Do I have difficulty asking for help?
- Do I often feel guilty for not doing enough?
- Do relationships seem unbalanced to me because I give more than I receive?
- Do I derive my greatest satisfaction from helping others?
- Do I pride myself on being sensitive and intuitive about others' feelings?
- Do I see myself as a people pleaser?
- Do I need to be needed?
- Do I often feel controlled by the expectations of others?
- Do I have a nagging sense of being taken advantage of by people?

PATH TO HEALING: MAKING YOURSELF A PRIORITY

If you are a caretaker, you are not likely to go to a therapist for help unless you are feeling desperate. You see yourself as competent and well-practiced in caring for others. You hold yourself to high standards of care. People depend on you, you don't depend on them. But at some point the imbalance in your relationships becomes an impossible burden. You become so drained that you cry out, "I can't do this anymore." Often your body tells you before your mind fully realizes it. You cannot sleep and you suffer aches and pains. Your stomach churns, your back hurts and you have headaches. You feel a deep restlessness and cannot relax. Your mind whirls with a confusion of thoughts that will not stop. It may reach the point that you believe you are having a nervous breakdown before you ask for help.

Sessions with caretakers often go like this. "I had a good week," they offer as an opening.

I return, "What made the week good?"

"I felt better and didn't have any problems," they respond.

"What makes feeling better and not having problems so good?"

"It's better than feeling worse and having problems," they say defensively. Then, I invite them to notice how quickly they judge themselves, rather than just simply being curious about their experience. All feelings, even the unpleasant ones, are valuable paths to self-awareness. And problems open our minds and hearts to self-exploration.

I welcome those burdened with caring for others and judging themselves so quickly, inviting them to relax with themselves and find refreshment. I tell them they are not going crazy; by coming for help they have taken a huge step toward recovery. As the therapy unfolds, I help them understand that they have become addicted to the role of caretaking, which has drained them of life. Like any addict, they will change only when they realize that the trouble their caretaking behavior causes them outweighs the benefits. There are many benefits in caring for others. You feel satisfaction and enjoy the admiration of others. You take pride in your accomplishments on behalf of others. But the hidden cost can be considerable.

When you feel so drained by caring for others and resentful that no one pays attention to your needs, listen to your pain. If no one seems to make you a priority, consider making yourself a priority.

Because caretakers are natural-born fixers, they are drawn to those who are broken and "need fixing." They possess an unfailing intuitive sense of others' needs and respond immediately and generously. But do they include themselves among the people they help? Are they as perceptive of their own needs as they are of those close to them? Do they even see themselves as needy?

Another name for caretaking is codependency, a term used in substance abuse recovery circles. Caretakers, like codependents, become so preoccupied with attending to the needs of others that they become disconnected from their own needs. In fact, attending to others becomes a way of avoiding themselves. They become astute at discerning what others need but out of touch with their own needs. In sacrificing themselves to care for others, they lose themselves. Another image of the caretaker/codependent is the martyr, who sacrifices his life for a noble purpose. But if you scratch below the surface of the caretaking role, you uncover a huge reservoir of anxiety, low self-esteem and the need to control, much like any addict.

You might be surprised to learn that the twelve-step program of Alcoholics Anonymous (AA) applies equally to family members of alcoholics who are codependent as well as to caretakers. As the alcoholic is addicted to liquor, the codependent is addicted to controlling the alcoholic's behavior. In similar fashion, the caretaker is addicted to the role of helping others. His self-esteem rises and falls according to the reaction of others.

You might ask, "What's so bad about wanting to help others?"

I respond, "Nothing, unless it becomes compulsive and too exclusive." Caretaking becomes compulsive when it leads to self-neglect and efforts to exert a godlike control over others. You exclude yourself from the circle of care. The freedom to step back from the role, from helping behavior, disappears. You feel driven to help and assume responsibility, even if it does not make sense to you. You may feel guilty when you do not help, set limits or say "no." You feel like you can never do enough for others and do not know how to relax with yourself. In the face of such addictive behavior, recovery begins with acceptance. To paraphrase the first step of AA: "I admit that I am powerless over my caretaking and that my life has become unmanageable because of it."[6] What a relief to step back and begin focusing your attention and care on yourself.

When the pain leads you to admit your addiction, you can begin to let go of your compulsive behavior and come to understand it. As a good-hearted caretaker, you are driven by a rescue fantasy. You want to save others as a way of saving yourself. Your religious upbringing may have reinforced that way of thinking. Loving God and your neighbor summarizes the essence of religion. But read the love commandment more carefully. It reads, "Love your neighbor as yourself." The key word is "as," not "more than" or "less than" yourself. In other words, love others in the same way and to the extent that you love yourself. Caring for others naturally overflows from healthy self-care. The command to love implies a balance in loving yourself and your neighbor. What you have lost is that sense of balance, caring for others at your own expense. Caring for others is a wonderful quality, but if you have lost yourself in the care-taking role, you have not sufficiently included yourself.

To help achieve a realistic sense of balance, I recommend that you reflect on the Serenity Prayer: "Grant me the serenity to accept the things I cannot change, the courage to change the things I can and the wisdom to know the difference."[7] You are limited in your ability to change other people and many circumstances in your life. It takes honesty and humility to accept those limitations and not give in to compulsive guilt. However, you have the ability to change your own attitudes, behavior and life, needing only the courage to face yourself with honesty.

I recommend a four-step process—stop, look, listen and talk—to help restore a sense of balance and control over your own life.

1) STOP RUNNING IN CIRCLES.

First of all, force yourself to stop. Your whole life has revolved around taking action to assist others. You live your life in constant motion, if not in acting, in making plans of action and evaluating your performance. "How can I help? What do I need to do next? How can I get this job done and do it better?" you keep asking yourself. You hardly recognize the anxiety that is driving your need to stay busy and focused on caring for others. Staying busy distracts you from yourself. You feel restless and guilty when you stop, so you stay busy to avoid the discomfort. However, recovery will not begin until you make a firm decision to cease the obsessive thinking and compulsive behavior. Face the discomfort of stillness and quiet and see what emerges.

2) LOOK AT YOUR LIFE.

Next, make the effort to look carefully at your life. You are so accustomed to acting that your actions in caring for others, without taking sufficient time for reflection, have become automatic. You may think you plan well what you do, but in reality your behavior is more programmed than you imagine. You want to please others and make them happy. What you do not see so clearly is your need for approval and the anxiety it provokes when others are disappointed in you. You may identify the feeling as guilt for not living up to your standards. But in reality, you risk losing the approval of others if you do not do what they expect of you. Anxiety drives you, which you attempt to manage by caring for others.

When you stop to look closely, you will notice the patterns of behavior in your relationships. You will immediately observe how much more you give to others than you receive from them. People expect you to offer your services and may become demanding of you. In turn, you grow to expect much of yourself, never asking if those expectations are realistic. Furthermore, you will observe your own hesitancy to ask for help and discomfort in accepting compliments. Consequently, people, caught up in the image you portray, see you as being strong and never needing help. They do not see your lonely heart crying out for nurturing. In overextending yourself to help others, you notice that they become dependent on you, not making the effort to care sufficiently for themselves. Some call it "idiot compassion" when caregivers persist in doing for others what they can do for themselves. In their dependency, those cared for both love and hate the person they rely on.

3) LISTEN TO YOURSELF.

Third, listen attentively to the stirrings of your own heart. You are so accustomed to focusing your gaze outward, sensitized to the needs of others, that you never listen to the desires within you crying out for attention. You know exactly what is best for others, but are clueless about your own needs and desires. I encourage you to extend your natural compassion and generosity to yourself, and not be so exclusive in your love. Let your all-embracing love include you. After all, you deserve care as much as those you serve. However, knowing accurately what you need will require effort, determination and a shift of focus. You will need to learn to listen to yourself and take your desires seriously.

4) SHARE YOURSELF WITH ANOTHER.

Finally, talk with someone—your partner, a close friend or a counselor. Share with that person what you are experiencing and learning about yourself. It may be a new experience for you to rely on someone else. Take the risk. After overcoming your initial resistance, you will be amazed at how relieved you feel to be understood and supported by another. You may also be surprised at what you gain from the feedback of others who can confront some of your distorted thinking. In the interaction, new insights and perspectives may emerge, leading you to self-learning. Remember how good you feel helping others, listening to them, offering support. Can you imagine that others may want to do the same for you and would feel contentment doing these things for you?

You will struggle in your recovery and have many relapses. The rewards for being a caretaker are considerable. Caretakers sense their power and importance in being needed. Knowing what is best for others and doing for them fills them with pride. They enjoy the admiration, gratitude and approval of others. It fills an unrecognized void in their lives. Your addictive mind will keep you chasing the high of proud accomplishments and enslaved in your addictive behavior. Yet your rational mind will see clearly the emotional and physical cost of your caretaking and how you enslave others by making them dependent on you. You feel exploited and victimized. Your rational mind will guide you in the search for a healthy balance in your life, neither neglecting yourself nor others.

PATH OF HEALING: STEPS TO SELF-CARE

1) **Stop all your running around and judging.**
2) **Look carefully at your life.**
3) **Listen attentively to the stirrings of your heart.**
4) **Talk with someone about what you discover.**

As you progress in the practice of stopping, looking and listening, you will let go of your disguised caretaking pride and grow in honesty and humility. You will see more clearly and accept more willingly your limits in rescuing others. The lines of responsibility, where yours end and others' begin, will become more evident. You will bring more wisdom to your compassionate behavior. Knowing the truth about yourself and putting it into practice will set you free. As you grow in honesty, humility and compassion, you will find it within yourself to forgive your parents, who deprived you of the nurturing you needed because they were caught up in their dance of infidelity.

EXERCISE: DISCERNMENT OF SPIRITS

Since you have been so busy taking care of people, you may have been neglecting yourself without being fully aware of it. Consequently, you will need to find a way to become better acquainted with yourself. Your lack of self-awareness will likely become painfully evident when you are faced with important life decisions, like whether or not to stay in a relationship or whether to change residences, a job or church affiliation. If you are a believer, as I am, in the presence of a higher power, our next exercise can be of special help. We'll focus on a practice from the Christian spiritual tradition to become more aware of the deepest desires of your heart to aid in decision-making. It is called "the discernment of spirits," a practice taught and used on retreats by St. Ignatius Loyola, the founder of the Jesuit religious order. In making decisions, you must know yourself, your deepest desires, in order to make a wise decision in your best interest.

The everyday practice of stopping, looking and listening begins the process of self-awareness and of taking yourself seriously. Paying attention to what arises when you are quiet and still reveals many thoughts, feelings and beliefs that are below the surface of your normal consciousness. The practice of "discernment of spirits" can reveal deeper levels of your consciousness for those who are religiously inclined. You do not have to be Christian to benefit from this exercise, just someone open to a "higher power" in life. That "higher power," whom some call God with a variety of names, can guide your decision-making.

Begin by placing yourself in the prayerful presence of God, however you conceive him. Some view God as a supreme being who stands above the universe, overseeing and directing events. I see God as a mysterious, hidden presence in our hearts that is one with the universe. God is intimately involved in our lives, not as separate from us as we may think. He speaks to us in the stillness of our hearts. Find a quiet place with no distractions, possibly a place you consider sacred. That sacred place is where you are accustomed to praying. Ask God for enlightenment so you may see clearly what he wants for you, how you can best serve him. According to all religious traditions, God desires our eternal happiness. Thus our personal happiness corresponds with giving him glory and doing his will.

Next, bring your decision to God in prayer. In preparation for this prayerful moment, it is helpful to write in a journal your reflections on the change you are considering. Take two pieces of paper and draw a line down the middle of each. On the first page, write the advantages of remaining where you are on one side, and the disadvantages on the other. Try to be as honest as you can about your thoughts and feelings about the proposed change, whether it is about your relationship, job or overall state in life. Write freely, letting the thoughts flow. On the second page, write the advantages of making the change on one side, and the disadvantages on the other. Now reflect prayerfully on the alternatives you are considering, asking God for honesty and courage in making the decision. Consider carefully the costs and benefits of your proposed decision.

Seek clarity in your decision. If clarity does not emerge after this initial time spent in prayer, think more deeply about which decision is more consistent with the movement of your own life history. Step back and look at the flow of your life up to this point. Typically, clarity will emerge slowly out of darkness and will require patience. Despite continuing doubt, make a tentative decision and pray about it, asking God for confirmation. Live with the tentative decision for a while in your mind and see how it feels. A sustained sense of inner peace will normally follow a wise decision, even though you may feel considerable anxiety about following through with the decision.

If you do not experience a sense of inner peace, repeat the process at a later date. Repeat the practice as often as you need until you arrive at a place of serenity. Persistent turmoil indicates that you are not yet ready for the decision. Following the spirit of your true self leads to feelings of courage, strength, consolation and peace. Following the spirit of your false self results in anxiety, sadness, confusion and inner disturbance. Peacefulness cannot be forced but it will come with patience and confidence in God's loving presence in your life. Remember that you were born to be happy and at peace with yourself and the universe.

Entering honestly and courageously into your own struggles to know yourself and make wise decisions will help you understand your parents. They obviously struggled with a life-or-death decision about their relationship because of the affair. Whether or not it is evident to you, your unfaithful parent faced inner turmoil in deciding to have the affair. Both your parents faced a crisis in deciding whether or not to stay together. Your own laboring at decision-making may help you to have compassion for them and eventually to forgive them.

Part 3

Those Who Disengage in Relationships

Chapter 7

The Grasping Avoider— Hanging On in Quiet Desperation

Jake fulfilled his lifelong dream when he moved to an island and built his own home. He had lived in the big city all his life, hating the pandemonium and confusion. "I can't think clearly with all those people around making so much noise," he complained. So when the opportunity came for him to buy a small piece of land on a nearby island, Jake jumped on it. He bought a plot in a wooded area that was secluded from any neighbors. Not married, Jake devoted all his free time to planning and building his dream house. He designed the structure himself, making it environmentally sensitive. His plan also included bringing in the natural beauty of the surroundings with large windows and skylights. He bragged that he built his home without incurring any debt, completing projects only as the funds became available and doing much of the work himself.

Jake had always loved the outdoors. As a child, he wandered through the woods surrounding his subdivision, getting to know them like the back of his hand. By temperament he was an explorer and he carefully observed the animal life and changing natural environment. The wildness, savagery and fighting for survival fascinated him. Curious about how the natural world worked, he asked adults countless questions. He identified with the American pioneers who ventured West seeking adventure. As a teenager, he eschewed joining any organized group, but preferred camping on his own. He developed considerable outdoor skills and challenged himself with journeys to remote, rugged places as an adult.

In high school, Jake was shy and had few friends. The only classes he enjoyed were biology, where he could indulge his passion to learn more about nature, and an auto mechanics class. Jake was fascinated by how things worked and developed a talent for fixing things. He avoided dating, claiming, "No girl would be interested in me." He had long hair and a scraggly beard and wore tattered jeans. Jake had no interest in looking like everyone else or being part of "the mindless crowd." Jake marched to the beat of his own drum. His few social connections were with the "burnouts" who smoked marijuana at parties.

After a few years of community college where he studied science and mechanics at his own leisurely pace, he joined the working world. He was hired at a factory as a quality assurance inspector, a job at which he excelled and received many promotions. The factory was his frontier, where he wandered freely, spotting and resolving problems. He had an eye for any imperfections in the parts he observed and gained a reputation as the "go to" person to resolve quality control problems. Jake took pride in his work. He loved his job but found it exhausting working around so many people. Building his own home on an island where he could escape after work was the place of refuge he needed for his own sanity.

Like-minded people lived around him: those who did not fit in conventional society and avoided the crowd. Each Thursday night, Jake gathered with a small group to discuss current political and economic issues surrounding the environment. All those in the group were suspicious of big business and government which they saw as exploiting people and abusing the environment. At one of their regular sessions, something happened that rocked Jake's complacent world. A group member introduced him to his sister, Nancy. Jake and Nancy made an immediate connection. Both had avoided the world of dating and never intended to be married. Both loved their solitude and independence. Both relished their freedom to pursue their wide-ranging interests.

Jake came to therapy because he was falling in love with Nancy and it frightened him. They had been dating for several months and Jake found himself caught in a painful pattern. As Nancy expressed feelings of closeness with him, he withdrew, which hurt her deeply. He could sense himself sabotaging the relationship with the only woman he had ever allowed himself to have feelings for. He did not want to lose her but did not know what frightened him so much.

Exploring his childhood, Jake recalled his parents were always fighting. His father was a quiet, shy, introspective man like himself. But he turned into a different person when he drank. Jake's mother, an outgoing, assertive, sociable woman—his father's opposite—nagged Jake's father relentlessly because of his laziness. When sober, he withdrew in seething anger at his wife's onslaughts. When drunk, he fought back with screaming and occasional punches. The fights went on throughout his childhood and Jake could not remember exactly what the reasons were. "They just seemed to fight about everything," he said. When the battles occurred, Jake wanted to be invisible, and he hid in his bedroom, daydreaming about wandering in the woods. A sensitive person, Jake could hardly tolerate the daily tension in the home, so he stayed away as much as possible.

Jake remembered an event which helped him make sense of the turmoil in his parents' marriage. One dark night he looked out his bedroom window and was shocked to see his mother kissing their neighbor. The veil began to lift as memories of what his parents argued about emerged. His father suspected that his mother was having an affair, which she vehemently denied and he could not prove. The atmosphere of mistrust that permeated his childhood home had seeped into his adult psyche. Jake only felt safe being a loner, in his own world, pursuing his own interests.

Reflecting on his childhood and his constant running away from home, Jake recognized that deep down, he felt ashamed of his family because of the fighting and his sense that something was terribly wrong. "The shame was like a stain that penetrated me to the core," he observed sadly. Growing up, he did not invite his friends into the home as he did not want anyone to know what was going on in the family. The sense of shame consumed him. Not only was he hiding from his family and others, he hid from himself, not wanting to face his shame.

Having learned to understand himself and his past as we counseled together, Jake decided to take a stand and not run away in fear. He courted Nancy and married her. They had a child together who was their pride and joy. Jake broke free of the chains of shame.

CHILDHOOD CONNECTION: SURVIVING IN A JUNGLE

After your parents' affair(s), your home becomes a jungle in which all the members fight for their own survival. The betrayal interrupts the serenity and regular routine of your home life. The normal tensions of living together escalate with occasional, often frightening, outbursts. Your unfaithful parent attempts to defend herself against the suspicions and attacks of her partner. She may also be absent physically and emotionally, leading a double life with a second family. Your betrayed parent tries to nurse his wounds and somehow manage to keep the family together. He fights for his own emotional survival, often overwhelmed by feelings of depression, anxiety and anger. His world is falling apart and he puts all his energy into just hanging on. Both parents become preoccupied with the affair and how to adjust to this new reality in their marriage. In the wilderness of their marriage, only the strong survive. In their life-or-death battle, what energy is left for the care of the children?

Consider what it takes to be an effective, nurturing parent. Parents create a home environment to help their children grow to mature adulthood. That is their task and noble calling. For that to happen, they provide a secure base for their children to explore the world and return for nurturing. It requires that they be attuned to the varied individual needs of their children and be generous in accommodating to those needs. They encourage their children to become independent and create their own worlds, yet remain connected by maintaining intimate relationships. To assist them in growing to maturity, they make rules which are flexible enough to allow for inner-directed growth and firm enough not to let chaos reign in the home. Parents foster a healthy intimacy in their children, staying involved yet not taking over, neither disengaged nor hovering. They must know when to hang on or let go, as the child requires. Most of all, they provide a model of healthy living. Being a good parent is a fine art that requires keeping a delicate balance so that the children are neither spoiled nor deprived. Parenting is like a violin string that can be neither too loose nor too tight to make the best music.

If your parents are involved in a fight for their own survival, what energy is left for the demanding work of parenting? If they feel so overwhelmingly insecure in their marriage, how can they provide a secure home environment for a child's growth?

In the jungle of your affair-disrupted home, you and your siblings have to fight for your own emotional survival. In normal circumstances, you could count on your parents being there for you, attuned and attending to your needs. But in their distraction, they are emotionally and physically absent in many ways. How do you survive the parenting void? It may begin to dawn on you as a child that you have to become self-sufficient. You have to take care of yourself, because you cannot depend on your parents. Furthermore, sensitive to your parents' dilemma and for your own protection, you want to stay out of their way and not be a trouble to them. So you become invisible. You try to blend into the background and wander off into your own world, perhaps the world of your imagination. Aware of your aloneness in a big, dangerous world, you begin to teach yourself survival skills. You develop hobbies and interests to entertain yourself. You learn to cope with disappointments and frustrations by withdrawing into yourself, the only person you can count on. Your strength is in your self-sufficiency.

As self-sufficient as you become, this strength is tainted by a sense of shame. Your parents have failed you and engaged in shameful behavior. You want to hide from others, not only to protect yourself from being disappointed, but also to keep others from knowing you. Deep down, you feel terrible about yourself because of what your unfaithful parent did to your family. The betrayal reflects on you, that somehow you were not good enough. You also fear others will judge you for what your parents did. So you stop talking about your family and do not invite your friends into your home. The shame spreads like a black stain on a white carpet, penetrating deeply and making it ugly and worthless. Your self-esteem suffers. In all your relationships you begin to hide yourself, fearful that if people get to know you they will see how awful you are and reject you. You hide to spare yourself the pain of anticipated rejection. The more you withdraw defensively, the more alienated and isolated you feel.

Growing into adulthood, your aloneness, separateness, shame and self-sufficiency become a fortress and way of life. After all, you learned, you have to look after yourself. You feel you cannot count on others to be there for you. Your shame makes you hide. Your self-sufficiency keeps you alone and safe. You may choose never to marry, afraid of recreating the pain and confusion of your parents' marriage, determined never to be a cheater or a victim. However, if you choose to become involved in a committed relationship, you keep your guard up just to be safe. The resulting emotional distance may propel your partner to seek comfort elsewhere. Then you become a victim like your betrayed parent.

Here are some questions that may help you be aware of your tendency to withdraw from intimacy for self-protection.

Do I Withdraw from Intimacy?

- Do I like to spend a lot of time in solitary activities?
- Do I protect my privacy at all costs?
- Am I proud of my ability to stand on my own?
- Do I keep my emotions under tight restraint?
- Am I an observer of the world around me, not a participant?
- Is it important for me to always be in control?
- Do I like to keep my world predictable?
- Do I take pride in knowing what's going on and how things work?
- Do I like to avoid being the center of attention?
- Do I hate crowds, preferring to be alone?
- Am I able to compartmentalize my life, keeping my activities separate?
- Am I afraid at times of being overwhelmed by my feelings?
- Do I believe strongly that everyone must learn to take care of themselves?
- If I am honest with myself, can I admit that I am afraid to get close to people?
- Do I see myself as alone in the world?

PATH TO HEALING: CONNECTING WITH OTHERS

People ask me what I do all day as a psychologist. I respond, "I listen to stories." I add, "Truth is stranger and more fascinating than fiction." We all tell ourselves stories about our lives as a way of making sense of the chaos of our experiences. The stories we tell ourselves take on the weight of truth and we use them to guide our lives. Without stories to guide us, we would feel lost in a confusing world, not knowing who we are, why we are here or where we are going. Our story-telling is normally an internal dialogue, because we realize we are the authors of our lives, constantly writing and revising the script that enables us to act. Sometimes, when we feel lonely, we share our stories to escape and to connect with others. People come to me because the stories in their minds are tragedies that have become overwhelmingly painful and hopeless.

When my clients tell me their stories, I listen carefully for underlying assumptions and beliefs. When they tell me, for example, that they see themselves as "a loser, worthless, alone and unloved," I remark, "That's an interesting way to think about yourself." Inviting them to step back and observe their stories, I further encourage them to explore, "Where did that way of thinking come from?" I tell them, "Just because you think it, it does not mean it's true." That comment usually takes them aback. Then the work begins of disillusionment, of examining closely the assumptions and beliefs they have constructed about themselves and the illusions that have guided their living. Along the way, I invite them to consider, "What purpose could it serve you to think that way about yourself?" We probe more deeply into what they really think about themselves.

When people begin to share their stories, something important happens to them. They learn they are not alone. They had imagined that no one had ever shared their experiences of pain and sorrow. When they take the risk of revealing their inner thoughts, their experiences are often unexpectedly validated by the other person. "So I'm not really as crazy as I thought," they can tell themselves. Telling others their stories opens their minds and hearts to the understanding and compassion of others, which leads to greater self-acceptance. They also receive feedback regarding their stories which enables them to assess their truthfulness and hold them less tightly. Their stories are only one version of the truth that can be altered, refined and made more coherent with their present experience.

Are you aware of the stories you are telling yourself about your life and who you are? Do you ever share your most personal stories with others? Do you take these stories as Gospel truth? Or could they be illusions you create about yourself to serve some purpose? Is your life story a comedy or a tragedy? If you are reading this book, there are likely tragic elements to the story. If a parent has been unfaithful, you may identify with some of the themes we have been exploring. A theme may emerge that is common in our culture, "You have to look out for number one." A second theme may be, "You can't count on anyone being there for you," and a third theme is "You have to hide yourself to be safe." If you personally resonate with these common themes, you need to step back and look at things from another perspective, from a "big mind" perspective.

1) MEDITATE ON THIS BOOK.

Consider for a moment this book you are holding in your hands. How did it come to be? First of all, unless you purchased the eBook, it is made from paper, which comes from trees. Trees come from seeds that fall to the ground from other trees and this process of regeneration goes back to time immemorial. The growth of the seed depends on the fertile ground formed from decaying plants and other life forms. The seed can only grow with the warmth from the sun and the rain that comes from the clouds in the sky. All the forces of nature collaborate to make the seed grow into a tree which is then used to make paper.

And how is the paper made? It is manufactured with the work of many hands. Lumberjacks cut the trees with equipment made in factories of steel from ore deposits in the earth. Drivers transport the logs on trucks made in other factories, with many workers on the lines. Those employed in paper mills make the wood pulp into paper, which is sent eventually to printers and then to book binders.

Before the book comes into your hands, it passes through the hands of distributors and booksellers. In the process, you cannot forget how the words come to the page from the ideas of an author who has been influenced by many sources. His ideas originate in a mind connected to the consciousness of the world. When you stop to consider it closely, the book you hold in your hands contains the universe.

2) MEDITATE ON YOUR BODY.

Now consider your own body that is holding this book. It is not as solid as you think, because it is made up of billions of cells. These cells are in continuous exchange with the world. Science reports that nearly all the cells in our bodies are replaced roughly every seven years. That corresponds with the traditional religious idea that we come from the dust of the earth and return to it, but not just at death—also continually throughout life.

We constantly regenerate ourselves. How does that happen? We nourish ourselves with the plants and animals around us. The farmers gather what we eventually eat after it is processed in mills and slaughterhouses, packaged and transported to markets. Countless people are involved in the processing and preparing of food, not to mention the person who may cook for you. The sun and rain participate in the growth of the food we eat and in maintaining the health of our bodies. As the saying goes, we are what we eat. In fact, the cells of our body come from and return to the earth, from which they are utilized as the material for new plant and animal life. All of life springs from the earth.

Furthermore, our bodies are sustained by the love and care of our parents and loved ones, who have been supported generation upon generation. Furthermore, our bodies are the storehouse for our minds which enable us to read and comprehend the books we hold in our hands. In short, the universe is present in the body that sustains your life.

3) MEDITATE ON THE EARTH.

Finally, consider the earth that is supporting your body. Some see it as a spaceship hurtling through the void that is outer space. However, it is a vehicle in which we are becoming more aware of how we live in close quarters, sharing not only an increasingly small area with population growth, but a common destiny. What happens across the world affects us all and we know about it almost instantaneously through Internet communication. A famine, flood, earthquake or war across the globe sooner or later affects everyone, demanding that our limited resources be used for the benefit of a few for the survival of all. We realize as never before that our planet will survive or perish as a whole. One part cannot die without eventually killing the whole.

Closer inspection reveals that we not only share a common destiny, but we are not as different as we seem. Most people share the same desires and fears. We all wish to be happy and to avoid suffering and we depend on each other to increase our contentment and diminish our sorrow.

Stepping back further to consider the position of our earth in the universe, we realize we are a speck in space in an ever-expanding universe of unknown dimensions. In ways we little understand, our earth is in a process of constant exchange with the material of the entire universe—the molecules, atoms, electrons and quarks. And there may be some spiritual connection that we dimly intuit and the religions of the world preach. Our earth mirrors the universe as a whole.

Taking the "big mind" perspective, we realize we are not as separate as we imagine. In fact, we are so connected that whatever we do for others, we do for ourselves. And whatever we do for ourselves, we do for others. That is the marvelous secret of the universe expressed in all the spiritual traditions and slowly dawning in contemporary psychology. If we genuinely love ourselves, that love will overflow into all our relationships, causing a ripple effect to the ends of the earth. Conversely, if we nurture a sense of personal worthlessness, we will not believe we have anything to offer others. Our world, then, shrinks to the measure of our self-evaluation. Giving ourselves openly and generously to others reverberates in peace and happiness for ourselves. Hating others only tears us apart.

PATH OF HEALING: THOUGHT EXPERIMENTS ON INTERDEPENDENCE

1) **Consider the book in your hand.**
2) **Consider your body holding the book.**
3) **Consider the earth holding your body.**

You may see yourself as a separate being because of your experience of being alone and neglected as a child. You may seek safety in solitude and self-sufficiency, believing that you can find safety in building walls around yourself. But your castle, as splendid as it may seem to you, will eventually become a prison that suffocates you in loneliness. The reality is that you are not alone or disconnected in the world. The whole universe and everything within it cries out its oneness. You do not have to hold onto yourself and your possessions so tightly. Your pain and fear of being further hurt caused you to build the walls around you and grasp yourself so strenuously. Appreciating your own fear, pain and desire for safety may help you to understand your broken parents who likewise withdrew to protect themselves. Their emotional absence was likely in the service of protecting themselves and not to neglect you as a child. Your understanding may open the door to forgiveness.

EXERCISE: KINDNESS MEDITATION

Albert Einstein reportedly said that ultimately we come to view the universe as either hostile or friendly. There is no in-between attitude. Because you experienced so painfully the emotional absence of your parents, you naturally learned not to trust others to be there for you. Your drive for self-preservation led you to rely only on yourself, to avoid the further pain of disappointment. You likely came to view the world of interpersonal relationships as hostile. To avoid being hurt by others, you withdrew within yourself for safety. However, in the process of disconnecting from others, you began to feel the pain of loneliness.

I recommend a practice that will help you escape the prison of your mistrust. It comes from the Buddhist tradition of Lojong, which provides fifty-nine exercises to cultivate compassion through training the mind. You can benefit from reflecting deeply on maxim number thirteen: "Meditate on the great kindness of everyone."[8] You may be startled by this suggestion because you have not experienced an abundance of kindness from the most significant people in your life. However, it is a matter of perspective. Perhaps you have developed the thinking habit of focusing on the negative, on what has been missing and hurtful in your life. Without realizing it, you have ignored what has been positive and enabled you to grow and become the person you are today. You are a survivor of a difficult childhood. How did that happen? Who and what enabled you to survive and thrive?

Begin your meditation by thinking about your parents. They were suffering people, caught in the throes of a troubled marriage. You felt neglected because they were so preoccupied with their troubles. But if you look carefully, you will realize that they also extended great kindness to you, in the best way they could under the circumstances. Despite their problems, they cared enough for you that you survived. They fed you, changed your diapers and provided a roof over your head. They took you to school, to the doctor and to visit your friends.

They provided for your physical well-being enough that you are alive today. Furthermore, they cared enough for you emotionally that you desired a better life for yourself. From a larger perspective, even their inadequate parenting was a blessing for you. The hardship you experienced as a child enabled you to develop strengths you might not have otherwise. Strength only comes in working through adversity. Furthermore, your parents had many good qualities that you inherited that make you the person you are today. Appreciate their goodness and kindness and do not focus on their faults and limitations.

Take a moment to reflect on the many people who have touched your life over the years. Think of the relatives and friends who supported you. Think of the teachers and family friends who encouraged you. When our parents were absent, many of us found substitute parents, like our friends' parents, who filled the void. Along the way, we found mentors in adults we admired who gave us guidance. Allow yourself to feel grateful for the many people who showed you some kindness. Appreciating their kindness and generosity with you can help you give up your self-obsession and become kind and generous with others. Let your gratitude overflow into generosity.

Many observe that there have been few times in the history of the world in which there was no war. They use this observation to confirm their belief in the natural aggressiveness and self-centeredness of the species. From another point of view, it is amazing that we have survived all these millennia as a species. We have not destroyed ourselves. In fact, we have progressed in astounding ways, coming to view ourselves as a global village. Meditate on the great kindness of a multitude of people around the world, from every age, that enabled our planet and species to survive and thrive. It is only through the natural cooperativeness of people that we continue to exist, both personally and globally. Allow yourself to see the universe as the friendly place that it is, despite occasional outbreaks of hostility.

Chapter 8

The Withdrawn Melancholic— Nobody Suffers Like I Do

The bedroom was Rachel's place of refuge for as long as she could remember. At the end of the day, she looked forward to retiring to her bedroom where she watched television, read her magazines and played on her computer. Rachel was a night person. She stayed up late pursuing her solitary interests and enjoyed sleeping in late whenever she could. She claimed, "I luxuriate by myself in bed, alone." There were other times that Rachel felt driven to her bedroom, the only safe place in her world. At those times, she was overwhelmed with a sense of sadness and sorrow, yet didn't know where the black mood came from. She climbed under the covers, hid herself, and fell asleep. Sometimes, when at the bottom of that black hole, she could not sleep. Her mind raced with worrisome thoughts, mostly about her children.

Rachel and her husband Tom had two boys. She loved children and had always wanted more, especially a daughter with whom she could bond. But a premature hysterectomy had prevented her from having the large family of which she dreamed. As much as she loved her husband and her boys, she felt like an outsider in their male interests. "I just don't fit in," she complained. While the boys were in school, Rachel kept close by volunteering to help in the lunchroom. The boys secretly enjoyed her presence in the school but complained that she was "hovering." Rachel admitted that she was a "worry-wart," especially about her children. Those worries often kept her awake at night.

A second worry also intruded into her sleep. She worried about her husband, who travelled frequently. Tom was the vice president of a large corporation with offices around the country. They had met in college, Rachel pursuing a degree in psychology while Tom majored in business administration. They dated for several years. Rachel was cautious about getting involved, because she had been hurt in a number of relationships with men who cheated on her. She saw Tom as mature, stable and ambitious, very unlike the other men she had dated. Facing her fears, she took a leap of faith in accepting his proposal. Within the first few years of their marriage, the boys were born and became Rachel's responsibility and preoccupation. Tom worked long hours and was away often on business trips, leaving Rachel alone with the children. When he was home, he was attentive to Rachel and the kids, but she never got used to his absences.

As close as she felt to Tom, Rachel never felt secure in their marriage. She always sensed that something was missing. She complained that he never paid her enough attention, never really listened to her and never anticipated her needs. She often became enraged with him when he appeared to ignore her or criticized her. She had temper tantrums, slammed doors and broke things. Later, she felt overwhelmed with guilt, apologizing profusely. Rachel admitted that she was a sensitive, insecure person who needed much reassurance. But Tom could never give her enough of what she thought she needed, as hard as he tried. Rachel was also tormented when Tom was away on business trips that he was having an affair with his secretaries. She screamed at him, "You'd be better off with another woman."

Rachel came to therapy complaining, "I can't get out of this black hole; something is terribly wrong with me." She felt she had lived her entire life within a well of sadness and sorrow. At times she could climb out of that hole, especially when she felt connected with her husband and children. She did not trust other people. But inevitably, she fell back into the darkness and seemed to dwell there. In a moment of candor, she admitted, "I think I'm addicted to my sadness and worry. If I wasn't sad and worried, I don't know who I would be."

Exploring the roots of her depression and anxiety, Rachel confessed that she had never been happy. As a child she called herself

Cinderella because she felt so much like an outcast. Her older brother was the prince, because he was so popular and performed so well in school. In contrast, Rachel was anxious, impulsive and hyperactive. She could not compete with him and felt doomed to failure in her attempts. She could not sit still in school or pay attention; her grades suffered. Her father called her "retarded" and her mother told her, "You're rotten to the core." In school, the nuns threatened that she was "destined for purgatory" because she was so restless and disruptive. Rachel believed that she was fundamentally defective and irredeemable.

Rachel never understood why her parents acted so mean and impatient with her. Her parents argued frequently. Her father screamed constantly and her mother withdrew into the bedroom. Rachel wanted to be invisible at those times and had nowhere to hide except her room. Her family kept many secrets and Rachel knew little about the background of her parents. Then one day when Rachel was twenty, her aunt broke the silence. She told her that Rachel's father was not who she thought he was. Her mother had had a brief affair during an unhappy time in her marriage and she was born. Suddenly, as if scales fell from her eyes, Rachel understood her father's rage and her mother's guilt, all of which became focused on her. Her fate was to be the family scapegoat, which she did not believe she could escape.

Aware of how she had become invisible and voiceless, Rachel redoubled her efforts in therapy and met with a psychiatrist who prescribed medication. Her depressed mood slowly lifted. She became involved in her church, where she finally felt she had found a home.

CHILDHOOD CONNECTION:
FEELING NEGLECTED AND LOST

When your parents are unfaithful, a sense of loss dominates the home. Consider for a moment all that is missing. Most conspicuously, a sense of closeness disappears within the family. Your parents are at odds with each other in a bitter struggle for survival. The hot anger of arguing and the cold anger of withdrawal replace the warmth of intimacy and affection. Bitter silence and hostile shouts replace free-flowing, spontaneous, happy conversation. All trust is lost, not only between your parents, but within the family as a whole. Secrecy reigns throughout the household. Your betraying parent hides his shameful activities, covering them up with lies. Both parents want to protect you from the shameful truth. You do not know what to believe anymore or whom to trust. You feel the tension, the loss of tranquility, but no one tells you honestly what is going on. You see your parents as angry, depressed and worried, but do not understand what they are going through. Their happiness has evaporated like mist, along with your own sense of security and contentment.

As a child in that family, you are not a passive outside observer but an involved participant, whether you like it or not. You have no choice in the matter. After all, you did not choose your parents and are not responsible for their behavior. Yet as a child, you feel a sense of responsibility for the tragedy that is unfolding. Young children normally think of themselves as the center of the universe, the cause of all that happens around them. That is called "infantile omnipotence," which normally fades as the child matures and develops realistic boundaries, separating from others. As a child, you blame yourself for what is missing in your parents' marriage. Somehow, you believe you caused their problems and feel helpless to solve them. The more you entertain the childlike fantasy that you are responsible for their failure, the more you feel inadequate and defective as the problem continues. You internalize their loss as your own, coming to view yourself as defective. In your youthful mind, your parents' failure becomes yours.

When one parent cheats on another, blame is thrown around. Both parents may accuse each other of causing the problem and portray themselves as blameless. You witness their blaming in loud accusations and hostile silence. As a child, you become an innocent participant in their blame game and may feel pressure to take sides. You suffer yet another loss—the loss of childhood innocence.

When you grow up and leave home, you still live in the shadow of sadness and guilt. You cannot completely escape your past, as hard as you try to forget it. Running away from your past is like trying to outrun your shadow. You dodge around to escape it until you fall down in exhaustion. The shadow is still there. As an adult, you have an ever-present feeling that something is missing in your life. You may suspect that it has something to do with the loss of a sense of security as a child, but you do not completely understand your intense moodiness. You identify with the depressed mood of your parents, especially the one who was victimized. When the black mood overtakes you, you withdraw from life to nurse the wound. You may wonder what is wrong with you, thinking yourself crazy or defective, because you feel so helpless to escape the moods. You may secretly relish the intense feelings, even though they are painful, because it makes you someone special, a tragic hero.

If you decide to marry, hoping to find happiness and redemption, the dark moods follow. You may look for some Prince Charming to marry who will rescue you from your sadness. But the sense of loss never leaves, and eventually you begin to notice and focus on what is missing in your marriage. To protect yourself, you withdraw behind the apparently safe barrier of your moodiness, leaving your partner alone and vulnerable to the seduction of an affair. Or, disappointed with your partner, you may look outside the marriage for another Prince Charming.

Here are some questions you can ask yourself to identify your tendency to be a withdrawn melancholic.

DO I WITHDRAW IN MELANCHOLY?

- Do I tend to focus on what is missing in my life, rather than what I have?
- Do I often compare myself with others?
- Am I particularly sensitive to being abandoned?
- Do I see myself as a moody person?
- Do I feel deeply any losses in my life?
- Am I attracted to those who are distant and unavailable in my relationships?
- Am I especially sensitive to the suffering of others?
- Am I angry at being abandoned by significant people in my life?
- Do I tend to withdraw into my black moods?
- Do I see life as more a tragedy than a comedy?
- Am I preoccupied with regrets from the past?
- Do I experience my emotions as dramatic and intense?
- Do I long for perfection in my relationships and focus on the negative?
- Does a mood of melancholy often consume me?
- Do I usually direct my anger inward in self-criticism?

PATH TO HEALING:
ENTERING THE HEART OF DARKNESS

When you are in the black hole of depression, you feel helpless and hopeless and think you will never be able to climb out of the hole. Drained of energy and motivation, all you want to do is sleep. Yet often sleep eludes you or is available only in brief snatches. The night, which reflects your mood in its blackness, seems to last forever. Your mind races with anxious thoughts and you ask the question, "When will this pain ever end?" You cannot help worrying about everything, imagining terrible things happening to you and your loved ones. Your heart is heavy with a sense of loss and emptiness. As you discover aches and pains you never felt before, you imagine even your own body betraying you. All joy and pleasure in life has fled. You lose your appetite, not only for food, but for all the activities that once gave you pleasure. Your mind is in a fog. You see yourself as worthless and your life as meaningless. Your only desire is to escape the pain, so you withdraw and wait. In your despondency, you may even think that the only escape from your misery is death.

In the depths of your pain, you want someone to understand, but you do not believe anyone can truly appreciate the extent of your misery. Those who are depressed sink to different levels of depression, from feeling completely consumed by the mood to a passing sense of loss. When people come to me overwhelmed by their moods, I try to comfort them and offer hope. They usually want a quick escape but I implore them to be patient with themselves. They wonder aloud, "What's wrong with me? How can I ever fix myself?" They feel dead inside.

I assure them, "You are very much alive, because you still feel pain. Your pain has a message. Let's see if we can decipher it together."

Sometimes I use the analogy of a frostbitten hand to show the value of pain. When our hand is frostbitten, it is numb and we feel no pain. We might think, inaccurately, that there is no problem because we are painless. However, as the hand thaws out we feel terrible pain and may think our condition is worsening. The opposite is true. Pain indicates that feeling is returning, and we are on the road to recovery.

As I explained earlier, pain serves a purpose. It helps us survive. It alerts us to a problem and draws our attention to it. Pain, both physical and emotional, grabs our attention and makes us focus on it. Pain indicates a place of woundedness that must be cared for. Ignoring it could be life-threatening. Because of our natural instinct to seek pleasure and avoid pain, we want to get rid of it as quickly as possible. If the wound is a surface scratch, it will heal quickly, and the pain will disappear with little effort on our part. However, if the wound is deep and pervasive, healing will take time plus much effort and patience. I tell my clients, "For the emotional wound to heal, you cannot go around the pain. It can heal only by going through it."

What is depression? There are biological roots to some depressions that are genetically inherited. Mood disorders run in families and can be treated with medication. Other depressions arise from our struggles with the changing realities of life. Depression is a natural reaction to the loss of something or someone important to us. The sadness expresses love's longing for fulfillment. It reveals a sensitivity to loss and indicates what we consider important. The natural sadness at the passing nature of life can become a programmed reaction to life and deepen to a depressed mood. That happens when we begin to dwell on the losses of the past, blame ourselves for them and lament, "If only it were different." We become trapped in thoughts about what we have lost and what is missing in our lives. The preoccupation with the gap, the difference between how life is and how we think it should be, becomes a habit of thinking. We begin to brood about it, feel sorry for ourselves and see ourselves as losers. Naturally, we hate the painful sadness and become critical of ourselves for being in a mood, perhaps thinking, "I have no reason to feel this way." The longer the mood persists, the more helpless and self-critical we feel. Exhausted by the sadness, we want to withdraw from life to nurse the wound. In that retreat from life, the process of healing can begin.

If you feel overwhelmed with sadness, I invite you to enter into the heart of darkness and not run away from it. Ignoring or rejecting the sad mood will only deepen it. Trying to distract yourself from your painful sense of loss will only give temporary relief. The sense of inner emptiness will remain and gain a firmer hold on your life. Instead, contrary to all your instincts, I encourage you to embrace the emptiness and deadness to see what new life can emerge from it. I suggest following a five-step process for healing:

1) ACKNOWLEDGE YOUR SADNESS.

First, recognize that you are sad. That may seem surprising to you. However, many people do not accurately identify their feelings of sadness because they are disguised in many ways. Sometimes your body is wiser than your mind. Your sadness may reveal itself in aches and pains, a sense of fatigue, a loss of appetite or difficulty sleeping. You may notice that you are more irritable and easily angered. Things that never bothered you before now irritate you. For many, anger hides sadness. Your thinking may be more negative. You criticize yourself and others more readily. Anxious thoughts that imagine the worst creep into your mind. You may notice that you are less interested in activities that previously gave you pleasure. You do not feel like being around people and spend more time alone, perhaps playing video games. All these are signs that you are feeling sad and may be depressed, if the feeling is prolonged.

2) ACCEPT—DO NOT FLEE FROM—THE PAINFUL FEELING.

Second, accept that you feel sad. Do not pretend otherwise if it is true. You are entitled to all your feelings. When you are sad, you are reacting to a loss of something important to you. Do not be tempted to tell yourself, "My life is good; I have no reason to be sad. Other people have it much worse than me." Your sadness indicates an area of sensitivity, a tender spot, that experiences something missing. Unfortunately, people may dismiss your mood and tell you, "You are just too sensitive. You are overreacting." Do not listen to them. There is no such thing as being "too sensitive." People have different levels of sensitivity. It is important that you recognize your tender spots so you can protect yourself from further hurt. Opening your mind in accepting your sad or depressed mood can launch you on a path of self-discovery, healing and growth.

3) EXPLORE THE CAUSE OF YOUR SADNESS.

Third, investigate your sad mood. Become well acquainted with it, like with a good friend. If you have physical pain and go to a doctor, he will ask you many questions so he can understand it and make a diagnosis to guide his treatment. He will want to know when it began, where you feel the pain and under what circumstances it occurs. He will ask you to describe the pain in detail, whether it is chronic or passing, sharp or dull, still or moving. He may even prescribe some tests to get a clearer picture of the cause. A competent doctor will not undertake a treatment until he knows with some certainty the cause of the pain. You can become your own healing physician by asking yourself similar questions about your mood. Become a careful observer, a scientist of your own mind. You will know how to relieve your suffering when you know what is causing it. Your sadness tells you something is missing. You will not know how to begin the recovery process until you know that clearly. Remember that your mind possesses considerable depth and can reveal many untold riches. It is a treasure house waiting to be discovered.

4) LEARN FROM YOUR SADNESS.

Next, learn the wisdom of your sadness. Your sadness reveals your tender spots and is an avenue to self-awareness. As a natural reaction to loss, it tells you what you value when you realize that it is missing. Its absence cries out to be noticed. Your reaction reveals your attachments and aversions, what you love and hate. Sadness lets you know when you are not getting what you want in life and, instead, are receiving what you don't want. For example, you may notice that you miss emotional closeness in your marriage. When you realize what is missing, you can begin working at getting what you need. You may feel a sense of dissatisfaction in your job. Your sadness may propel you to look for another job. Or you may be missing relaxing or creative activities in your life because you are so consumed by your work. Awareness of what is missing may then lead you to take care of your need for relaxation. On a deeper level, your sadness may make clear your resistance to the unavoidable, impermanent nature of life and your tendency to cling to pleasures that can never last, like money, status or power. "If only" thinking dominates: You imagine that if only something or someone were different in your life that you would be happy, which makes your contentment dependent on conditions outside yourself. You can stop and assess with a wise mind what is really necessary and important for your happiness.

5) DO NOT ISOLATE YOURSELF.

Finally, share your sadness with another. Your sadness is a whirlpool that spins your mind and drains the joy from your heart. As you sink deeper into your mood, you become more and more isolated and alone, and you drown in the emotional swamp. You need a companion to pull you out of the quicksand, someone just to listen and understand your overwhelming sense of loss. The kindness of someone making the effort to understand you can help release you from drowning in your depression. You are not alone, not as isolated as you feel in the depths of your depression.

PATH OF HEALING: STEPS TO ENTERING YOUR HEART OF DARKNESS

1) **Recognize your sadness.**
2) **Accept and do not flee the sadness.**
3) **Investigate your sad mood.**
4) **Learn the wisdom of your sadness.**
5) **Share your sadness with another.**

Entering into the heart of the darkness of your mood can open your heart in many ways. You can become a more compassionate person, able to identify with the suffering of others through accepting your own. That sensitivity can then motivate you to work for their happiness and, in the process, find relief from your own mood. Focusing on the sorrows of others and comforting them brings you joy. Working through your own depressed mood can also help you to shift your focus from what is missing in your life to what treasures you possess. An attitude of gratitude may arise that will dispel the darkness of depression. You will feel more even-tempered and emotionally balanced in facing the inevitable challenges of life. Finally, you may begin to feel some compassion for your parents, who suffered great sorrow in their relationship because of the betrayal. That compassion plants the seed of forgiveness for them.

EXERCISE: EXCHANGING PLACES

When caught up in a dark mood, you withdraw into your own world of suffering. You feel like a helpless prisoner of churning emotions you cannot control. Instead, your emotions control you. In a strange way, you may gain a sense of insecure safety by withdrawing into your mood state. For a moment you escape the pressures of life and disconnect from others, whom you do not believe could ever understand the depth of your pain. Imprisoned in your black mood, you may push those closest to you away, thus increasing your suffering in isolation. How can you break the cycle?

Shantideva, a Buddhist monk, introduced the practice of exchanging places with others to confront our tendency to become self-absorbed and build walls separating us from others. It is an exercise in empathy that can enable you to become more aware of the suffering you cause yourself by comparing yourself with others. He describes the practice in a few verses:

> Take others—lower, higher, equal—as yourself,
> Identify yourself as "other."
> Then, without another thought,
> Experience envy, pride, and rivalry.[9]

Retreat to a quiet place where you can relax and be alone. Breathe deeply to still your restless body and mind. Just relax. Now imagine you are a homeless beggar on a busy street in New York. Feel the hard pavement on which you are sitting and see the rush of people passing by, staring at you. Notice a businessman wearing a three-piece suit who stops in front of you. You detect a hint of disgust in his gaze. You have nothing, wear tattered clothes and beg for a handout. He seems to have it all, well-groomed and handling important business. Feelings of envy well up within you. "If only I could enjoy the money, power and success that he has," you lament to yourself, "then I would be happy." The difference between his condition and yours increases your sense of misery and self-pity. You also notice another emotion arising—hatred. You hate him because he possesses what you lack and long for. As much as you want his help, his giving you money would be humiliating. Dwell on the scene for a few moments, allowing yourself to feel the pain of envy, hatred and humiliation. Feel the suffering that results from your self-pity as being less than the person you envy.

Next, imagine yourself changing places with the wealthy, successful businessman. Walking down the busy street, you come upon a beggar in tattered clothes who smells. You stop for a moment and your mind wanders. He looks so filthy and disgusting, you hesitate to get too close. You think, "I wonder how he came to be so poor and miserable?" You think about how fortunate you are and grateful that you are not in his position, reviled by so many. Further reflection leads you to congratulate yourself: "I worked hard for everything I have and deserve it. Was he willing to work as hard?" You may even feel insulted that he would beg from you, someone who earned every penny he possesses. You have earned the respect of others through your accomplishments. "What has this man done?" you ask. Linger for a moment on the scene, allowing yourself to feel your arrogance and disdain.

Finally, on that same street, imagine yourself as another successful entrepreneur who encounters his fellow businessman. You are competitors, selling the same product and vying for the same customers. You look him up and down, assessing his measure of success. You compare the suit he wears with yours and how stylish he looks. You think to yourself, "I am the best in the business and will beat him at his own game. I welcome the challenge and will get great pleasure in winning and seeing him fail." You even begin planning how you will bring about his downfall. You will advertise your good qualities and hide your weaknesses. At every opportunity, you will gossip about his character flaws and minimize his accomplishments. All will see your superiority and flock to buy your product. You think about the times he outperformed you. What sweet revenge to excel and put him in his place. Allow yourself to feel the competitive fires burning within you, your desire to push yourself to be the best and your wish to destroy your rivals.

As Evelyn Waugh observed, "Comparisons are odious."[10] This exercise can help you experience the truth of that saying. Comparing yourself with others only leads to inner turmoil, envy, hatred and pride. Our illusory sense of separateness creates the need to fight and protect ourselves from others. It puts us at odds with others and with ourselves. Relief comes from surrendering our desire to be unique and special. It comes from recognizing our true equality with all. We are not as separate as we think.

Chapter 9

The Laid-Back Outsider—
Going to Sleep on Oneself

Timmy daydreamed from as far back as he could remember. As a child he was fascinated with superheroes and imagined himself fighting against earth's enemies. A shy child, he often played alone in his bedroom. He also liked to draw pictures, developing a real talent for reproducing lifelike superhero figures. In grade school, he won prizes for his creative writing skills. He dreamed of writing and illustrating science fiction comic books or young adult fiction about the adventures of superheroes saving the planet from alien invaders.

Timmy had few friends in school. Because he did not enjoy sports, he did not join in with the other boys who played catch or basketball during recess. Instead, he wandered about alone or went to the library to read. His teachers saw him as a gifted student and praised him for his imaginatively written stories in English class and his colorful drawings in art class. They admired his creativity and encouraged him to develop his skills. "Timmy, one day you will be a great author or artist," they said. His teachers recognized the exceptional abilities behind his quiet façade.

In high school, Timmy felt like he never fit in with any of the social groups. The popular group saw him as too weird. The jock group ignored him because he was so uncoordinated and uninterested in sports. He did not use drugs or belong with the burnouts. Some called him a geek, because he excelled in writing and drawing, but Timmy took pride in his appearance and dress, which set him apart. "I march to the beat of my own drum," he exclaimed with a quiet pride. Timmy never dated in high school, but he had several friends who were girls. The girls appreciated his sensitivity, which distinguished him from the other boys who tended to be crude, immature and self-centered. It did not bother Timmy that he was an outsider to the normal social groups. In fact, he relished being different, his own person. The casual but careful way he chose to dress expressed his uniqueness and invited more teasing that he was "girly."

After graduating from high school, Timmy was uncertain about what he wanted to do with his life. He always enjoyed writing and drawing, but he did those activities for his own entertainment and had never thought of pursuing a career with these personal interests. He attended a junior college, taking general courses. His advisor suggested that he major in English and become a teacher. Not knowing what else to do, Timmy followed that suggestion, took literature courses and graduated with a liberal arts degree. Sheer momentum and not any deliberate decision led him into a graduate program in English. Timmy never cared to find a job and work like everybody else, so he just continued in school because it was easy for him.

After completing the graduate program, everybody told him he should be a teacher. Following their advice, he looked for a job in a market flooded with teachers. Unable to find full-time employment, Timmy settled into being a substitute English teacher in local high schools. Never ambitious to work too hard, he worked three or four days a week as the spirit moved him. He had no great financial demands, because he lived at home with his mother. He was thirty years old and had no ambition to leave home. He nested in his room where he spent nearly all his time reading science fiction and occasionally writing and drawing superheroes.

Timmy had a long-term assignment in a rowdy class where he felt he was losing control. One day he could hardly breathe, had chest palpitations, had a panic attack and thought he was having a heart attack. A physician examined him, told him he was suffering from stress and referred him for counseling. During therapy sessions, Timmy became aware of an underlying anxiety that was controlling his life. Exploring the roots of his fears led back to his childhood.

Timmy had an older brother, Tom, who was always in trouble. His teachers complained that Tom was disruptive in class. He associated with the drug-using group in high school and was arrested for under-age drinking, marijuana use and shoplifting. Tom was the rebel, while Timmy was the good child. His mother, a high-strung, complaining woman, raised the two boys herself while working full-time as an office manager. Their father ran off with another man when Timmy was four years old. His mother never seemed to recover from the trauma of dis-covering her husband was gay. She complained constantly to whom-ever would listen about how she was deceived, how humiliated she felt and how hard her life was. Timmy listened, trying futilely to console her. When she had her regular crying spells, Timmy embraced her and offered words of reassurance. He also tried to mediate the numerous fights between his disappointed mother and rebellious brother. "I sup-pose I stay home to take care of my mother, who could not survive without me," Timmy rationalized. He slowly grasped the truth in ther-apy that he had withdrawn from life into the slumber of helplessness.

Over time, with the help of the therapist, Timmy moved into his own apartment. A full-time teaching position became available at the local high school. With some trepidation, he applied. Timmy found a home teaching creative writing and he was surprised by the accep-tance he received from his students.

CHILDHOOD CONNECTION: THE UNSAFE HOUSE

When a parent is unfaithful, your home becomes a house of toil and trouble, not a place of refuge. The secure and predictable routine of family life is disrupted. Your parents' energy is poured into coping with their problems and with the uninvited intruder of a third per-son in their marriage. The specter of that third person possesses the home. Your parents fight, either openly or in silence. They may com-plain loudly or secretly. They withdraw into their own worlds just to survive. As a child, you sense how troubled they are without being able to understand or help. You feel alone and frightened, a spectator as they destroy each other before your eyes.

How do you cope with their trouble? You may go in two differ-ent, opposing directions. You may outwardly express the trouble your parents experience, becoming the bad child. You express with your outward behavior the outrage at your loss of security; you are pro-testing through disruptive acting out. Or you may become the good child, secretly trying to rescue your parents with your admirable behavior. You do not want to add to their problems and may even look for ways to be a peacemaker. You want them to be proud of you so they can forget, at least for a moment, the turmoil of their ruined marriage.

As the good child, the compliant child, you receive rewards by being praised, if your parents even notice. You gain a sense of pride in doing the right thing that others tell you to do. You may enjoy the sat-isfaction of many accomplishments in following the rules and doing your duty. However, whether or not you recognize it, you pay a huge emotional price. In steadfastly following the expectations of others, you begin to lose touch with your own desires. You begin to sacrifice yourself in the service of bringing peace to others. Over time, you do not know what you want in life and may not even care. A sense of helplessness and passivity begins to seep into your life. Without knowing it, you identify with the parent who was betrayed and iden-tify with her sense of helplessness.

Desperate not to be a troublemaker or contribute to your par-ents' burdens, you withdraw into invisibility. You may become like Peter Pan who never wants to grow up. Instead of taking on the challenges of leading an adult life, you may prefer to live in a fan-tasy world in which you are the master. That fantasy world can be rich, colorful and entertaining. It is a world created by your wishes, an escape from the harsh reality of your family experience. That fantasy world is an intoxicating source of pleasure and a way of avoiding pain.

Your preference for this fantasy world may lead you to withdraw from engagement in the real world, which involves hardship and con-flict. The real world is a messy place, as you experienced at home as a child. You may also prefer to live alone and withdraw from the strug-gles to establish an intimate relationship—the give and take and the uncertainty. After all, you do not want to risk recreating the pain and failure of your parents' marriage. You prefer the security and tran-quility of the world you create in your own imagination. The danger is that you may become so immersed in your fantasy life that you lose touch with reality. The result becomes complete isolation. Another possibility also emerges, however. In developing your fantasy life, you nurture a creative imagination that can inspire you to produce great art. You see things others do not see, which can awaken extraordinary insight in others.

As you grow into adulthood, a sense of helplessness may dominate every area of your life. You would rather withdraw into inactivity than risk the dangers of working to make an independent life. To be independent, you have to know what you want and fight for yourself. Others may disagree with you, oppose what you want and disappoint you. You witnessed within your own family the pain and suffering people can inflict on each other. You do not want to make waves and prefer to be left alone. Or perhaps you wish for someone wiser and stronger on whom you can depend to guide and nurture you. If you risk entering a committed relationship, you sacrifice yourself to your partner's wishes to avoid conflicts. You willingly lose yourself to gain a sense of security that eventually proves to be false.

Here are some questions that may help you identify a tendency to withdraw from life into helplessness or your own self-created fantasy world.

AM I LIVING IN A FANTASY WORLD?

- Do I feel distant from my own desires and needs?
- Do I have difficulty making decisions about what I want?
- Am I more focused on others' opinions rather than my own?
- Do I tend to withdraw into my own comfortable world of routine?
- Do I cultivate a rich fantasy life?
- Do I avoid making commitments with people?
- Do I keep myself busy with many activities that do not lead to a concrete goal?
- Do I tend to waste time daydreaming?
- Do I avoid conflict at all costs?
- Do I keep a tight hold on my anger or express it indirectly?
- Do I tend to procrastinate and sidetrack myself with busy work?
- Does the law of inertia rule my life?
- Do I have difficulty standing up for myself?

- Do I tend to be stubborn?
- Am I a lazy person?

PATH OF HEALING: TAKING CHARGE OF YOUR LIFE

Unhappiness drives people to make appointments with me. I pose an opening question in my first session with my clients, "What made you decide to come to see me?"

They proceed to tell me about their pain and conclude, "I just want to be happy." When I ask them what they think will make them happy, most respond that they do not know.

Then I explain, often to their dismay, "You can't make yourself happy. Seeking happiness is like chasing the wind. It is a byproduct of being yourself and doing what matches your deepest desires." Or I may turn the question around: "What keeps you from being happy?" Responding to their "I don't know," I tell them my conviction that, whether they believe it or not, happiness is their natural state and something within them is keeping them from being themselves. If they choose to accept this mission of self-exploration, we begin the work.

I am amused that many people refer to me as a "shrink." They assume that I am perpetually analyzing people, shrinking their minds and behaviors into bite-size, comprehensible categories. When we are together at a social gathering, I respond, "The meter is not running." The truth is that I am in the business of helping people expand, not shrink, their minds. I encourage them to open their minds and hearts to love rather than pulling back and closing up in fear.

We reap what we sow. Do you ever ask yourself what kind of seeds you are planting in your life? Your intentional actions are seeds that eventually bear fruit. What fruit is your life bearing at this moment? It is by your fruits that you will be known and rewarded.

When people come to me for therapy, they have a story to tell, but they often do not know how to put their experience into words. They may come to sessions week after week insisting that nothing is new. I respond, "How can that be? Every moment is new and your mind is never at a standstill." Instead, they focus on what goes on outside themselves and on the routines of their lives. No wonder they feel stuck, because they are caught in emotional programming and habits of thinking from the past. Without knowing it, they dwell in the past, shaped by their repetitive thinking, and not in their present experience. I urge them to pay close attention to whatever arises in their minds in the moment. I instruct them, "Speak about whatever comes to your mind, any thoughts, feelings or experiences. We'll then sort it out together." Often, I detect a confused look on their faces, as they wonder how talking about what is on their minds can resolve their problems. I tell them, "You have the answer already within you, but may not know it. When you understand yourself, you will know what to do for yourself." We listen together, attentively, to whatever emerges.

When they begin to formulate their stories, we notice that they are often riddled with the idea that they are powerless over their lives and helpless in the face of overwhelming circumstances. They see themselves, even as adults, as helpless children. I point out these notions of helplessness and comment, "Isn't that an interesting way to think about yourself. How did you come to see yourself that way?" They proceed to tell stories about their past, what experiences led them to the conclusion that they are helpless in a dangerous world. I then ask, "What purpose could it serve you to think that way about yourself?" That question stops them dead in their tracks. It never occurred to them that seeing themselves as helpless, a painful thought, may have some benefit. We explore how a self-image of helplessness may justify them withdrawing from life and not making the effort to work through problems.

I see the goal of therapy to be facilitating the self-awareness of my clients through our dialogue together. Knowing themselves, they become free to be themselves. Transparency leads to liberation. Each of us is like a glass of muddy water. We lack clear direction in our lives because the mud obscures our vision. In the calm self-reflection of therapy and its aftermath, the silt settles and allows light to shine through. The inner light of our true selves shines through, is recognized and acknowledged. The silt is the conditioning of our past experience, all the passions, compulsions, distorted thinking and false beliefs. The shining light of awareness reveals the muddy impediments to our being our true selves.

Self-reflection may reveal the murky waters you are currently negotiating. If you see yourself as a helpless person, telling yourself stories of pain and powerlessness, I suggest some steps to overcome the inertia that results from such storytelling. The first four steps—to stop, look, listen and talk—were suggested previously. Now I add three more steps: to decide, act and savor.

1) STOP TO NOTICE.

First, I recommend that you stop. Stop for a few moments from all the activity that distracts you from paying close attention to yourself. Be still and quiet. Notice how thoughts and stories of helplessness arise spontaneously in your mind. Observe how much you hold your-self back to play it safe. Notice how often you use the words "I can't." Banish those words from your vocabulary if they are used in reference to your state of mind.

You may not be able to change some of the circumstances of your life, but you can change your attitude toward those conditions. That "I can't" way of thinking will likely become a self-fulfilling prophesy, reinforcing your sense of powerlessness. Recognize and also stop your daydreaming and wishful thinking about how your life could be. Shift your focus to the present moment of your immediate experience.

2) LOOK AT YOUR LIFE.

Second, look honestly and carefully at what you are doing now in your life. What desires and goals are guiding your life? Notice in particular how you are using your time and energy. What you do reflects what is important to you. Your feet reveal who you are more accurately than your lips.

I suggest you take a notebook and write out a time sheet of your activities. Start by keeping track of your daily activities on a single page. Watch your activities for a week and then extend it for a month. What do you observe about yourself? How do you choose to spend your time? For example, how much time do you devote to watching television programs or playing video games? How many hours have you dedicated to serving others? Some patterns in how you choose to invest your time and energy may emerge, which will then reveal your values.

3) LISTEN TO YOURSELF.

Next, listen to the stirrings of your heart. Do you ever stop to listen to yourself? What do you think will make you happy? It never ceases to amaze me how many of my clients draw a blank when I ask them this question. I should not be so surprised, because our culture is driven by noise, speed and greed which militate against quiet self-reflection. Our culture promotes living on the surface and ignoring the depths. If you look honestly at yourself, what do you see as your strengths and your weaknesses? Observing your interaction with others will reveal your gifts and your faults. Our relationships are the mirrors in which we can see ourselves most clearly.

Also ask yourself what is most important to you in your life: your family, your work or your community? What values guide your living? Captivated by a sense of powerlessness, you may easily overlook your own higher power within. Your "higher power" does not dwell in the heavens, outside you, shaping your life. Rather, that power resides within the deepest recesses of your heart and it's waiting to be acknowledged and released. Remember that you are the author of your life and no one else. What kind of story do you want to write and live out?

4) SHARE THE NEWS.

Fourth, tell someone you trust what you are discovering about yourself. Your isolation breeds a sense of helplessness and disconnects you from the real world. Alone in your own mind with your fantasies, you can become a prisoner within the four walls of your perceptions of yourself. Take the risk to venture out. Your rich fantasy life and unique perspectives make you an interesting person who can enrich the lives of others. Share yourself and your story. You may be amazed at how others value your gifts.

5) DECIDE FOR YOURSELF.

Fifth, decide what you want to do for yourself and others. Many of us are paralyzed by the routines and rituals of our lives. We act out of habit on autopilot without making a conscious decision about what we really want to do. Addicted to routines, we eventually lose a zest for life and feel dead inside. Many of my clients are depressed, because they feel so empty not living out of what makes them joyful. Some people avoid making conscious decisions to interrupt their routines because they fear making a mistake or suffering a loss. I remind my clients, "Whatever you decide, there is a gain but also a loss. If you choose one path, you enjoy the benefits you find along the way, but you also give up what you might gain on the other path." Because life is constant change, loss is inevitable. It takes courage to make a decision.

6) TAKE ACTION.

Next, take action. Based on your awareness of your own desires and decisions about what you want to do, choose to act in a concrete way. Your personal reflection may lead you to conclude that you have been neglecting yourself or your loved ones in some way. You can change your behaviors and overcome a sense of inertia. For example, you can schedule an appointment with the doctor for an exam, begin a diet or give time and money to some charitable work. Consider some action that you consider will be of most benefit to you and others. Choose an action that will break you out of your habitual self-absorption. There are many possibilities about what you can do for yourself and others. Just remember to use your heart as the guide.

7) SAVOR THE RESULTS.

Finally, savor the benefits of the activity you chose. You may think you are too tired or busy to undertake some new behavior. But if the action comes from your heart, it will energize you in unexpected ways. Activity also wakes you up to your own aliveness. For example, when I work with those who are addicted to substances, I am inspired by how their sobriety gains momentum. They are doubtful when they begin that they can survive without their drug of choice. Once they decide to be sober and begin to change their lifestyles, they feel better than they ever imagined. Their mental fog lifts and they start to feel their emotions. Shame and guilt begin to dissipate and they feel good about themselves. They enjoy the fruits of being sober, which reinforces their decision and new behaviors. In the same way, when you undertake new activities for yourself, notice the good thoughts and feelings that are generated.

There is a danger in focusing prematurely on the results of your efforts to change your behaviors. Preoccupation with the results of your actions can inhibit you from acting freely and spontaneously. You get caught up with what might happen as a result of your actions and do not pay close attention to what you are doing. You can also become impatient that your actions have not yet produced the desired results on your timetable, tempting you to give up the effort if you do not see the results you want. When you plant seeds, it takes time for them to grow to full flowering. Choose your actions well and let their consequences unfold in due time. After a while you can assess the results and alter your approach.

Path of Healing: Steps to Taking Charge of Your Life

1) **Stop to pay close attention.**
2) **Look honestly at what you are doing now in your life.**
3) **Listen to the stirrings of your heart.**
4) **Share yourself with another.**
5) **Decide what you want to do for yourself and others.**
6) **Take positive action.**
7) **Savor the benefits of your action.**

When you face your sense of helplessness honestly and courageously, you open the door to understanding the feelings of your parent who was betrayed. Your unfaithful parent may also have suffered from a sense of powerlessness in his or her marriage which he or she tried to overcome through involvement with another. Compassionate understanding, beginning first with yourself, is an important step on the path to forgiveness.

EXERCISE: TONGLEN

If you are caught up in a sense of helplessness, the world has become a dangerous place for you. No wonder you feel the need to withdraw into fantasy or your own busy work to feel safe. The outside world is too threatening, so you retreat within the walls of your own imagination or routines. You notice then how much you are ruled by fear.

You also observe how much your life has shrunk in order to feel safe and secure. What a tradeoff! You withdraw into a small world, which can eventually suffocate you with loneliness, to avoid engaging in the larger world, which feels too overwhelming for you. You exchange safety for aliveness.

Fortunately, there is a way out of this dilemma. It is the way of embracing your fears, discovering their emptiness and opening your heart to courage.

Your greatest fear is of being hurt deeply to the core of who you are. That is the pain you avoid at all costs. Your natural instinct is also to chase after pleasure which gratifies your desires. Furthermore, you want to hang onto the pleasure you acquire, because in your dangerous world it is in scarce supply. A traditional Eastern practice to cultivate fearlessness and a connection with the whole world is called "'Tonglen," which means "sending and receiving."[11] In this exercise, you act against your natural, fear-based tendencies to flee pain and chase pleasure. Instead, you intentionally breathe in the suffering of yourself and others and breathe out peace and joy for the benefit of all. Let me describe the practice.

First, sit comfortably in a quiet place. Perhaps you have found a place of refuge, a sanctuary, in your own home where no one will disturb you. Withdraw to that place of peace. Breathe slowly and consciously and become aware of a sense of peace and relaxation filling your body. With each breath, feel a sense of openness and spaciousness within your heart. You breathe the same air as all living creatures. The air, which is the breath of life, connects you with the whole universe. Breathing reminds you that you are alive and not alone in the world.

Second, from your place of peace and tranquility, imagine that you are breathing in hot, black smoke that almost makes you gag. You feel the discomfort—your repugnance—as you breathe in the burning blackness. As you breathe out, imagine you are exhaling a cool, fresh breeze. Imagine the lightness and freshness of the great outdoors being expelled from within you. Breathe in black smoke and breathe out fresh air, just as the trees take in carbon dioxide and release oxygen.

Third, visualize a person you know who is in pain and sorrow. You can start with yourself. Feel deeply your pain and confusion in the moment. Do not hide from or minimize your suffering. Be open to the full force of the pain. As you breathe in, feel that suffering as if it were hot, black, filthy smoke. Breathe it in deeply but do not hold onto it. As you breathe out, imagine exhaling peace and contentment, like fresh, clean, exhilarating air. With each inhale, touch the pain and sorrow. With each exhale, let it go and send out joy and tranquility.

Finally, imagine all the living creatures in the world. They experience both pain and pleasure. They, like you, want to avoid sorrow and seek happiness. Sense your oneness with all the living. Your pain is theirs and theirs is yours. All are united in suffering and in the desire for relief from it. As you breathe in, imagine all the suffering of the world. As you breathe out, feel yourself extending joy and peace to the whole world. Sense your willingness to embrace compassionately the suffering of all and your desire to bring them relief. Be aware of your heart expanding and opening with love for all creatures.

You can use this exercise to embrace the suffering of anyone you choose—a close friend, a stranger or even someone who has harmed you. The practice of Tonglen helps you to cultivate a compassionate, fearless heart. It also strengthens your self-confidence that your suffering and the suffering of others will not destroy you. You take in the suffering, refusing to run from it out of fear. In facing your fear of pain, you overcome it and transform fear into a way of peace.

When you are ready, you can breathe in the suffering of your parents who harmed you through their infidelity and breathe out love and forgiveness.

Part 4

Ineffective Ways
of Parenting

Chapter 10

The Controlling Parent—
Father Knows Best

Roger, whom we discussed earlier in chapter 5, came to therapy when his second wife of ten years suddenly left him. With deep remorse and a sense of helplessness, he admitted that his temper drove her away. "I deserved what I got," he lamented. Roger believed he earned the punishment of her abandonment, despite his pleading with her that he was sorry and would change. After each angry outburst, he would apologize and, with white-knuckled effort, would keep a relative calmness for a few weeks until the next explosive episode. Anger controlled him. In therapy, he came to admit his powerlessness over his temper and acknowledged himself to be a "rage-aholic."

Roger had two children from his previous marriage to Rhonda. Roger and Rhonda had met in the military and married after a whirlwind romance. Rhonda soon gave birth to a daughter, and a year later became pregnant with a son. Roger beamed with pride at having two children and imagined a glorious future for both of them. In the early years of their marriage, the romance and dream of a shared life in the service seemed to keep the anger in hibernation. But with the financial stress of raising the children and his wife less concerned about money matters than he, the suppressed rage seeped out. Soon the venting became explosive outpourings. Although he prided himself at never being violent like his parents, he went off on tirades like the drill sergeant he was trained to be. He believed it was his responsibility to keep the troops at home in order. And he enforced the home rules with an iron hand.

After several years, Rhonda left Roger for another man whom she met while on assignment overseas. Roger was devastated. She abandoned him and their young children. Priding himself on his sense of responsibility and resourcefulness, he succeeded in raising them to be mannerly, good students who were well disciplined and responsible. Roger had the help of his second wife, who cared for his children as her own, until she could not tolerate his temper either and left. Roger was alone and miserable, consoling himself, "At least I have my children."

Roger felt heartbroken when his daughter, Jennifer, went away to college. She was an honor student in high school and a cheerleader, a lovely girl whom all admired. She left with Roger's blessing, a tribute to his no-nonsense parenting with a firm hand. "Discipline pays off," he bragged to his co-workers. When summer vacation came, his daughter decided to live with her mother across the country. Roger felt betrayed and asked, "How could she leave me for her mother, that woman who abandoned her?" Humiliated, he secretly wondered why his daughter did not want to stay with him.

A second blow came when his son, Jason, who was a senior in high school, was arrested for theft and drug possession. Roger was in shock. His son was his pride and joy. Like his sister, he was an honor student, popular and his class president. Roger entertained dreams of him pursuing an honorable military career, reaching heights greater than his own. With that arrest, Roger's dream collapsed like a house of cards. "How will you ever go to an outstanding college and pursue a successful career with a felony conviction?" he asked his son. Roger blamed himself, asking, "Where did I go wrong?"

Roger had maintained strict rules at home, encouraging his children to live the disciplined life that helped him advance his career. He tolerated no foolishness and reacted with quick anger to any backtalk or questioning of his authority. His children followed all the rules with minimal grumbling, according to Roger. They did well in school, had many friends and performed their chores at home according to his regulations and standards. Roger believed that other parents envied him for how well-behaved, respectful and accomplished his children had become. Their teachers complimented him for the quality of their schoolwork and deportment in the classroom. They were both model students. Roger beamed with pride and reasoned, "I'm only doing my duty as a parent."

Roger never had even an inkling that his son was using drugs and stealing to support his habit. His son lived a double life, keeping a hidden wall between Roger and himself. It never dawned on Roger how little he really knew his children. He kept going over what he felt was his good parenting but in therapy began questioning the past. They were obedient and followed his rules but never really talked about their thoughts and feelings. He demanded obedience from them, which they appeared to give him, but little else. He had a surface relationship with his children. As we explored his relationship with his children, Roger realized that his temper held them captive as it had his two wives. "But I never hit them like my parents hit me," he rationalized. However, Roger could not sense the fear that lurked beneath their respectful behavior.

As a child, Roger and his two siblings lived under a reign of terror and he considered himself a victim of his father's wrath. His father was an angry man who punished even the most minor offense severely. He yelled at the children and freely used the belt for any backtalk or B grade in school. He was the sole authority in the household, expecting all to submit to his wisdom and guidance. His mother followed the strict program of discipline for many years until she suddenly left to live with another woman.

Roger feared and hated his father because of his violence but admired his strength in keeping law and order in the house. Because he was not violent like his father but kept firm discipline, Roger believed he was a good parent. He minimized the impact of his anger on those around him because he exercised some restraint in how he expressed it. As we explored further, Roger became painfully aware of how frightened his children were of him and how he had unwittingly become their persecutor like his own father.

The next Thanksgiving, before the guests arrived, Roger asked his children to come into the den because he had something important to tell them. He did something he had never done before, expressing from his heart, "I'm truly sorry for how I hurt you with my anger. Please forgive me."

CHILDHOOD CONNECTION: THE WAGES OF WAR

You may be realizing that growing up with an unfaithful parent has affected the way you relate to others in intimate relationships. You may feel driven to become unfaithful, marry someone who cheats on you or be mistrustful of intimacy and disengage emotionally. What may not be so clear is how your parents' infidelity affected your relationships with your own children and impacted your own parenting style. That should not come as a surprise. After all, your parents were your first and primary role models. Your model of marriage, for better or worse, was your parents' relationship. As a child, without being aware of it, you learned how men and women relate and followed their example. What other example did you have as a child? When you were older, you observed other couples and thought about what you wanted in a relationship. Then you began a process of discernment, picking and choosing what you believed suited you as a person. Undoubtedly, you sometimes surprised yourself at how often you reacted just like your parents in a particular situation, thinking, *I'm just like Mom (or Dad)*.

The same process occurred in becoming a parent. Who was your model? Your own parents. As a child interacting with them, you learned how parents and children relate and developed your own internal template for that relationship. That template was deeply ingrained and mostly unconscious. You grew up with what you thought was normal. It was only when you got older and observed how your friends and their parents interacted that you learned there were other ways of relating. You may even have realized at some point that something was missing in your relationship with your parents, that somehow it was abnormal. When you had your own children, if you were a consciously aware person, you began to decide what kind of parent you wanted to be. That choice, however, was always made against the background of how you were raised.

Infidelity may produce a unique kind of devastation for children in undermining the natural development of trust in relationships—between adults and between parent and child. Further research will have to show the uniqueness of its harmful impact on childhood growth and development. However, what is becoming clear in clinical experience is the common ground of the harmful effects on children who grow up in homes with an alcoholic and/or abusive parent and, as I am suggesting, live with unfaithful parents. Research and experience demonstrate consistently how children suffer long-term effects as a result of having a parent who is alcoholic or who physically or sexually abuses them. These children grow up with developmental deficits that may be disguised for many years and erupt later in life. Working with adults, I am observing the long-term impact of growing up with an unfaithful parent that mimics the harmful effect of alcoholism and abuse.

CAUGHT IN THE CROSSFIRE

How does your childhood with an unfaithful parent affect the way you parent your children?

In a home in which a parent is unfaithful, rage rules. The anger of betrayal either simmers below the surface or erupts with a vengeance. One parent engages in an affair, justifying it because he feels discontent and resentment in the marriage. The offended parent is outraged at being betrayed. The home, which was always intended to be a safe haven, is transformed into a battlefield where the children suffer collateral damage. The parents shoot darts of anger at each other, both in disguised and plainly visible ways, and the children get caught in the crossfire. They feel the tension and shudder at the wrath that is prevalent in the home. And worse, the parents too often direct their anger and frustration at the children. On edge because of the wreckage of their marriage, they show little tolerance or patience for those under their care.

Growing up in an atmosphere of hurt and anger, you have been deeply affected. Your parents were both wounded by the infidelity and you share in their wounds. As much as your parents desired to be loving, their preoccupation with the affair and the aftermath of overwhelming feelings interfered with their ability to be fully present for you. They were caught up in a personal battle of which you may have been unaware. However, you experienced the tension of the war that was taking place on the home front. This was no foreign war on distant shores. It was a civil war, tearing apart the home and family.

How did your parents cope with the insecurity of the affair and the intrusion of a third person into their marriage? That person was also brought in as an unwelcome guest into your family, the unseen ghost that affected how everyone interacted with each other. How did this intrusion affect the way your parents related to you as a child?

"My life is so chaotic now, I'll at least try to keep order in the home," your parents may have told themselves. One way of compensating for the disruption and chaos created by the affair is the attempt to maintain order at all costs. Embroiled in a battle for the survival of their marriage, often feeling overwhelmed by hurt and anger, parents may try to create a measure of peace by making and enforcing rules. That is only natural. If you feel out of control, you try to regain it. If you feel powerless, you seek ways of exercising power.

Perhaps to establish at least a fragile sense of peace for you as a child in the midst of their personal war zone, your parents may have become more controlling. They tried to restore order by establishing more rules and routines to give a semblance of peace. If your parents tended to be strict, their rules and routines may have become more rigid and inflexible than they previously were. There were no exceptions to bedtime and curfew. You could not procrastinate with chores. Computer and TV time were strictly limited. No fall-off in grades was tolerated. Arguments and fighting with your brother or sister were abruptly stopped. You sensed that your parents' anger at each other was being redirected toward you in impatience, less tolerance and more severe discipline. Time-outs became longer, yelling more frequent and there was even an occasional slap that had never occurred before. Your parents may have tended to be stricter than the parents of your friends, but the intensity of the discipline ramped up for no apparent reason. And their temper outbursts frightened you.

Another change also occurred. With their growing impatience, your parents spent less time talking with you and enjoying your company. You did not play together or at least less than before. You did not feel as close to your parents and felt less free to express your opinions to them, especially when you disagreed with them. You stopped asking for reasons why they wanted you to do something. You sensed that they were more easily angered and fear crept into your relationship. You began withdrawing more into your own activities. You shared less with your parents about what you were doing, afraid of their disapproval. Without realizing it, you were developing a secret life that reflected their secrecy.

To cope with the chaos and insecurity of their crumbling marriage, your parents may have become more controlling and developed an authoritarian style of parenting. That model of parenting has directly influenced how you relate now to your own children. What are some signs that you have followed in their footsteps?

PARENTING QUESTIONS

- Am I impatient with myself and my children?
- Do I lose my temper easily?
- Do I expect unquestioning obedience from my children?
- Do I resent them asking for explanations of the rules?
- Are rules especially important in my home?
- Am I intolerant of my children procrastinating?
- Do I tend to be stricter than other parents?
- Are my children free to disagree with me?
- Do my children talk openly with me?
- Do my children see me as a dictator?
- Am I quicker to punish than give rewards?
- Do I hesitate to ask my children's opinions about the rules?
- How often do I say, "Because I said so?"
- Am I demanding of high performance from my children and intolerant of failure?
- Do I monitor their activities closely?

PATH OF HEALING: LEARNING TO LISTEN TO OTHERS

Maintaining order and discipline in the home is a necessary quality of effective parenting. Making clear rules and enforcing them consistently provides children with a needed sense of security. As much as they protest, children do not want unlimited freedom to do whatever they want. Such unguarded openness would generate too much anxiety. Children need guidance and structure. However, focusing so much on rules, order, discipline and obedience can be stifling for a child, particularly if it is not balanced with affection and understanding.

Your children may react by becoming compliant and lose a sense of their own competence, strength and self-esteem. Or they may rebel, either secretly or openly. As they grow into adulthood, their intimate relationships will tend to follow your example and may become power struggles in which one dominates over the other. Such tension may lead to an emotional disconnection that provides fertile ground for infidelity. They will also tend to mimic your parenting style, becoming controlling with their children. And the cycle continues, creating an environment ripe for unfaithfulness to occur once again.

Wisdom teaches us that a fault is usually an excess of a strength. Your path to healing from the devastating effects of your parents' infidelity is to find a balance in your life that works for you, instead of overcompensating. They compensated for their trauma by focusing on regaining control over you as a child. Consequently, you learned to be controlling as a parent with your own children. You can learn to find balance in your parenting style by being more aware of yourself and following these steps, preferably in conversations with your spouse. Remember, effective parenting is always a team approach.

1) OBSERVE YOURSELF CLOSELY.

First, become an observer of yourself and recognize your tendencies in parenting. "No one is a perfect parent," you tell yourself, "but I try to be one anyway." Perfection is an idea in the mind and does not exist in reality. See yourself as you are interacting with your children, not as you wish you would be or as you think you should be. Imagine yourself as an observer invited into your home to watch how you relate with your children. What would that objective person see? All of us have our own unique personalities and we operate out of our needs, desires, wishes and habits. Our personalities and upbringing shape the way we interact with others, including our children. How controlling do you see yourself? How open to the opinions and feelings of others? How emotionally close do you feel with your children? How open and honest are you with each other? How tolerant of differences? You can ask yourself the same questions regarding how you interact with your spouse. Do you dominate or are you a team player?

2) ACCEPT WITHOUT BLAMING.

Second, accept what you see without blaming. As you take a moral inventory of your parenting, you may say to yourself, "I don't like what I'm seeing." What is lacking may become apparent. It takes a great deal of humility to be honest with yourself and then to accept what you discover. Instead of condemning yourself or your parents for not showing you a more effective way, rejoice in discovering the truth. You may observe a tendency to judge yourself or others quickly against some imagined standard of perfection. Your pride is hurt. Resist the urge to judge and let it go. Blaming either yourself or your parents serves no purpose except to keep you stuck in your anger and resentment. Anger divides and paralyzes, especially the anger of self-criticism. Acceptance opens you up to new possibilities and brings people together. The freedom that acceptance brings will allow you to heal the wounds of your childhood, accepting the loss of not having perfect parents.

3) INVESTIGATE WITH AN OPEN MIND.

Next, investigate the patterns you observe with an open mind. Think of yourself as a curious scientist who is excited to understand more in the quest for truth. The laboratory is your own home and you, your partner and your children are the subjects of the truth-seeking experiment. Become an accurate observer of yourself and look closely at your behaviors, your children's reactions and your interactions with each other. Also notice your feelings, automatic thoughts and beliefs about being a parent. Pay special attention to how your children react to you. The truth emerges in the interaction. As you sift through your observations, you will begin to see patterns in the way you and your children interact. For example, you may notice how much you like law and order, expect obedience, resist compromise and hate to explain yourself. You may observe that your children do not freely express disagreement with you, keep to themselves, just follow rules and do not take initiative.

Is what you observe familiar? Your way of thinking and acting as a parent is derived from your earlier experiences. The realization may strike you, "I'm more like my parents than I care to admit." Allow yourself to explore your own childhood, your interactions with your parents and how you felt as a child. You may be embarrassed at the extent to which you imitate your parents, despite your proclaimed desire to be different from them. And you may be proud at the many ways you followed in their footsteps because you admired what they did. When you appreciate the source of your parenting style, you understand better what your children are experiencing with you as their parent. At one time, you were in their shoes.

Consider your motivations for continuing the patterns of parenting you learned from childhood. Because of our tendency to deceive ourselves, meeting with a therapist can help to uncover hidden motives and desires. You may discover, as many do, that your behavior in some way compensates for what was missing from your childhood. For example, you may be concerned about power and control in dealing with your children because you felt so powerless and helpless with your parents. Acting like your parents, who were domineering, may also be a way of connecting with them, especially when you have suppressed anger toward them.

4) EXPLORE ALTERNATIVES.

After investigating the patterns, explore alternative ways of parenting that will be more beneficial and balanced. Your spouse can be especially helpful in exploring alternatives, because your partner has his or her own parenting style that likely will have significant differences from your own. The differences can lead to tension and conflict but also to enlightenment. In many ways opposites attract in marriage and create friction, heat and passion. If you tend to be a strict parent, it is possible that your spouse leans toward leniency. If you find that you tend to have an authoritarian style in parenting, you may discover some internal resistance to listening to what your partner has to say, particularly if his or her opinion differs from yours. But be open for the benefit of your children and yourself.

If you have an authoritarian style, you may need to become more democratic in your approach with your children. That means talking more openly with them and listening to what they have to say. Value and do not dismiss the disagreements. You may have to learn how to negotiate with your children and compromise on your rigid rules and routines as long as safety is not compromised. You may have discovered that emotional closeness was sacrificed for the sake of an orderly household. To correct that imbalance, you may begin to spend more time with your children and become more of a friend and not just a parent. Show your children that you care about what they think and feel. Let them know you as a person and not just in a role as a parent. Alternative ways of parenting are as unlimited as your imagination and willingness to change.

Consider also alternative ways of living for yourself. You cannot be a relaxed, effective, loving parent unless you experience inner peace. In the long run, you will nurture your children to the extent that you genuinely, not obsessively, care for yourself. Behind your authoritarian façade you may discover deep longings for intimate connections with others, including your children. You may also discover a hidden quest for power, control and competence in your own life. Instead of trying to exert so much control over your children, shift the focus to yourself and pay attention to your deepest needs and desires. Allow yourself to pursue your own passions in life and engage in activities that make you feel alive, creative and competent. Reclaim power over your life and ease up on your children. They will eventually have to find their own passionate pursuits that match who they are as people. Your role modeling in that pursuit can help them immensely.

5) LET GO AND MOVE ON.

Finally, after all the exploring, try to let go of the past and move on. The exploration will be ongoing, because life is constant change. But you will have more confidence that you can adjust to the changes. Undoubtedly, many hurts and resentments from your own childhood will emerge in reliving your memories of interactions with your parents. This can be an opportunity for you to better understand your parents' struggles. You never really understand your parents until you become a parent yourself. Then you have a glimpse from the inside of what their life was like—all the joys, worries and uncertainties. Understanding them and yourself helps you to give up the image and longing for the perfect parent and humbly accept the ordinary, with all its magnificence. It opens the heart to forgiveness.

STEPS TO HEALING THE IMBALANCES

1) **Recognize your parenting tendencies to control.**
2) **Accept, don't blame.**
3) **Investigate the patterns, your hurt and anger.**
4) **Explore alternatives; be more democratic.**
5) **Let go, forgive and move on.**

EXERCISE: JESUS WITH A LITTLE CHILD

A traditional practice in Christian circles is meditating on a passage from the Bible to deepen faith and become more loving. Through meditating on the life of Jesus, Christians believe they can "put on the mind and heart" of their Lord and come closer to God. Even if you are not a professed Christian, you may be able to appreciate the wisdom of the message contained in the Bible. The Bible presents universal truths that enrich human life. Jesus lived a fully human life, exemplifying self-sacrificing love. Following his example, anyone of any faith persuasion can come to a healthier, more wholesome life.

Here is a story from the gospel of Matthew (18:1–5). Pay careful attention to these words and let them engage your mind and heart. Use your active imagination to enter the story and transport yourself into the situation. Observe and admire how Jesus interacts with a little child to the dismay of his disciples, who had a more authoritarian attitude toward children. Such an attitude characterized the Jewish culture of the time.

> At that time the disciples came to Jesus and said, "Who is the greatest in the kingdom of heaven?" So he called a little child to him and set the child in front of them. Then he said, "I tell you solemnly, unless you change and become like little children you will never enter the kingdom of heaven. And so, the one who makes himself as little as this little child is the greatest in the kingdom of heaven. Anyone who welcomes a little child like this in my name welcomes me."[12]

Find a quiet place where you can be alone and reflect. Sit comfortably and relax. Close your eyes for a moment and follow your breathing. Think of nothing but the inhaling and exhaling of your breath. Your breath is life, the spirit of life flowing through you and out into the world. Feel your body relaxing and your mind quieting. Now, when fully relaxed, open your eyes and reread this brief story from the gospel of Matthew. Don't rush through the reading; let the words penetrate into your heart.

Now close your eyes again and imagine the scene you just read. Transport yourself into the time of Jesus. Imagine you are one of his disciples, arguing about greatness. That's easy. Who does not want to be great and powerful in their heart of hearts? You may criticize those disciples for talking so openly about their prideful desires, but admire their honesty. This was a serious discussion for these men who longed for the kingdom of heaven. They competed for greatness. Perhaps they were not embarrassed when Jesus asked them what they were talking about. But imagine their shock at Jesus's response. He brought a little child into their midst. In those days, children were to be seen and not heard. They were considered the property of their parents with no rights, privileges, power or prestige. They had no value because they were not yet contributing members of society. Feel the shock and confusion as Jesus tells them that they must change and become like this little child to even enter into the kingdom of heaven. What does that mean? Become as powerless and valueless as a child? And then Jesus adds that to be great you must become little like a child. What greatness does a child possess? Let your mind wonder and wander in the uncertainty of the meaning. Let the words sink in: "I must become like a little child." Ask yourself, "What can I learn from a child?" Let your mind roam freely and explore the possible meanings of true greatness. What does it mean to be childlike, not childish?

Now let your imagination transport you back to the present day to your life as a parent. How do you value and treat your children? Do you see them as models of greatness as Jesus did? What can you learn from your child? Do you even listen closely to them? Does your child embody a wisdom that you have not yet acquired or have received at one time and lost? Remember, you were a child once upon a time. Have you maintained the childlikeness that Jesus taught was essential to entering the kingdom of heaven, for leading a wholesome life? Be open to whatever you learn about yourself and the way you parent your children. And do not judge yourself. Jesus did not condemn his disciples for their preoccupation with being the greatest. Instead, he invited them to look more deeply and discover the truth for themselves.

Chapter 11

A Friend, Not a Parent— Finding Security in Love

Karen, a stay-at-home mom, devoted herself to her children. She came to therapy because she had found out that her fifteen-year-old daughter, Jill, was having sex with her boyfriend. "I have failed her as a parent," she moaned. Karen was stunned and felt betrayed when she intercepted an e-mail from Jill's boyfriend talking about their sexual encounters. She saw her daughter as quiet, studious and somewhat prudish. Ryan was Jill's first boyfriend and he had always impressed Karen as polite and respectful. Karen believed that there were no secrets between her and her daughter, because they could talk so openly about almost any subject. Karen had warned Jill about the dangers of sex and the need to be always on guard. She brought her children up in a strong moral environment. A few years earlier, the whole family had joined a born-again Christian church where they became active members.

Karen prided herself at being close to her two children, Jill and her younger brother, James. She chose to give up her job when her daughter was born. It was important for Karen to be there for her children and not entrust their care to anyone else. She was a mother first and foremost. She wanted to be with her children for all the important events in their lives, unlike her often-absent parents.

Karen enjoyed being a lunch mom at school and attending her kids' sporting events. James played soccer while Jill loved basketball. Karen and her husband rarely went out, because they did not want to leave their children with babysitters. She particularly wanted to stay close to home, because James suffered from diabetes and his sugar levels had to be monitored closely. Worry for her children never left Karen completely.

Her husband Mark had a good job with a law firm. He worked long hours and was often tired and crabby when he got home. He relaxed with a couple of drinks and Karen worried that he had a drinking problem. When she confronted him, he denied it vehemently: "Can't a man just relax with a drink?" Mark was a good, caring father, but was often preoccupied with work. For the most part, he entrusted the care of the children to Karen and she appreciated that he made enough money so she could stay at home. She never wanted to be a career person. Her children were her life. While Karen considered her husband a good parent, she was concerned when he became overly strict with the children. He could be demanding, especially when they procrastinated with their chores. Mark wanted things done right and had little tolerance for half-heartedly done tasks. When the children did not behave as he expected, his temper showed, although he never hit the children. Karen would never stand for that. She always stepped in to protect her children when she thought Mark was being too hard on them. Actually, James and Jill were a little afraid of their father. They gathered around Karen like chicks around a mother hen.

Karen had been sensitive as a child, easily hurt, and her parents did not understand her. Karen was determined to be a parent different from her own. She encouraged her children to talk and listened carefully to the undertones and unspoken messages. Jill and James came to her with their problems and Karen always offered wise counsel. "You can tell me anything and I will understand," she reassured them. She carefully monitored all their activities with their friends and at school. At teacher's conferences, if she sensed the teacher was unfair or too demanding, Karen quickly spoke up in her children's defense. Her husband chided her, "You baby the kids." But she ignored him as "too strict and out of touch." After all, she knew her children better than anyone. When her son, a sensitive child, was picked on at school, she decided to home school him for two years.

Karen wanted, more than anything, to keep her children safe. She never wanted them to feel as insecure as she did growing up. An undercurrent of fear and desperation coursed through her childhood home. Her parents had both been previously married and had an affair together that broke up their marriages. They subsequently married each other. Her mother was a weak woman who complained all the time about how hard her life was. Her life was difficult because of the choice she had made. Karen's mother married a man who drank excessively and worked sporadically. Many days he sat home and drank. When he was drunk, he became embarrassingly sexual, made lewd jokes and comments and tried to fondle Karen and her sisters. At times he walked around the house half-naked in a drunken stupor. "I felt disgusted and there was nothing I could do," Karen said. Her mother stood back and ignored what was going on. She withdrew into watching television soap operas. Karen asserted, "I couldn't rely on either of them."

Karen felt alone and uncared for growing up. Her stepfather paid attention to her only when he was drunk and felt sexual. Her mother complained that the children were a burden to her, moaning, "Why did I ever have children?" Karen became a sounding board for her mother's ceaseless complaints. However, nobody ever listened to Karen or paid any attention to what she wanted.

Karen was the oldest of five children. As her stepfather withdrew into alcoholism and his own sexual fantasies and her mother increasingly ignored the harsh reality of their home life, Karen assumed more and more responsibility for her younger siblings. She made sure the younger ones were clean, fed and ready for school. She helped them complete their schoolwork. They looked to her as their mother. She found a role that gave her a measure of satisfaction. Karen reasoned, "If no one would protect them and care for them, I would step up to the plate." She assumed the role of the responsible one until the burden became too much. One day, at the tender age of fifteen, she ran away from home, never to return.

Suddenly, it dawned on her that Jill was doing what she had done: "She was running away from me. I was smothering her by being overprotective." As she learned to relax with herself, she loosened her grip on her children.

CHILDHOOD CONNECTION:
AN OUT-OF-TUNE SYMPHONY

Raising children is a fine art, like conducting a symphony. The conductor knows the musical piece thoroughly, with his whole heart, soul and mind. The music lives and breathes through him. He needs to be absolutely and confidently attuned to the music in his heart before he can lead the orchestra, which depends on him. The members of the orchestra look to him for direction and to combine their individual contributions into a whole and produce a beautiful, harmonious sound. The orchestra members know how to play their own instruments after years of lessons and practice. But they rely on the conductor to enable them to work together and produce the most beautiful music. Alone they are musicians; together they are a symphonic orchestra.

Parents are the conductors of the orchestra that is their family. What is unique about their directing the orchestra is that they are a twosome who must work together to produce harmony. Not only must they be attuned to the role of being parents, but they must be attuned to each other's differing parenting styles to successfully accomplish this task. Furthermore, they need to be attuned to the members of the orchestra, the children who play their own instruments. No two children are alike, just as each instrument produces its own unique sound. What a daunting task it can be to bring out the best in each of the children and to facilitate their interacting together to make a family. Each family member, and the family as a whole, work together to make a beautiful melody.

Effective parenting is also like a finely-tuned instrument. All the keys of the piano must be properly tuned and balanced with each other to make music that soars. Similarly, an effective parent cannot be too strict or too lenient regarding the rules and roles in the family to promote the growth of the children toward a healthy independence. Furthermore, they cannot be too enmeshed or disengaged emotionally in order for their children to develop a capacity for healthy intimacy.

If your parents experienced the disruption of an infidelity, they lost the capacity to create beautiful music together and make the family sing. Torn apart by the betrayal, your parents were unable to work together to be effective, nurturing parents for you. The cacophony in their relationship reverberated throughout the family. You picked up on the discordant feelings—the anger, sadness and anxiety. Consequently, you lost your sense of peace, safety and security. Instead, confusion and inner turmoil reigned. Furthermore, because your parents were so embroiled in their own problem, they had few emotional reserves to attend to your needs. They may have continued keeping you fed, clothed and with a roof over your head. They may have taken you to school and other events. However, something essential to your well-being was missing. To some degree they were emotionally absent, drained by the demands of surviving the wreckage of their marriage. They lacked the energy to be fully attuned to you emotionally and to respond consistently to your needs. The emotional chaos they experienced in their personal lives spilled over into your life.

A MUSIC MAKER

How did you cope with the emotional chaos and your parents' inconsistent care for you? Even as a child you were remarkably resourceful in finding a way to survive. You created an oasis of safety and security for yourself in which you made your own music and danced to your own tune. Perhaps as a child, like Karen, you assumed a responsible role with your siblings. You found a sense of purpose that bolstered your self-esteem in caring for the other children in your family. In becoming their caretaker, you filled the void left by your parents.

As you grew into adulthood, you found that you gravitated to that familiar role when you became a parent. You were resolved not to be emotionally distant and inconsistent like your parents. Your choice was to go in the opposite direction, immersing yourself in the lives of your children. You could direct their lives in a way that produced harmony, according to the musical piece that ran through your mind. Furthermore, if you happened to choose a partner who was emotionally distant like your parents, you found refuge in caring for the children. In short, you discovered a way to make up for what was lacking in intimacy in your marriage by engaging emotionally with your children. And you could avoid the dangers of getting too close to an adult, dangers you saw played out in your parents' marriage.

What are some questions you can ask yourself to determine your tendency to be more a friend than a parent to your children?

QUESTION YOUR PARENTAL ROLE

- Does my life revolve almost exclusively around my children?
- Do I need to be needed?
- Do I take pride in how close I am to my children?
- Do I have trouble saying no to them?
- Do others accuse me of babying my children?
- Am I reluctant to make too many demands on my children?
- Do I tend to avoid confrontation?
- Does my spouse see me as too lenient?
- Do I share my whole life with my children?
- Are my children my best friends?
- Will I give up almost anything to help my children?
- Am I afraid to let go of my children and let them grow up?
- Does my mood and self-esteem rise and fall with the reactions of my children?
- Do I feel like a martyr because I sacrifice so much for the sake of my children?
- Do I fear the disapproval of my children?

PATH OF HEALING: LISTENING TO YOURSELF

Children long for a strong emotional bond with their parents. Your desire to be close with your children and to keep the lines of communication open reap tremendous benefits for both you and your children as you all grow older. You teach them to be openly expressive of their feelings and to listen to each other. This validates their feelings and they come to know and trust their own emotional reactions. You are the mirror in which they find themselves. However, if they come to rely too exclusively on you for emotional support, they may never develop enough self-confidence to trust themselves completely and reach out to others. In your enthusiastic caretaking, the message they receive is that they cannot care for themselves adequately. If you do not set appropriate limits with them and hold them accountable for their behavior, they may not learn to control themselves or work up to their potential. They may not learn how to respond appropriately to those in authority outside the home.

If you unwittingly foster too much emotional dependence, your children will struggle to develop a healthy independence, self-confidence and ability to assert themselves. They never grow up. As they move into adulthood, they may be attracted to a strong, dominating partner whom they hope will parent them. The clinging may become desperate and a burden to their spouses, leading to marital dissatisfaction. Affairs arise from such discontent. Furthermore, following in your footsteps, your adult children may become more friends than assertive parents with their children. Thus another link is added to the chain of infidelity.

"How can I break that chain and spare my children?" you may ask. Instead of becoming addicted to the role of caretaker, which you developed in reaction to the emotional wasteland of your childhood, you can learn to find balance in your parenting style. That will require taking an honest look at yourself and your parenting behavior. Working with your spouse will be invaluable in the process.

1) OBSERVE YOURSELF CLOSELY.

First, observe yourself closely in your interactions with your children. What do you see? Because you felt ignored by your parents who were preoccupied with their own problems, you may not be used to anyone paying attention to you, particularly yourself. What I observe over and over with my clients is the tendency to treat themselves the way their parents treated them as children. They dismiss themselves just as their parents ignored them. "I don't want to be selfish," they object. They may come, then, to crave the attention of others because they never learned to attend to themselves. Resist that tendency and take yourself seriously.

What do you observe? How much does your life revolve around your children with few other hobbies or interests? How much do you ignore yourself? When you feel invisible to your spouse, do you then focus your energy more on your children? Do you look to them for emotional support? In your desire for closeness, you may recognize a tendency to avoid being strict or demanding with them. Are you reluctant to reprimand them or enforce rules? Do you expect little of them and excuse their bad behavior?

Try to be honest with yourself and be aware that self-deception is a constant companion. We cannot be completely objective with ourselves because we have no platform outside ourselves from which to observe. Our subjective biases and desires, often unconscious, shape our perceptions. Nonetheless, with the help of those who know us well, we can gain a measure of accuracy about ourselves. Ask your spouse, close friends or trusted family members what they observe. Listen attentively with an open mind to what they say. You may not like it if their observations contradict your self-image as a caring, selfless parent. But listen anyway, realizing that the truth will set you free, even though it may make you miserable for a time. The alternative—remaining in an illusion—will harm you and your children in the long run.

2) ACCEPT WITHOUT JUDGING.

Next, accept without judging what you see. Perhaps, as a child, you felt judged harshly and unfairly by your parents. You may have inherited from them a tendency to be quick to judge yourself. Resist indulging the urge. Just notice how thoughts of self-blame for not being a good enough parent pass through your mind. Let the thoughts come and go without trying to stop them. Be gentle with yourself and resist the urge to beat yourself up as your parents did. Recognize the harshness and unfairness of the judgment and release the anger it expresses. Hostility toward yourself will only close you up. In contrast, acceptance will open your mind to embrace the truth about yourself. It will also expand your heart to be more compassionate with yourself and your children.

3) INVESTIGATE WITH LOVING CARE.

Third, investigate carefully the pattern of the behaviors you observe. You may notice that you behave with your children similarly to the way you do in all your relationships. Perhaps you observe how accommodating you are to their wishes while ignoring your own. You want harmony in all your relationships, tending to hide any dissatisfactions or conflicts behind a façade of being nice. Loving others and maintaining family closeness are your most important concerns and you are willing to sacrifice your personal agenda, even yourself, to achieve them. Perhaps you notice an imbalance in your relationships, that you give more than you receive. Helping others excites you and you entertain a secret fantasy of rescuing others in need. "I just want those I love to be happy," you tell yourself. If they are happy, you are happy. Your happiness is dependent on them.

Does that pattern of caring for others while sacrificing yourself seem familiar to you? Trace its roots back to childhood memories. Allow your mind to wander, letting any thoughts, images or sensations emerge spontaneously. You don't have to force the memories to come. Just let yourself go and daydream for a while about the past. What you will discover is the past is not as finished as you think. It lives on in the present in the ways you think, feel and react. You recreate the past every day in the way you interact with others. In many ways, sometimes gratifying and sometimes frightening, you become your parents in mimicking their behavior and attitudes.

What memories emerge? Perhaps one of your parents or a close relative whom you admired modeled that caretaking behavior to you. If you were a religious person, your faith, praised service and self-sacrifice may have influenced you. Even if your parents were not models of selfless service, you may have relished the recognition from others for your dedication to caring for your siblings. You noticed a particular sensitivity to praise and criticism, to how others reacted to you. Being responsible and caring brought you recognition.

If you notice a pattern of being permissive and indulgent with your children, explore the possible motivations for the behavior. Listen to yourself and to the subtle murmurings of your heart. "I don't want to push them away," you tell yourself. Perhaps you fear your children will not like you if you correct them or that they will withdraw from you. You do not want anything to interfere with the emotional bond you are creating with them. You think correcting them will be hurtful, rather than helpful, and may drive them away from you.

Looking more closely, it may dawn on you how much fear underlies your parenting style. You are afraid of the disapproval of your children that would eventually lead to them abandoning you. So you cling to them, avoiding conflict at all costs. You may also cling desperately for their love, because you fear being alone. Feeling insecure in yourself, you do not believe anyone will love you as you are. Love must be earned by self-sacrifice.

Many clients confide in me, "I can't stand being alone."

I ask, "What's so terrible about being alone?"

"It's just so lonely," they respond.

I then invite them to explore the experience of being alone, pointing out, "Being alone and being lonely are two different things." Often our explorations lead to the experience of feeling empty or abandoned when not distracted by the companionship of another. They relive childhood experiences of being abandoned and feeling rejected. I encourage them, "Learn to enjoy your own company. Only then can you be a good companion to another."

4) EXPLORE ALTERNATIVES.

Next, explore alternative ways of parenting that may be more beneficial to your children. The honest investigation may reveal how out-of-balance your parenting has become for your children and the possible harm it may cause them in the long run. It keeps you dependent on each other, too entangled in each other's lives to allow healthy growth. Again, consulting with your spouse can be immensely helpful. Likely, his personality and style differ from yours. You are not mirrors of each other. However, together you can work out creative solutions.

Because of your fear of conflict, you may not believe that disagreement can be productive, as you saw in your family of origin. One parent may have submitted to the will of the other, or both lived parallel lives without attempting to resolve differences. You may fear that disagreement inevitably leads to arguing and a disruption of the relationship. You want peace to reign in your household. However, a peace that ignores differences of opinion and suppresses conflict is really a fragile peace. It produces a false harmony at the expense of honesty.

The truth of the matter is that conflict is a sign of maturity and life. Individuals possess their own minds with their own opinions, desires and agendas. In a relationship, unless there is forced conformity, conflict is inevitable with people of independent thinking. At times their opinions, desires and agendas will overlap and at other times they will collide. Efforts to resolve the differences through honest communication create intimacy in the relationship. Both parties must state clearly what they believe and value and try to understand each other. Furthermore, both parties must then negotiate with each other in a give-and-take process to resolve the differences. This intimate dialogue sparks creativity in coming up with alternatives never before considered. The fruit of this effort to resolve differences is a more intimate, mature relationship and new solutions.

If you have a permissive style of parenting, you may need to learn to be more honest with yourself and more assertive. Instead of focusing on what you imagine your children need and mindlessly imposing your agenda on them, you will have to listen openly and honestly to yourself and recognize your hidden desires. You will have to confront your need to be needed and how you use that hidden desire to control your children. Without fully realizing it, you keep your children close and dependent to assuage your fears of being alone. Love is associated with being needed. If you are needed, then you have value. And they will not abandon you.

Realizing that your own unrecognized neediness underlies your indulgence of your children, you can feel freer to assert yourself. Recognize that your children need rules and expectations to guide them. They need to be held accountable for their behavior and challenged in order to develop to their true potentials. At times you will need to confront them for inappropriate behavior and impose consequences. In assuming more control as a parent, you will also need to find a balance in letting go. Children learn from their mistakes and life itself eventually becomes their primary teacher, not you. As they grow older, gradually release your grip on them. Recognize that the center of their emotional lives will naturally shift from you to their friends and then to their life partners.

If you discover how much your life has been wrapped around your children, your challenge will then be to create a life for yourself. Over and over, I hear my clients admit sadly, "I don't know what I want for myself." Perhaps you were so focused on caring for your children and for others that you did not know what you wanted. You may be surprised at how much you lost yourself in your role as a parent. Learn to listen to the deepest desires of your heart. Pay attention to your dreams for your own life. What do you want for yourself? What activities would make you feel alive? Looking back at your childhood interests that you have let go over the years can give you some clues to what you really enjoy. Allow yourself to be that child again. What hobbies would you enjoy? Hobbies are things you do simply because you enjoy doing them, not because the activity produces anything or serves some other purpose. Do you do anything simply because you love doing it? Can you think of anything you would like to do to better yourself? Take an art class, join a gym, start a diet?

5) *LEARN TO SURRENDER.*

Finally, after all the exploring, learn to surrender. Let go of the tight emotional rein you hold on your children. Let go of the fear of being abandoned and alone and allow yourself to live fully in the present moment. Living in the present simply requires you to pay full attention to yourself and your deepest desires. Expand your caretaking to include yourself. If you are fully alive and enjoying your own life, you will extend that happiness to others. Open your mind and heart to your spouse and your children. The joy of being yourself cannot be contained. Your openness will extend your care to others in a more authentic way and you will gradually embrace your parents in the arms of forgiveness.

STEPS TO HEAL YOUR PARENTING IMBALANCES

1) **Recognize your tendency to cling to your children.**
2) **Accept yourself without harsh judgment.**
3) **Investigate the pattern and fear of being alone.**
4) **Explore alternatives; be more assertive.**
5) **Learn to surrender to the present moment.**

EXERCISE: WRITE YOUR OWN BIOGRAPHY

You have lived your life focusing on others, especially your children. In the process, you may have lost yourself. In the movie *Flight*, an alcoholic pilot crashes a plane, but saves many lives because of his skillful maneuvering. During the investigation of the crash, his alcohol and drug abuse are discovered and then covered up. While being investigated, the pilot undertakes a self-scrutiny and realizes how much he has lost because of his addictions. He is estranged from his ex-wife and son and he has built a web of lies about himself. When he has the opportunity to lie once again to save himself, he tells the truth about his drinking. His honesty results in his imprisonment and sobriety. Incarcerated, he exclaims, "I am now free for the first time in my life." His son comes to visit him in prison because his counselor asked him to write a paper about the most fascinating person he ever met. Sitting across from his father, he asks, "Who are you, Dad?"

After a thoughtful pause, the pilot responds, "That's a good question."

Without fully realizing it, you may have become addicted to your caretaking role and become a permissive parent. Like the pilot, in your addicted state, you forgot yourself. Undertake this exercise to become more acquainted with yourself. I am inviting you to write a biography of your life. You may protest, "I'm not a writer. I don't even like writing." You don't have to be a great writer to do it. No one has to read what you write. It makes no difference if your sentences are complete or your grammar correct. What is important is taking a long, careful look at your personal history.

You can begin by looking through family photo albums and gathering pictures of the most significant people in your life: your parents, grandparents, siblings and so forth. Look carefully through the images. Do not rush. When the pictures provoke thoughts or memories, let your mind linger for a while. Do not hold back. Let the thoughts, feelings and sensations emerge freely. Let your mind wander from event to event. Look at pictures of yourself at different ages and recall what was happening at the time, what you felt. Take a long look at pictures of your parents at different times in their lives. Notice the feelings that arise. Viewing pictures of your grandparents, aunts and uncles, imagine what your parents' lives were like growing up.

Do not rush the process. Look at the pictures whenever you have a free, quiet moment. Take several days or even weeks to ponder the images. Create a collage in your mind of your life's events. Jot down some thoughts, memories and reactions. When you are ready, get a notebook and begin writing. You might have some loose time frame, like early childhood, grade school, high school, marriage and so forth. Begin writing down the collage of memories without being too concerned about order, without analyzing. Put your analytical mind at rest for the moment. Write for as long as you want, whenever you feel inclined. Let the memories flow onto the page.

Your biography will never be complete, so don't try to make it perfect. Your life is ongoing and your mind will always bring up new material. At some point, though, stop to review what you have written. This time imagine yourself as a neutral observer reading your work. What would that neutral person think? Would that person feel compassion for the suffering you endured? Would he admire your resourcefulness in coping with adversity?

If you were raised in a family with an unfaithful parent, the suffering and turmoil were considerable. Can you feel some compassion for yourself as you read your own life story? Can you feel some compassion for your parents who were trapped in a painful drama? Allow the balm of forgiveness to cover yourself and your parents. See yourself and your parents as the beautiful but imperfect human beings we all are.

Chapter 12

The Absent Parent—
Flight to Safety

Steve came to therapy because he was arrested a second time for driving under the influence (DUI). "The lawyer said I should see someone about my drinking. It would look good when I stand before the judge," he responded to my question about his reason for therapy. Steve related that he began drinking as a teenager and experimented with many different drugs. When he worked as a fireman, he drank after work with his friends. His first DUI arrest happened driving home after a night of drinking with the boys. He stopped for several years and attended Alcoholics Anonymous for a period of time. Steve admitted that he'd resumed drinking the previous year because he was retired and felt bored and lonely. He claimed he had learned his lesson not to drink and drive, but confessed, "One night I was just stupid and after drinking for hours drove home from the bar. That's when the cop pulled me over."

Steve had been divorced for fifteen years. "That was all because of my drinking," he explained. His ex-wife, Julie, had been a teacher who loved children when they married. Steve never wanted to have children, because he said, "I didn't believe I would be a good parent, after the way I was raised." Nevertheless, Julie pleaded with him to have a child and he reluctantly agreed. Soon she became pregnant, giving birth to a son. Julie quit work to care for their son, while Steve continued his routine of long hours at the firehouse and his second job in home improvement. Two years later, they had a surprise, much to Julie's delight and Steve's dismay, when a second son was born. Steve was enraged and believed that Julie had tricked him, secretly not taking her birth control. He withdrew more in protest.

Feeling betrayed at the birth of his second child, Steve's drinking increased. He spent more time away at work. During his free time, he went to the bar. As the children grew older, his attitude toward them began to soften a bit. "I agreed to watch the kids on occasion and be their driver," he said. He never talked with them about what was going on in their lives. Communication was Julie's department. He just watched as an observer in the few hours he was home and spent little time with his children. He and Julie established a fragile peace. She immersed herself in caring for the children and the home, while he was the provider. Steve loved his job as a fireman. He enjoyed the thrill of putting out fires, all the excitement and danger. Afterwards, he liked meeting his coworkers at a bar and rehashing the adventure.

Then the fragile peace on the home front fell apart. As the kids grew older, Julie felt lonelier. She had devoted her life to the children and now they were spending more time with their friends. She wanted Steve to be more of a companion to her. The more she demanded attention from him, the more he withdrew. They bickered and these became full scale arguments. Steve displayed a temper which had been dormant for many years. He spent more time with his friends drinking at the bar and came home intoxicated. Finally, Julie had had enough and filed for divorce.

Steve moved out of their home to an apartment and had visitation with his sons every other weekend. As teenagers, his sons protested, "We would rather be with our friends," and refused to come to visit him. Steve futilely insisted, but eventually gave up. He maintained infrequent contact with them, mostly on birthdays and holidays. He called the children occasionally but they refused to talk with him. They blamed him for the breakup of the marriage. And besides, they had never felt close to their father.

Alone in retirement, Steve began reviewing his life. He felt deep regret for the trouble he had caused his wife and for neglecting his children. He felt helpless and hopeless to overcome the estrangement from his children, who were now adults and raising families of their own. "I wish I could do it all over again," he lamented.

Talking about his childhood, Steve began understanding his discomfort and aversion to being a parent. He was an only child. His father was a traveling salesman who loved his beer. When he was not working, he spent time on his boat with his drinking buddies. Every weekend during the summer, Steve's parents boated and left Steve with his grandmother. His mother was employed as a teacher, and she enjoyed partying with her husband. Alcohol was the one thing they had in common. When they both drank, the atmosphere around them grew tense. They began bickering and arguing. As a young child, Steve wished they would stop fighting and often hid in his room under the bed covers. As he grew older, he stayed away from home as much as possible, involved in school activities and sports. He ran track as a long-distance runner and practiced throughout the year on long, lonely runs.

One summer night when Steve was twelve years old, his parents brought him along on an overnight cruise in their boat on the lake. While half-asleep, he heard them arguing about a woman his father was seeing. The next morning, an icy silence shrouded the boat. Only the alcohol drinking later melted the silence with the heat of resumed arguing. Steve obsessed about his father being unfaithful, but was afraid to ask his parents or talk with anyone about it. The secret lay heavily on his heart.

Steve related that while visiting his aunt many years later he had a moment of awakening. She told him that both his parents had been married before to other partners and had a torrid affair with each other. His father refused to divorce his wife. Then, the unexpected happened. His mother became pregnant with Steve and his father decided to leave his wife at the time. Both his parents divorced their spouses and married each other. Steve thought of himself as the "unwanted bait child." He felt like an outcast in his family, an intrusion. When his father did pay attention, it was only to yell at him for doing something wrong. His mother kept busy with her chores, took him where he needed to go and waited for happy hour. Steve had done the math and knew he was the unexpected surprise package before they were married. What his aunt revealed helped him make sense of the estrangement he felt growing up. He knew something was not right between his parents. A shameful secret occupied the house, like an elephant in the living room. "My childhood was all lies and deception, a big façade. I always knew I could not trust them," he said sorrowfully.

Lonely and regretful, yet hopeful, Steve picked up the phone and called his sons. "I can start over," he told himself. "It's never too late."

CHILDHOOD CONNECTION:
AN EMOTIONAL WASTELAND

What can grow in a desert? Only the hardiest plants thrive in the harsh, dry conditions. Only plants that need little water and few nutrients can grow in the heat and strong sunlight, like cactus, sagebrush and wildflowers. These plants have a beauty all their own, particularly in the moonlight, when they stand as stark, majestic sentinels. Much of the desert vegetation, to protect itself, has a tough outer skin and a moist, soft inside. They also have spines and needles to keep away any dangerous intruders. The plants fight back. Darwin's theory of natural selection is most evident in the desert, where only the fittest survive in a life-and-death competition.

Being a parent is like being a gardener. Children are the flowers that grow healthy with the constant, caring attention of the gardener. Without proper care, the flowers in all their beauty wilt and die. Weeds overwhelm them and rob them of nutrients. Some flowers might survive neglect, but they are tiny and fragile. Aware of what is needed for proper growth, the gardener tends his garden with loving care. He prepares the soil and plants the right seeds for the climate of the region. You don't plant delicate orchids in the Antarctic. The gardener plants the seeds and monitors their growth with the proper amount of water, fertilizer and sunlight. He weeds the garden and protects it from invading insects and animals. He gives special attention to sick plants, carefully nurturing them back to health. What pride and joy the gardener feels when the plants are in full bloom, in all their colorful glory. He is proud of the fruits of his labor and joyful at the gift of new life. Flowers blossom through both effort and grace.

If your parents suffered the trauma of infidelity, their ability to be constant, nurturing gardeners was compromised. Because they were so distracted trying to keep their marriage together, they could not give full attention to you and your siblings. Their energy was being sapped by the turmoil in their relationship and they could not work together to nurture you properly. They may have cared for your physical needs, but undoubtedly something was missing regarding your emotional needs. Their care was at least inconsistent. And, as the sensitive child you were, you absorbed their chaotic feelings and sense of insecurity.

Your home was more like a desert wasteland than the Garden of Eden. You were a survivor who got by in the harsh condition of emotional neglect. But you paid a huge emotional price.

A FLOWERING CACTUS

How did you survive in that emotional wasteland? You became a flowering cactus that developed an outer toughness that disguised your inner tenderness. You coped by becoming self-sufficient and valuing your freedom. You learned at an early age that you could not rely on your parents to satisfy many of your needs, so you began to depend on yourself. Many would describe you as a resourceful person who found satisfaction pursuing many interests. Because you learned you could not trust people to be there for you, you turned to activities, keeping yourself busy to find fulfillment. Activity became a substitute for intimacy. All your needs for emotional closeness and dependency were buried beneath a tough façade. You tried to convince yourself, "I don't need anyone."

As you grew into adulthood, your resourcefulness and energy bore fruit. You probably became a productive member of society, valued for the work you did. Finding it difficult to relax and feeling lonely, you may have turned to alcohol or drugs, like Steve, in order to escape the pain and feel some comfort. Not feeling secure enough to trust anyone, you remained distant in your marriage if you chose to marry. If you had children, you related in the only way you knew how, with attention to their physical needs and neglect of their emotional ones. If anyone became too demanding, you withdrew into your world of interests and activities. After all, what you grew up with was normal for you and you repeated what your parents taught by their example.

Here are some questions you can ask yourself to identify your tendency to be an absent parent.

ABSENT PARENTING

- Do I have difficulty trusting people?
- Do I keep my thoughts and feelings to myself?
- Am I unaware of what is going on in my children's lives?
- Do I have difficulty having conversations with my children?
- Do I resent requests for help as intrusions on my time?
- Am I extremely involved in pursuing my own interests and hobbies?
- Do I need to keep busy almost all the time?
- Do I have difficulty sitting still or listening to others?
- Does my partner complain that I am absent?
- Do my children tend to ignore me?
- Do I spend a lot of time away from home?
- When I am home, am I engaged in my own thoughts or activities?
- Do I prefer to be alone rather than with family?
- Am I out of touch with my own feelings?
- Do I make few demands on my children?

PATH OF HEALING: ENGAGE WITH OTHERS

Lovers believe that if their love is true it will endure and actually grow stronger through separation. Adversity strengthens the heart and nourishes desire, they reason. If you are a parent who tends to disengage, you may have a secret belief that somehow your absence is beneficial to your children. As you experienced growing up with the emotional distance of your parents, you became self-sufficient and imagined yourself a stronger person for it. You became the tough cactus that can survive the harshest conditions. Similarly, you may reason that your emotional absence can strengthen your children to endure the inevitable trials of life. You imagine that disengaging as a parent will help to build character or somehow make them fonder of you.

If you consider your emotional distance to be beneficial, you are mistaken. It is true that the tragedies of life cause children to endure many unwanted and unexpected hardships, like the death of a parent, serious illness or job loss. In many difficult circumstances, children find the resourcefulness to survive and thrive. However, being uninvolved in your children's lives as a parenting strategy is seriously off the mark. Children, like delicate flowers, need constant care to blossom into the healthy, confident, independent adults they are meant to be. They need good enough parents who provide structure, guidance and the proper amount of emotional sustenance. Such nurturing gives them the foundation to cope with the inevitable frustrations and hardships of life.

Being an uninvolved parent will have a detrimental effect on your children. They will grow up feeling unwanted, have difficulty managing their emotions and behavior and will not feel competent and confident in themselves. Even if they maintain a strong façade, inside they feel worthless, insecure and weak. Much of their behavior is an attempt to prove their own adequacy. As they grow into adulthood, they may choose to remain alone and not trust anyone. If they do marry, they may remain emotionally aloof, which can drive their partner into the arms of another for comfort. Your children will tend to imitate your disengaged parenting style with their own children.

MAKING A DESERT INTO A GARDEN

How can you transform your parenting style so your home resembles a lush garden more than a desert? You grew up as an invisible child and now you may have become an invisible parent. Your household is a garden neglected by you, even though your spouse may be a very involved parent who attempts to make up for your absence. How can you now become an equal partner in parenting? Again, I recommend following a few steps toward self-awareness and self-acceptance. I believe that authentic change grows naturally from the cultivated soil of self-awareness and self-acceptance.

1) SEE YOURSELF CLEARLY.

First, recognize your tendencies to withdraw and become uninvolved with others and with life in general. "I like to watch people," you may observe about yourself. Now watch yourself. Notice how often you use the word "no" with your spouse and your children when they ask you to do anything with them. Over time they will stop asking you. Is that what you want? Observe, too, how often you withdraw into your own world. It might be into the world of your thoughts or the world of your interests and activities. How often is your family included in your activities? How often do you participate in theirs? Do you consider it a hassle to discipline your children, help them with homework or play catch with them?

Observe the impact of your aloofness on your children and on the family. Does your spouse tend more and more to leave you alone, because she has gotten the message? Do your children also receive the same message? They have given up asking for attention from you and now avoid you. They do not talk to you. Instead, they speak more with your spouse, each other or their friends. You are left out of the loop. Your children begin to ignore you as you ignored them, and as your parents ignored you.

The word *ignore* is interesting. It is the root for ignorance. The word comes from the Greek which means "not knowing." Your path to healing is to become aware and make the effort to know and overcome ignorance.

By temperament, you likely appreciate knowledge about many things but have not yet turned the searchlight onto yourself. Introspection does not come easily for you. However, you may be a natural scientist. Being objective is your strength. You are probably more accustomed to looking at life as an observer rather than as a participant. Use your strength of observation to help yourself by becoming more aware of yourself, especially your hidden depths. Be as open to learning about yourself as you are to learning about the world around you.

2) ACCEPT WHAT YOU SEE.

Next, like a good scientist, accept all that you see without quickly passing judgment on its value. Many of my clients beg me, "Just tell me what to do. You are the expert and I'm paying you for your advice." They want me to make a value judgment about how they should live. Instead, I encourage them to be good scientists themselves. I ask them to pay close attention to themselves and reserve judgment. When they have gained enough information, analyzed the data and come to understand themselves, then they will be in a secure position to make a decision about what to do. They will make well-informed personal decisions based on their own values and priorities. As you move through this process of discernment, be patient about rushing to make any decisions about what to do or not do as a parent.

3) ANALYZE WHAT YOU FIND.

Third, having gathered much data, now try to make sense of what you observed. Even a superficial investigation may reveal that your tendency to withdraw into your own world is repeated in many situations, not just in your home. In fact, that pattern of emotional withdrawal is likely a lifelong pattern from childhood. It has become a deeply ingrained habit. It may quickly become clear to you that you are repeating a familiar behavior from childhood. You learned well from your parents how to disengage.

Viewing behaviors from the outside may be within your comfort zone. Now look inside and inquire, "What purpose could acting this way serve?" Asking yourself the reason behind such behaviors may take you into uncharted waters. You see surfaces clearly, but the depths remain murky for you, especially the realm of emotions. Like a Greek philosopher, you rely on reason and put passions aside to stay reasonable. Nonetheless, you will never come to deep and accurate self-knowledge unless you venture to look more deeply at your possible motivations for acting.

Your emotional detachment serves a purpose. Like the animal you are, it serves a survival function. In the face of a threat, animals fight, flee or freeze. What you do is flee from perceived danger. Growing up, you perceived emotional closeness as dangerous because your parents let you down so often by not being there for you. They may have criticized you harshly, not listened to you and even discouraged you from speaking up. Perhaps you were punished for expressing your feelings. To protect yourself, you withdrew your expectations of nurturance from them so you would not suffer the hurt of disappointment. You withdrew trust from them because you experienced them as untrustworthy. There may also have been lies and secrets about their affairs and your image of reliable, committed parents was shattered by the revelation of the infidelity. You then generalized your mistrust to the whole world of personal relationships and found safety in self-directed activities.

4) EXPLORE ALTERNATIVES WITH YOUR PARTNER.

Next, explore alternative ways of being a parent with your children. Aware of your tendency to withdraw and the harm it causes your children, you have the motivation to look for different, more effective ways of parenting. If you look beneath your aloof, tough, rational surface, you will realize a tenderness and unfulfilled longing for connection with people. Only your fear of being hurt stands in the way. Your children also long for connection with you. You have a special, irreplaceable, biological relationship with them along with your spouse. Your children cry out for attention, guidance and nurturing from you. Deep within yourself you have the capacity to love them deeply and passionately.

The path to healing takes you where you would prefer not to go, because of your fears. The best way for you to come to know yourself and explore alternative ways of parenting is through honest communication with your co-parent. Understandably, that may seem to be a daunting task for you, because you have avoided such intimacy your whole life. Furthermore, in your parents you lacked good role models of honest communication. But the only way of overcoming the stranglehold of fear is to face it and see it for the illusion that it is. Make the effort to speak openly and honestly with your partner about ways of becoming more involved with your children. You may feel awkward talking about your feelings and may not have a clear idea about what you believe or feel about parenting. Just dive into it. Bumble along the best you can and see what emerges. Even the effort to communicate is an act of love that breaks down the barrier of separateness you feel in relationships.

If you have been an uninvolved parent, you may ask your spouse to suggest ways of becoming more engaged. Allow yourself to be present, physically and emotionally, at family gatherings. Make an effort to communicate more with your spouse and your children. Spend some quality time with each of your children alone in some activity that they enjoy and choose. Let them decide what they want to do and just go along with it. Make time with your spouse to talk about the rules of the house and the expectations you share regarding your children. These are just a few ideas that may stimulate your imagination and desire to explore further with your partner ways of becoming involved.

You grew up in a house of lies. Your parents lied about their infidelity. They were dishonest with themselves, with each other and with you, because of their shameful behavior. No wonder you learned to be dishonest, especially with yourself, and not to trust anyone. Not only did you become disengaged from others to protect yourself, but in the process you became distant from yourself. You lost intimacy with yourself. Furthermore, you came to mistrust both your perceptions and your feelings. What your parents told you did not match your experience. You believed their distortions rather than your own truth.

Aware of what has been missing, you can make it a goal to pay closer attention to yourself, particularly to the feelings that arise spontaneously. Make it a habit to pause frequently during the day to consult with yourself and ask, "What am I feeling now?" Pay close attention to your physical reactions. So accustomed to living in your head, you probably ignore your body. Notice your body. Because you are so used to ignoring your feelings, you may not even be able to identify them. You can begin by noticing your physical reactions— the tension in your neck and back, the churning in your stomach and shallow breathing, for example. Feelings are expressed through these subtle, and not-so-subtle, spontaneous physical reactions. Let your scientific mind focus on your own body and see what you learn.

There is another benefit. Getting in touch with your feelings will enable you to be more attuned to the feelings and needs of your children and your partner. You can break the chains of isolation.

5) STAY OPEN.

Finally, be open with your mind and heart. Fear and mistrust have clenched your heart, clamped down your feelings and narrowed your vision. You have lived a constricted life, isolated from yourself and others. Allow yourself to gently open to yourself and others. Let them know you and the richness inside you. Allow the love you hold inside to radiate outward. Let that love embrace first yourself, then your family and then your parents who loved you the best that they could. Escape the prison of your fear. You have the key: It is the love you hold in your heart, a power beyond reckoning.

Steps to Heal Your Parenting Imbalance

1) **Recognize your tendency to isolate emotionally.**
2) **Accept; don't judge yourself.**
3) **Investigate the pattern of withdrawal and mistrust.**
4) **Explore alternatives; engage with others.**
5) **Open your mind and heart.**

EXERCISE: DIALOGUE WITH YOUR PARTNER

Self-awareness and self-acceptance heal. The healing begins when you make a commitment to pay close attention to yourself and to take yourself seriously. Meditation facilitates the process, but can only take you so far. Having been wrapped up in yourself in fearful guardedness, you need another step to move forward. You have lived long enough in solitary confinement. The presence of another with whom you can share yourself in honest communication can open the prison door. You cannot come to know and accept yourself fully alone. The loving communication of another can help to set you free.

The Marriage Encounter movement was founded in the 1950s to help couples enrich their relationships. The movement is affiliated with the Catholic Church and has the further goal of deepening faith. However, you do not have to be Catholic, Christian or even religious to appreciate its benefits. Through weekend retreats, Marriage Encounter brings couples together to explore, rediscover and reconnect with their partners. The heart of the program is a structured dialogue that encourages the couples to share themselves by sharing their feelings. Couples are taught a process of communication in which both reveal their feelings without being judged or analyzed. They are encouraged to express their honest feelings without blaming or criticizing. The sessions are not used for problem-solving or pressuring partners to change. The goal is simply to help couples listen and speak from their hearts.

The rules of the dialogue are simple and straight-forward, using the acronym WEDS:

1) Write for ten minutes a love letter focusing on feelings.
2) Exchange the letters and read them twice, once for the head, and once for the heart.
3) Dialogue for ten minutes on the strongest feeling in one of the letters.
4) Select a question for your next dialogue.[13]

Each of the dialogues focuses on a question of personal concern in the relationship. For example, some questions for dialogue might be: What is my strongest feeling today? What is the most difficult situation facing us as a couple now and how do I feel about it? What did I most look forward to today and how do I feel about it? What is my dream for tomorrow? When did I feel closest to you today? Please forgive me for what I did. How did I feel about it?

You get the idea about the questions. They aim directly at your heart and feelings and not your head. The dialogue is also intended to be a regular feature of the couple's life together, making them more attuned to themselves and each other.

I encourage you to engage in this dialogue process to help open your heart. It may appear contrived, because in a sense it is. However, you may need to utilize a technique which you can make a regular practice to release you from the long-ingrained habit of withdrawing into yourself. Spontaneous, heartfelt communication does not come naturally for you and it's possible it never will. Nonetheless, you can open yourself a crack by going against the grain with this practice. What is natural (but shut down in fear) is the love you hold in your heart and long to express. The practice can assist you in expressing that love and connecting with your partner. In connecting with your partner, you can allow yourself to be closer to your children.

Part 5
Challenges of Offending and Offended Parents

Chapter 13

The Offending Parent—
The Truth Will Set You Free

Bridget, an attractive Irish redhead, came to therapy a month before her wedding. "I thought my wedding day would be the happiest day of my life, but it is turning into a nightmare," she complained. Both she and her fiancé, Paul, had been previously married to partners who were mismatches for them. Paul and Bridget agreed that they were "soulmates" and wished they had found each other many years before. What prevented the upcoming wedding day from being perfect was the reactions of their children. Paul had an eighteen-year-old daughter who refused to attend the wedding.

"It's all a sham and I won't have any part of it," she protested. Bridget had two teenage sons. The younger son was thrilled his mother was marrying, while the older one despised the idea. The older son, who lived with his father, refused to spend weekends with his mother and pretended that the wedding was not happening.

Bridget acknowledged that she could understand the anger of the children, although it still hurt. More than anything in the world, she wanted to establish a harmonious family with Paul. When she was newly married to her first spouse, Bridget met Paul while she was working as a junior editor in the publishing company he owned. Bridget admired his energy, drive and creativity and looked forward to going to work each day. She secretly had feelings for him, but never pursued a relationship because both were married. However, they became good friends, talked often at the office and even went out as a foursome with their spouses.

Over the years, Paul became Bridget's best friend with whom she could share anything. They talked about their work, their families, their dreams and their marriages. Bridget had married her first husband, Brian, when she was twenty years old. He had been her high school sweetheart. But soon after the wedding, Brian changed. He began to drink more, spent more time away at work and became moody and sullen. With the birth of their children, Brian objected to the fact that Bridget wanted to continue working and put the children in daycare. Bridget loved her work, having advanced to a senior editor position, and she especially enjoyed working with Paul. Brian's moodiness escalated into temper outbursts, especially when he was drinking. He became a raging tyrant when intoxicated, demeaned Bridget and hit her on two occasions. Bridget felt trapped in her marriage. She was raised Catholic and firmly believed that she and her husband were sacramentally bound to each other "until death do us part." She would stay married, she believed, until it killed her.

Bridget shared her marital heartaches with Paul and he showed an empathy she had always longed for from her partner. At the same time, Paul related to her the stresses he felt in his marriage with a nagging wife. They commiserated with each other and they sensed a growing bond. Looking back, Bridget admitted that she was having an emotional affair with Paul as she felt more distant from her husband. Then, one evening after going out for a drink after work, they crossed the line and had sex.

Brian had suspected for a while that something was going on between his wife and her boss. Bridget stayed late at work more frequently. She received mysterious phone calls and texts at all hours. Then, one day he checked her computer and found a sexy e-mail from Paul. Brian was enraged and confronted Bridget. She denied anything except friendship but Brian did not believe her. He began monitoring her calls and activities. He secretly put a GPS tracking device in her car. The tension between them grew and their bickering escalated into full-blown shouting matches. The children witnessed the arguing and Brian complained to them that their mother could not be trusted.

Finally, the open hostility reached the point that Bridget blurted out, "I'm having an affair and I'm done with this marriage."

Bridget surprised herself that she had the courage to file for divorce after eighteen years of marriage. She had been so miserable for most of those years, feeling so demeaned and dominated, that she was relieved when she finally made the decision. However, it was a contentious divorce and the children took sides. The older son chose to live with his father, while the younger one, who hated his father, moved in with Bridget.

Paul, who had divorced his wife the year before, began dating Bridget secretly at first and then more openly. No one in the office was surprised. Everyone could sense the chemistry between them. After several months of a rocky courtship, torn between passion for each other and guilt, they decided to set a wedding date.

"I never envisioned my life would take these turns," Bridget reflected. She was raised in the country, where she enjoyed working hard beside her stepfather, whom she admired. He was a strong, quiet man. Bridget could not remember her father, who left when she was four years old. Only when she was an adult did her mother tell her honestly what happened in their marriage. She related that Bridget's father was a moody, passionate man who loved alcohol and gambling. He worked in a factory and spent most of his paycheck every weekend at the casino. One day he suddenly disappeared, leaving only a note which read, "I do not love you anymore and am leaving town with another woman." Bridget's mother was devastated and fell into a deep depression. She had never suspected that he was involved with a waitress at the casino he frequented every weekend.

For several years her mother struggled to raise Bridget and her sister on a meager salary as a secretary, until she met Jacob, a stable, hardworking man who owned a farm. After a brief courtship, they married. Bridget became quickly attached to her stepfather. Her mother, however, never seemed to fully recover from being abandoned by her first husband. Despite Jacob's trustworthiness and sensitivity, she harbored a deep suspicion that one day he would also leave her. Bridget realized, "I know now why I have always felt so insecure in relationships."

Bridget resolved that she would not let fear and guilt ruin her relationship with Paul and their children. "I will be patient with myself and them," she told herself.

IMPACT ON THE CHILDREN: BREAKING THE RULES

Children play, naturally and spontaneously. Watch an infant play with his hands, moving, grasping and sucking his fingers. Notice his delight when the parent plays peekaboo, hiding then reappearing. The repetition of the game never bores the infant, always bringing a smile. When infants become toddlers exploring the world, the games change. They play with dolls, action figures and other toys. Yet older, their imaginations take hold and they play house or cops and robbers. At a later age, they join other children like their siblings and play games together, creating their own worlds of make believe. The games graduate to higher levels as the children mature. They play board games, cards, checkers and other contests. These games have their own rules which children learn they must follow to avoid arguments and get along. The play extends to the outdoors with the rule-bound games of baseball, football, soccer, hockey, lacrosse and basketball. A sense of competition grows. Playing helps children develop their imaginations, social skills and a sense of rules and roles in a confusing, unpredictable world.

The playing does not end with childhood. Adults play their own games, some for fun and some seriously. Interacting with others in the social and work world, they must learn the rules of the game of life to survive, fit in and advance. They learn how to work within the rules to benefit themselves and others, realizing both their necessity and limitations. Unfortunately, some bend the rules to their advantage, causing others harm. They pay the price, suffer the consequences and may even end up in prison.

As a social institution, marriage has many rules that define it and give the family a sense of stability, predictability and security. Many expectations regarding marriage are explicit while others are implicit but well understood. One clear expectation for married couples is that their relationship is special and exclusive, emotionally and sexually. The boundaries are clearly defined, especially regarding sexual expression. No sex with anyone but your partner. If you have an affair, you break the rules of marriage in a serious way. The repercussions of that choice reverberate throughout the family and affect spouse, children, extended family and even society as a whole.

THE BETRAYAL BOND

How do children react to you if you break your marriage vow and have an affair? How does it affect your relationship with them? The short answer is that they feel betrayed and you as a parent must repair the damage. Let us look more closely at the ripple effect of betrayal.

"I'm scared because things aren't the way they used to be." When you break the rules by having an affair, you throw your children's world into confusion. Your marriage and the family are no longer a safe, predictable haven for them. Naturally, they react with anxiety. As your marriage crumbles, their sense of security is shattered. They may wonder if you will get a divorce and break up the family. "Who will take care of me?" they ask themselves. Younger children will not understand what is happening in the family, but they will soak up all the tension you and your spouse display during this crisis in your marriage. They may become more nervous, withdrawn or irritable. Distracted by the turmoil at home, their schoolwork may suffer. The older children also sense trouble but may be left in the dark if you hide in secrecy and deception. They may flee the tension at home by staying away and spending more time with their friends. If you are at all attuned to your children, your guilt may deepen. You realize the harm you are causing your children as well as your partner.

"If I can't trust my parents, who can I trust?" Your children suffer a loss of trust in you and in themselves. You broke your marriage vow and deceived the family. You have betrayed the family trust. Naturally, your children are disillusioned by your behavior when they eventually discover the truth. Your actions have not matched your words. Children find emotional safety by idealizing their parents. As they mature, they give up their illusions of perfection, that "my mommy and daddy are the best in the world." Normally, the illusion of the perfect parent is questioned during adolescence when the teen sees your defects more clearly and may rebel to establish independence. However, when your children learn about your affair, the natural process of disillusionment is short-circuited and fast-tracked. In fact, you may quickly become a devil in their eyes instead of the angel you used to be. With this loss of credibility, your children may become more oppositional, argumentative and defiant. They may challenge authority in school, become more rebellious or take drugs.

Your children may also come to mistrust themselves, particularly if the secrecy and deception persist. Children perceive much more than parents realize, even if they do not understand what they are experiencing. Like a spinning top, they are sensitive to shifting emotional ground and quickly lose their balance. They sense something is off kilter, but cannot grasp the reason. The more you keep secrets and concoct lies, the more confused and insecure they feel. Children need to trust their parents to feel secure in a confusing, frightening world. When your words and self-presentation do not match their experience, they begin to doubt themselves. "My parents would never lie to me," they tell themselves, "so what I feel must be wrong." The worm of self-doubt slowly eats away at their self-confidence. The chaos of the outer world invades the safe confines of the home.

"I'm so embarrassed about what my parents did; I don't want anyone to know." Because of your behavior, your children experience a sense of shame. As sexually open-minded and liberated as our culture pretends to be, we cannot escape our Puritan roots. In the hidden recesses of your conscience, you wear a scarlet letter "A" on your chest like Hester Prynne in Nathaniel Hawthorne's *The Scarlet Letter*. Your children absorb your guilt and shame. Young children especially tend to believe they are the cause of everything that happens around them, including your behavior. They are stained by your guilt and want to hide in shame. Embarrassed, they do not want their friends to know about the problems their parents are having. The veil of secrecy you brought into the family now covers them. Carrying the burden of shame, their self-esteem suffers. Your child may seem sad, more withdrawn and less willing to talk. He may not want to spend as much time with his friends or may want to keep busy with them to distract himself.

I am surprised that so little has been written about the impact of infidelity on children. So much publicity has been given to the affairs of prominent people, which has inspired a plethora of books, articles and talk shows on infidelity. Hardly anyone speaks openly about how the children are affected. I speculate that shame keeps the topic hidden. Those involved in affairs feel too guilt-ridden to consider deeply how their behavior affects their children. Adults, wanting to protect the idealized image of their parents, do not want to explore the possibility that their parents may have been unfaithful and hurt them by their behavior. That would open Pandora's Box.

"I'm so angry I can't stand it." Your children are angry, even enraged, at you because of the betrayal. That is understandable, because your infidelity disrupted the security of their world. Much of the anxiety, shame and insecurity they feel inside may be expressed outwardly in hostile behavior. Your children may refuse to talk with you or they may engage in verbal tirades against you. They may become more defiant, argumentative and deceitful. Their anger may extend outside the home and be expressed at school through skipping classes, not studying or being disruptive. They may become involved in delinquent behavior, stealing, destroying property or associating with troublemakers. As teenagers, they may express their rage in rebellious actions, such as drug use or sexually acting out. They may test limits, break the rules and ignore boundaries, as you did by stepping beyond the bounds of marriage. Your children observe you closely and, even if they reject what you offer as guidance, they imitate your behavior. Your actions shout so loudly that they cannot hear what you are saying.

"I feel so guilty for hating them." As enraged as your children may feel, their anger also generates anxiety and guilt in them. They fear pushing you out of their lives with their anger, when deep down they have a strong emotional bond with you as their biological parent. For better or worse, you will always be their parent. As young children, they need you for survival, physically and emotionally. As older children, they grow into adulthood identifying with you. Their anger also inspires guilt within them. Any thoughts of revenge rebound upon their own heads as a betrayal of their natural-born loyalty to you as their parent.

How your children react is influenced by their temperament. Those who tend to be more aggressive by nature may express their anger more openly against you. They may become more defiant at home and school, rebelling against authority that has failed them. The children who are more fearful and dependent may cling to you or your spouse, suppressing the anger they feel. Acknowledging their anger would generate too much anxiety about the family falling apart and their being abandoned by you. Shy, withdrawn children may become even more invisible in order to protect themselves and avoid making waves.

As your children grow older, they may verbalize more openly the hurt, anger, shame, mistrust and sense of betrayal they feel, making clear the impact of your behavior. Nonetheless, the behavior of the younger children also stands as a wordless protest against the injustice of the betrayal they suffered.

CHILDREN'S REACTIONS TO THE OFFENDING PARENT

1) **Increased anxiety about family disruption**
2) **Lack of trust in you and themselves**
3) **Sense of shame**
4) **Anger about betrayal**
5) **Guilt for being angry**

PATH OF HEALING: BE HONEST

An astute observer of the human heart, Jesus stated, "The truth will set you free."[14] Only facing the truth will free you and your family from the bondage of infidelity. Having constructed a network of lies to cover your affair, at some point it may have dawned on you how much you were caught in your own deceptions and entangled by your lying. Thrashing about, creating more lies to hide your shame about the affair, you may have come to believe your own falsehoods. You fabricated reasons for the affair in your own mind, blaming your spouse for your unhappiness in the marriage. Trapped in your own distorted thinking, you lost your sense of reality and didn't really know what was true. Truth became a stranger to you.

1) BE HONEST AND SEEK TO UNDERSTAND YOURSELF.

The first step in your own recovery is to open your mind and heart to the truth. You need to be honest with yourself before you can be honest with your family. Only honesty will repair the damage you have inflicted on yourself, your spouse and your children.

The first question to ask yourself is: "Why did I have the affair?" Working with couples who have been traumatized by infidelity, I discovered that most affairs are a symptom of a disconnection in the relationship. Affairs normally do not occur out of the blue. Often, many years of dissatisfaction and tension in the marriage precede them. Sometimes the extent of a spouse's misery is hidden from her partner until the affair is revealed. I have observed six kinds of affairs, which I describe in my book *Transcending Post-Infidelity Stress Disorder (PISD)*. I also describe a path to healing.

1) Some people engage in affairs because they fear emotional closeness. They often seek a comfortable distance from others in activities and isolation. They can be workaholics, married to their jobs and the pursuit of success. Interestingly, these emotionally disengaged individuals often marry someone who is emotionally needy. Because of their fear of intimacy and desire for freedom, they withdraw more when they feel pressured from their partners to relate. Their partners chase them while they run away. An affair becomes attractive because it offers an escape from the pressures of intimacy, often into the arms of another who is admiring and undemanding, at least for a while. Eventually, the pattern of flight is repeated with the new lover when the person feels smothered and then disengages.

2) A second type of affair occurs in marriages in which both partners fight desperately for control. Their relationship is like two scorpions trapped together in a bottle. They fear being dependent on each other or on anyone and create distance in their relationships through competition and hostility. Power struggles dominate their interactions. They tend to live parallel lives together. These often success-driven people mistrust others, seeking control and power to maintain a sense of safety. At the root, they fear intimacy and dependence. The affair may be a way of asserting their independence or retaliating against their partners. Eventually they repeat this power struggle with their lovers. They may try to dominate him or her, with a similar result.

3) A third type of affair arises from a fear of being independent. Some individuals long desperately to love and be loved. A romantic spirit possesses them. They appear to love just being in love. They exhibit strong needs for approval, affection and support. Behind their desire for love, however, lurks a fear of

being abandoned. They cling to their partners, because they do not believe they can stand on their own and survive, physically or emotionally. Too often, they choose partners who appear emotionally strong and tend to dominate them, so they withdraw into their own interests. When they feel ignored by their partners, who feel smothered by their demands for attention, these insecure people may look outside the boundaries of their marriages for someone to lean on. Over time, the pattern of clinging also drives the lover away.

4) Some affairs, the one-night-stands, are isolated events in which the involvement is limited to sex without any emotional intimacy. The act is impulsive and facilitated by a set of circumstances, often under the influence of alcohol or drugs. The unfaithful person believes he acted out of character, caught up in the moment. And the unfaithful behavior may never be repeated.

5) Some affairs exhibit a compulsive quality because they arise from a sexual addiction. With sexual addiction, there is little real emotional involvement in the encounters and the person has sex with many different individuals. This is your so-called philandering partner who is always on the prowl. Usually, this person has a long, hidden history of sexual behaviors like using pornography, going to strip clubs and frequenting massage parlors. He usually engages in multiple affairs.

6) The final type of affair signals the end of the marriage. It is an exit affair. The individual becomes involved with a lover, because he or she has decided to leave the marriage. Perhaps the person may not be fully aware of the depth of his or her dissatisfaction or decision to leave. These individuals may be reluctant to file for divorce. The affair is their way of saying that they are done.[15]

Stop to consider the ways you were disconnecting with your spouse and what led you to have the affair. Look closely at the timing, what was happening in your life and in your relationship. Perhaps you had unacknowledged feelings about the birth of a child, a job change or a recent move. Perhaps you held some unexpressed anger toward your partner. Try to be honest with yourself. You may need the help of a therapist to explore more deeply the patterns of your behavior, your hidden motives and the influences of your childhood. The truth, as painful as it may be, will set you free to move on with your life.

2) AVOID BEING ABSENT.

Second, resist the tendency to become an absent parent. You may have been so preoccupied with your lover, living a double life, that you were absent from the home. Now that you are dedicated to your own recovery, you may continue to be withdrawn but this time into your own moods and thoughts. Feeling depressed and ashamed, you may want to spend more time alone. The stress of arguing with your spouse about the affair may drain you. Uncertainty about your future, whether to stay married or not, whether to pursue the affair or not, may grip you. Resist the temptation to become so self-absorbed, remembering that your children need you as a parent. Manage your personal crisis as best you can but reserve time and energy for your children.

3) MAKE A WISE DECISION.

Third, make a wise decision about what you want. Initially, there are really only two choices: to stay or leave the marriage. If you leave, you have another decision: whether to continue the relationship with your lover or not. If you still love your spouse and believe there is a chance of repairing the damage in the marriage, couple's therapy can be helpful. Together, you and your partner can explore what went wrong in your relationship, decide what you both want and work to restore trust. The affair can be a painful moment of awakening to hidden cracks in the foundation of your relationship and to how much you really love each other. Realize that your partner has been deeply wounded, even traumatized. Her world has been turned upside down and she lives in the grip of uncertainty and insecurity. Recovery may take a long time for both of you, with moments of emotional upheaval and many fits and starts. Be patient with both yourself and your spouse.

Your children need you to make a clear decision—stay married or get divorced. Maintaining a relationship with your lover while still married causes your children nearly irreparable harm. You broke the most important rule of marriage in having an affair. The boundaries of marriage and the family were breached by your decision, causing your children pain and confusion. Continuing a double life only exacerbates their suffering and their mistrust of you. Consider the message you are giving your children about marriage and commitment if you stay connected with both your lover and your spouse. What impact will that have on their attitudes toward relationships as they mature? Remember, you are their primary role model. Therefore, it is essential that you end the affair. Furthermore, you will only be able to work on your marriage if you are fully committed, without distraction, to the process of reconciling.

If you decide to divorce, the children will recover far more quickly than if you continue the pretense of a double life for any length of time. If you are truly unhappy in the marriage and cannot reconcile the differences after a wholehearted effort, it is better to divorce. Continuing to be miserable in an unhappy marriage only teaches your children to tolerate the intolerable and to live a charade. The children will adjust over time, especially if you continue to be a responsible parent with them.

4) FORGIVE YOURSELF.

Fourth, forgive yourself and move on. Recognizing the harm that you have caused your family, you may be overwhelmed with guilt. Avoid becoming a prisoner of guilt. You can use that painful sense of remorse to transform your life and live more in accord with your most important values. As was described in a previous chapter, you can begin to heal through a process of honest self-confrontation. Begin with a moral inventory, acknowledging your faults and strengths. Look at yourself and avoid blaming your spouse for your behavior. Then confess your faults to another. Do not hide behind the veil of shame and self-deception. You exercise humility when you confess and acknowledge the truth about yourself to another. Next, with a firm intention to change your behavior, plan to make amends. Try to repair the damage you caused in a way that is beneficial to those you harmed. As you work through your guilt with honesty, you come to embrace forgiveness and surrender the need to punish yourself.

5) MAKE AMENDS.

Finally, make amends to your children by being honest with them. You cannot be honest with them until you have faced yourself with an open mind and heart. Making amends equires much effort on your part. You must consider carefully what they need and what will be helpful. You do not want to overwhelm them with too much information. That requires sensitivity to the individual personalities and ages of your children. How much truth-telling is appropriate for them? What do they need to know about the troubles in your marriage? How do you balance their need to know with your right to privacy? Only you can make these difficult decisions, knowing your children and yourself. You can begin to repair the damage of deceit by being truthful.

Here are some elements to consider in talking about the affair with your children:

- Your children need to know you are sorry and recognize the harm you caused them. Apologize to them from the heart. Acknowledge your wrongdoing without blaming your partner. Express to them your awareness of how you have hurt them, particularly if you made them collaborators in your crime by sharing the secret with them while the affair was ongoing. You must be sincere in expressing sorrow, or you will deepen their mistrust of you. Children are exquisitely sensitive to two-facedness.

- Confused by the turmoil in the family, children need to know its cause. Carefully explain to them, according to their ability to understand, the problems you have been having in your marriage. Speak generally, not in detail. Your children need to see you as human, with both weaknesses and strengths. The older your child and the more interest the child expresses, the more you can explain. Invite their questions and answer them honestly.

- Admit your affair in words your child can understand. For example, admitting that you were "too close a friend," "fell in love with," "acted inappropriately," or "kept secret a relationship" with someone other than mother or father. Again, avoid giving details.

- Children tend to blame themselves for what occurs in their world. Assure them that nothing is their fault. Take full responsibility for your behavior.

- Feeling insecure from the disruption in the family, children need reassurance that they will be cared for. Assure them with both words and actions that you will be there for them, no matter what happens. Assure them also that you and your spouse are working at resolving your problems. Promise them that you have learned from your mistake and will not let it happen again.

- You must be truthful with your children and cannot make false promises, even that the family will stay together when that is not the case. If you choose to divorce, you can tell them about it at the appropriate time.

- Listen to your children when they express anger or hurt. Do not be defensive or dismiss their feelings. Your children need to be heard and know that you understand their suffering.

Just as the truth will set you free to move on with your life, being truthful with your children will help free them to trust you again. Planting seeds of trust and nurturing them with love and honesty can help them not to repeat the mistake you made. You can begin to model a mature, truth-based relationship for them. Your recovery can begin to alter the family legacy of infidelity.

PATH OF HEALING: RECOVERING HONESTY

1) **Be honest with yourself.**
2) **Seek to understand the reason for your affair.**
3) **Avoid being an absent parent.**
4) **Make a wise decision to establish clear boundaries.**
5) **Forgive yourself.**
6) **Make amends with your children by being truthful.**

EXERCISE: A WALK IN THE PARK

If you have been unfaithful, your world has been closed up, shut down and needs to be opened up. You were caught up in passion, preoccupied with your lover and satisfying your desires. Greed and lust ruled. Now that you are involved in your personal recovery, you are again preoccupied—this time with your overwhelming sense of shame and guilt. You are aware of how you have betrayed the family and your own values. You see the pain in the eyes of your spouse and your children. "How could I have done this?" you ask yourself. That echoes the pleading questions of your family. As you open your mind to that question, realize the need to open your heart in compassion for your family and for yourself. You need a breath of fresh air to open you up.

A way of freeing up your mind and heart is by walking in the outdoors. Nature heals. Unfortunately, we have been so sealed within the artificial worlds we create for comfort through technology that we have gotten out of touch with our natural selves and with the rhythm of the universe that courses through us. We have disconnected from our deepest nature by our actions and need to restore balance again in our lives. Communing with nature can help.

Choose a favorite outdoor place. You may realize, sadly, that you do not have a favorite place because you have become such a stranger to the great outdoors. Try to find a place that holds beauty for you. It may be in a neighborhood park, along a lake or on a path through the woods. You may be fortunate enough to live near mountains, the ocean or a national park. These are ideal places to expand yourself. The natural beauty around you uplifts your spirit. Observing the beauty of a delicate flower, feeling the gentle power of the wind and warming yourself with the sun's heat draws you to the source of all that beauty. It puts you in communion with the majesty of the universe.

Begin simply by walking and paying close attention to your body as you take each step. Walk mindfully. Be aware of your leg muscles contracting and relaxing with each step. Feel the swing of your arms in rhythm with your steps. Feel your feet touch the ground—the heel and then the toe. Sense the rhythmic beating of your heart, its increasing pace. Experience the calming repetition of the movement. Allow yourself to relax completely in the moment. Let any distracting thoughts about your problems fade. Do not fight them. Just gently let them come and go, passing through your mind like the breeze.

Instead, focus on the movement of the various parts of your body and on your breathing. Sense the tension leaving your body. Through your body you are connected to the whole material world, from which you came and to which you will return.

Relax in your body and notice the splendor of your surroundings. Have you ever paid close attention to your natural environment? Listen to the birds singing and the sound of the rushing water. Feel the breeze on your face and the warmth of the sun. Looking up, let the deep azure sky draw you into its spaciousness. Observe the protean clouds floating above you. Notice the attention-seeking, colorful flowers and the trees offering shade. Watch the branches and grass sway in the wind as if alive. Smell the fragrance of the flowers and the freshness of the air. Perhaps you will catch a glimpse of a scurrying squirrel or a majestic hawk in flight. Allow your heart to swell with the wonder of all you see, feel, smell and hear.

Opening your senses to the richness of the world around you, you will be transported beyond yourself. What a wonderful world! That world exists within you and you within it. In comparison, how unfair to condemn yourself for your problems. After all, your heart contains the whole universe.

Chapter 14

The Offended Parent—
You Are Stronger Than You Think

Anne, an impeccably dressed woman in her sixties, came to therapy because her depression had become crippling. "I sleep all the time and can't motivate myself to do anything," she explained. Anne had always lived a quiet life, enjoying shopping and occasional outings with friends. But in the past month she never left her elegant suburban home. Depression was not new to her. She had periods of black moods throughout her forty years of marriage and raising her three children while her husband, Harvey, travelled for business.

Anne met Harvey while in college. She admired his energy, wit and ambition. He was a charming man whom all the women flocked to on campus. Anne, in contrast, was a soft-spoken wallflower whom men hardly noticed. What surprise and excitement she felt when Harvey turned his attention to her! No man had ever shown such interest in her. Her thrill knew no bounds when he asked her out on a date. That began a thoroughly unexpected, out of character, whirlwind affair. Soon they lived together on campus, much to the chagrin of her stuffy parents. A year after graduation, they were married in a stylish wedding reported in minute detail on the newspaper's fashion page.

Soon after graduation, Harvey was hired by an international corporation. Because of his intelligence, ambition and supreme self-confidence, he advanced rapidly in the company. He became the executive sales director in Europe and was required to travel there every month on business. Anne hated the separations, but consoled herself with the elegant, comfortable lifestyle his job provided. Within a few years they had three children and Anne occupied herself with caring for them. She enjoyed staying at home. She entertained herself with her interest in arts and crafts and decorating their home. She also enjoyed shopping sprees. Hiring a babysitter, Anne went out every week to browse the stores, looking for home decorating ideas or additions to her fashionable wardrobe. "I was a kept woman but I didn't mind it," she admitted.

Her world nearly fell apart, she reported, after they were married about ten years. Harvey had inadvertently left his personal computer on. Anne knew little about Harvey's business because he rarely talked about it. When he returned home from travelling abroad, he was usually exhausted and only told Anne about the trip in vague generalities. His business was technical and Anne had no interest in that. However, when his computer was left on and exposed, curiosity possessed her. Scrolling through his e-mail, she found a note with the subject "lover." Her heart almost stopped when she read the message from a woman in France recounting her and Harvey's wild sex together. Stunned with disbelief, Anne confronted Harvey when he got home. After hours of arguing, he finally admitted that he had a mistress in France whom he visited on nearly every business trip.

Anne's serene life exploded. She and Harvey argued constantly about the affair. He made promises about ending it but in reality became more secretive. Anne tried to monitor his activities more carefully but he only became more adept at deception. Clearly, the affair was continuing and Anne felt helpless. "Harvey was a runaway locomotive and I became a train wreck," she lamented. She considered divorce but felt frozen with indecision, stating, "I cannot accept the affair but I'm afraid to leave." She was afraid of being alone and unable to support herself. Besides, she enjoyed the comfortable lifestyle that Harvey provided. Anne survived by making a compromise with herself. "When I'm feeling down or angry with Harvey, I'll just shop," she reasoned with herself. She found comfort in her shopping and being with the children. She further protected herself by distancing herself from Harvey. They led parallel lives, side-by-side but separate and never touching.

However, the sadness and periods of crippling depression never left her. Often she stayed in her bedroom all day and her children then worried about her and catered to her. They learned to take care of themselves when their mother became depressed and isolated. Without being told, they knew that somehow their father was the culprit. They could see how their mother's mood changed during his absence and felt the chill between them when together. They saw him as a charming but emotionally distant man who ignored them. "I'm busy making money so you can enjoy this lifestyle," he explained to justify his absence. The children gathered around their depressed mother to comfort her and themselves.

During therapy, Anne talked about growing up in a fashionable area in the Midwest. Her parents were socialites in an upper class suburb, involved in church and the party circuit. Anne was their only child. She felt lonely with no siblings and little attention from her parents. Babysitters often cared for her, because her father was occupied running the factory he owned and her mother was busy with shopping and socializing. Anne attended private school and enjoyed all the finer things in life, but the sense of inner emptiness and unfulfilled longings never left her.

Exploring her parents' marriage, Anne commented, "They lived parallel lives and rarely spent time alone together. They attended parties together but both went their separate ways." She was always confused by their separateness. Then one day when she was already married, a close neighbor friend told her in a moment of drunken honesty that her father had a mistress throughout the marriage. Anne was shocked and fought with herself about how it could be true. She refused to accept the truth, dismissing it as just "drunk talk." She never asked her parents about it to avoid embarrassing them. She preferred to tuck that secret away in reserve and not delve more deeply into it.

But when she discovered Harvey's secret life, she knew instantly that what she had been told about her parents was true. "I have been living my mother's life," she saw in a flash of insight. Although in the early days she couldn't make up her mind to divorce Harvey, in therapy she decided to not continue the charade. It was costing her too much, not just to herself; now she recognized the impact on her children. She began making plans for how she could live on her own and support herself.

IMPACT ON THE CHILDREN: NO STURDY SHELTER

Children need a home in which to survive and thrive. Not only do they need a roof over their heads, but their home must be a sturdy shelter to provide safety and security. Most of all, children find solace in the strength of their parents. Parents provide a safe haven against the threatening world for their children in the stability of home life, predictable structure and constant nurturance. In their helplessness, children rely on their parents to be strong, loving and wise. They need to be able to put their trust in their parents to negotiate the perils of growing up in a confusing, frightening world.

When you are married to someone who cheats on you, your secure world falls apart. The shelter of your marriage collapses and you feel alone, unprotected and victimized. A childlike sense of helplessness may overwhelm you. After initial shock and disbelief, you may be overcome with a flood of emotions: fear, rage, sadness and a deep depression. You can easily drown in the sea of uncontrollable emotions if you do not find a life raft for yourself. Restful sleep eludes you, nightmares may disturb you and you feel exhausted. How will you cope with life? A once seemingly certain future has been destroyed and you feel lost. Floundering in the churning sea of emotional pain and uncertainty, you wonder how you will survive.

HOMELESS AND HELPLESS

While you are caught up in your marital storm, how do your children survive? They look to you as their parent to be a sturdy shelter. What happens to them when you feel broken and are looking for someone to support you? On whom can they rely? How do they react to you, the betrayed and broken parent?

"I feel so nervous all the time." Children are like Geiger counters that pick up subtle signs of radiating emotions. As much as you try to hide your feelings to protect them, they are aware of them at some level. They notice the change of mood, the different tone of voice and the increased time spent alone. They observe your red eyes, your tiredness and your distracted gaze. Psychologists tell us that as much as 90 percent of communication is nonverbal.[16] Your children, who may not as yet have developed verbal fluency, quickly pick up the nonverbal signs of distress you radiate without intending it. Your distress becomes their distress. They mirror your emotional state as they go about their business, playing with their friends or going to school.

"I want to help Mom and Dad." Your children sympathize with you, because they sense you have been victimized by the way you react. Initially, you likely think of yourself as a helpless victim because of the affair. You were betrayed and you had no choice in the matter. The more you think of yourself as a victim, the more negative feelings of helplessness you radiate, which your children soak up like dark sunshine. Your sympathizing children feel your anxiety about your crumbling world, your sadness at the loss of love and security and your rage at your betraying partner. They want to help relieve your pain.

Their sympathy for you and fear of losing you may cause them to cling to you more. They watch you closely and do not want to be too far away from you. You may wish to be alone but they want to be with you. Furthermore, you may cling to them more for comfort. Since you feel so estranged from your cheating spouse, their company fills the void of your loneliness. You may also rely more on the older children for help. Feeling exhausted from struggling with so many conflicting emotions, you may turn to them to help care for the younger children and keep everything running in the home. The older children may ask you directly what is wrong and you may want to tell them all about your marital problems and how hard life is for you now.

"You betrayed me too." Your children also pick up on your anger at their other parent. Whether or not they know about the affair, they sense accurately that your spouse is the violator and you are the victim. Their sympathy for you in your pain causes them to identify with your anger at being betrayed. Your rage becomes theirs. Attempting to protect you, they may become more defiant, argumentative and belligerent with the offending parent. They blame him for disrupting the peace of the house. If they know about the affair, the older children especially may become downright confrontational with the cheating parent. They may freely express the rage you feel. If your children do not know about the affair, you may desire to tell them so they can understand the reason for your distress. You may also want them as allies in your war against your betraying spouse.

"How could you be so weak?" Another reaction of your children toward you may be surprising. Instead of sympathy, some of your children may be angry with you. It may strike you as unfair to blame the victim. However, they are expressing a feeling that you may not acknowledge openly. At some level, you blame yourself for the infidelity. Somehow, you imagine you were responsible, because you were not good enough as a wife or husband. Furthermore, you may blame yourself for not seeing signs of the affair quickly enough. If you continue living with your cheating partner and tolerating the intolerable, you find another reason to berate yourself for your weakness and stupidity. Once again, your children mirror your thoughts, feelings and judgments. They see your weakness on display and resent you for it.

"Where are you? Can't I count on you?" The children may also feel resentment at being neglected and having to take care of themselves and you. As you withdraw to nurse your wounds, they are left alone to fend for themselves. And they do not like it. Your children depend on you to be the strong, guiding force on whom they can lean. They want you to take care of them and attend to all their needs. Children can be self-centered and demanding. During the crisis, you may not feel strong enough to support them in the ways to which they have grown accustomed. They resent that the established routine of care is interrupted. Children often do not understand that their parents have lives and needs separate from them. Children, even older ones, believe that the world revolves around them. They can be intolerant if your attention shifts to your own world. Yet their anger at you is not comfortable for them because they need you and risk alienating you.

As much as your children have sympathy for you in this difficult time, they may resent taking care of you. The role reversal burdens them. Some children may relish caring for you because it makes them feel needed and important. They grow up to become caretakers. However, other children resent adult-like responsibilities being foisted on them and intruding on their time just being carefree children. Even older children want to have their own lives and may resent the demands of your neediness.

"Who can I trust?" Also, your children may lose trust in you. It makes sense that they mistrust their unfaithful parent who broke the rules. However, their mistrust of you may make little sense and can even be hurtful. "What did I do?" you ask yourself. Ponder for a moment what your children have lost. They look to you to be a tower of strength to support them. They draw strength from you to overcome the helplessness of being a child. Your character shapes theirs. When you are overwhelmed by a personal crisis and display your deficiencies, their sense of security is shattered. They cannot rely on you as they did before. Remember, children idealize their parents when they are young in order to facilitate the process of internalizing your adult strengths. It takes maturity for them to see you as a human being with both virtues and vices. In the meantime, display of your emotional fragility undermines their trust in you and brings fear that you will not protect them.

Temperament affects how your children react to you. Children who tend to be more dependent by nature likely will show sympathy and want to help you. They are the budding caretakers. The temperamentally more aggressive children will be freer to express their resentment at being neglected or having to care for you. They will be less tolerant of your showing any weakness. Those who are more shy and withdrawn will try to stay out of the way. They will want to be self-sufficient and not cause you any more trouble.

CHILDREN'S REACTIONS TO THE OFFENDED PARENT

1) **Mirror your feelings.**
2) **Feel sympathy for you and want to help.**
3) **Anger at your weakness.**
4) **Anger at your neglect.**
5) **Loss of trust in you.**

PATH OF HEALING: BE STRONG

When you are desperate and down, where do you find a bridge over troubled waters? Some simply tread water, trying just to keep afloat. They may distract themselves by keeping busy, ignore the problem for a while or anesthetize themselves with alcohol or drugs. Many turn to others for support. That assistance enables them to survive until the waters settle. Most underestimate the strength they already possess and look outside themselves for that bridge. I suggest that adversity presents an opportunity for you to become more aware of your own inner strength and goodness. Discover the planks of that bridge within yourself. That does not mean that you build the bridge on your own. If you are being mindful in all of your relationships, then you will you come to know yourself.

In my book *Transcending Post-Infidelity Stress Disorder (PISD)*, I described how the offended partner is deeply wounded, even traumatized, and elaborated six stages of healing. Here are some important points summarized.

1) CALM THE EMOTIONAL STORM.

The first step in your recovery is to calm the emotional storm. If you are feeling so overwhelmed by your feelings that you have difficulty functioning, you may need therapy and possibly medication. You work through your feelings, not by avoiding them, but by facing them squarely. There are no shortcuts to calming the storm. You need to acknowledge all your feelings, accept them as your friends and make the effort to understand them. Your feelings of distress, as uncomfortable as they are, serve a survival purpose to help you cope. When you understand their wisdom, their intensity will decrease. Then you can figure out a wise course of action. You cannot help your children through their crisis until you are calm enough to work through your own.

2) UNDERSTAND YOURSELF.

The second step in your recovery, just as for your offending partner, is to understand yourself. That requires being truthful with yourself. Your strength comes from truth, which you already possess, but you may not be fully aware of it. Your truth-based strength will radiate to your children and help repair the damage of the infidelity. They will survive as you do.

The first question to ask yourself is: "Why did the affair happen?" In exploring this question, it is important that you do not blame yourself for the affair. Let me make it clear. You are not responsible for your partner's behavior, for his or her choice to have an affair. He or she alone is responsible. No matter how miserable he or she was in the marriage or how you contributed to your partner's misery, he or she could have responded in many different ways. The affair was his or her choice.

As we discussed earlier, an affair is a symptom of a disconnection in the relationship. You may have not been aware of the depth of your spouse's unhappiness or even your own. The affair can be a wake-up call for you that there are problems that need to be addressed. If you choose to stay together after the affair, addressing the underlying problems will strengthen your relationship. If you choose to separate, understanding yourself will prepare you for your next relationship. Unless you understand your part in the disconnection, you will repeat the same pattern with a different partner. What you learn about yourself in this self-discernment process you pass on to your children. That wisdom will strengthen them as they prepare to enter the arena of mature intimacy and parenting.

How did your behavior contribute to the dissatisfaction in the marriage? Parallel to what was explored in the last chapter, your style of interacting affected your partner. I have observed three typical patterns in relationships in which there was infidelity:

1) Some people tend to cling to their partners. When they have children, they tend to become overly involved emotionally with them too. These romantic individuals find the value and meaning of their lives in their close relationships. They live for love. They enjoy taking care of the family and the home. However, beneath this façade of selflessness resides a fear of being alone. They feel worthless inside and believe they can be reborn through the love of another. They crave attention, affection and approval. These insecure individuals choose as mates people they perceive as strong, independent and assertive, partners who possess the qualities they admire and lack within themselves. While initially being the caretakers of their partners, over time they lean more and more on their spouses, expecting to be cared for. When their spouses begin to feel smothered and withdraw, they then become more demanding of attention. The strangling mate may seek relief and emotional distance by having an affair. Those who cling to love often ignore the signs of infidelity or become hyper-vigilant, because of their deep fear of being abandoned.

2) The more aggressive types view relationships as power struggles. They seem to enjoy arguing, being right and proving others wrong. They present themselves as strong, assertive and independent. They want to be in control in every situation in their lives, especially in their relationships. The desire for power and control motivates them. However, beneath this façade of strength and competence often lurks a deep insecurity. These individuals fear emotional closeness and use their anger to keep others at a distance. Inside, they feel powerless and need to protect themselves from being exploited. They hide this inner softness behind a tough exterior. They may choose as a mate someone who is submissive, so they can dominate him or her and feel in control. Or they choose someone who will battle them and enjoy the fight as much as they do. "I fight, therefore I am" is their mutual slogan. The fighting keeps them connected but emotionally distant. The aggressiveness and consequent lack of intimacy can provoke the partner into having an affair.

3) A third group tends to become emotionally disengaged in their relationships. They flee closeness by keeping busy pursuing their own interests. They find substitutes for emotional intimacy in their love of work, projects or hobbies. They may be charming and sociable, but hold themselves back in relationships. Focused on the world of their own thoughts and interests, they may be oblivious to what is happening in their partners' lives. These individuals value freedom and being themselves at all costs. But deep down, they fear depending on others so they flee into self-sufficiency. They mistrust that others will really be there for them so they learn to rely only on themselves. For partners, they choose individuals who will not make demands on them and will be as self-sufficient as they are. Consequently, they live parallel lives in their marriage. Such an arrangement works until the other partner feels lonely enough—desperate enough—to look for love outside the marriage.

Consider carefully and honestly whether you exhibit any of these tendencies in your marriage. Be aware of how you spontaneously relate to people. You may even observe in yourself a combination of the above tendencies to move toward others and cling, to move against them and fight or to move away from them and flee. No one is perfect. We all learn our ways of relating from childhood experiences and what our parents modeled. Knowing your tendencies can help you work more effectively with them and not allow them to control your life unconsciously. Try to understand how your partner reacted to you so you can appreciate which dissatisfaction with you may have influenced his or her choice to have an affair. Knowledge is power. It will enable you to avoid making the same mistakes again.

3) AVOID CLINGING.

Third, don't clutch at your children. Feeling lost and abandoned by your spouse, you may observe a desire in yourself to rely more and more on your children for support. Feeling like a helpless victim, you may want to find allies in your children in the fight against your transgressing spouse. Resist the urge. Even though they sympathize with you and express concern for you, lean on others rather than your children. Letting them care for you reverses the parent-child roles in the family. Having them take sides with you against the other parent dismisses their need to be attached to both parents. Clinging to your children violates the boundaries in the family and will only exacerbate their confusion and resentment. Your partner violated the boundaries with the affair. You need to be strong in asserting clear limits.

4) MAKE A WISE DECISION.

Fourth, make a wise decision about the marriage. If your partner chooses to continue the affair and still wants to stay with you, have nothing to do with that. It will only cause endless heartache for you and the children. Staying with your partner while he or she lives a double life makes you an accomplice to the crime. You continue the charade and teach your children by your example to tolerate the intolerable. If your spouse will not end the affair, you need to stand up for yourself and your children and end the marriage. Your children need the example of clear boundary-setting for them to effectively negotiate the world of intimate relationships as they grow up.

If your partner ends the affair, is genuinely remorseful and is willing to work at rebuilding trust, a revitalized marriage is possible. However, you must decide whether or not you love your spouse enough to engage in the process of rebuilding a broken marriage. The affair can be an opportunity for both of you to rebuild your relationship on a firmer foundation. Working through the rubble of your relationship to restore love and trust can be a wonderful example to your children of the power of love and the strength of problem-solving.

5) FORGIVE FROM YOUR HEART.

Finally, forgive yourself and your unfaithful partner. You are undoubtedly enraged at your partner for betraying you and at yourself for becoming the victim. You are pissed. That is understandable. Yet stop for a moment to consider the consequences of your anger. Certainly, it protects you from being further harmed. It energizes you to stand up for yourself, and, if you deem it necessary, to persevere in pursuing a divorce. After that, what purpose does your continuing anger serve? It only harms you and those around you. Your cheating partner moves on with his or her life, with or without you. Anger is a poison that slowly eats away at you physically, emotionally and spiritually. It robs you of happiness. You cannot be tense, angry and ready for a fight while being relaxed, peaceful and content at the same time. Anger and contentment are opposing states of mind.

Forgiveness sets you free from the prison of your own hatred. Forgive for yourself and your children. It is no fun for them to be around an angry person. You heal from the wound of betrayal through the power of forgiveness. Forgiving is not a sign of weakness, a condoning of the wrongdoing or a forgetting of the harm done. Forgiveness is simply letting go of the anger and the desire for revenge. It does not happen overnight or with a simple act of will. Instead, forgiveness is a process that involves a journey of facing the hurt, understanding yourself and your partner and releasing the pain. You discover that you forgive as the wound heals and then you are free to love again. Model forgiveness for your children so they will be free to love their unfaithful parent.

You might be wondering how to approach your children about the affair. Trust yourself that you know best what your children need. Here are some ideas to serve as guidelines.

1) Your children need to know that you are not falling apart and will be able to take care of them. Be strong. Assure them that you are okay and will care for them, no matter what. Realize you need to take care of yourself before you can adequately parent your children. Get the help you need. Do not hesitate to consult with a professional. Admitting your need for help is a sign of strength.

2) Your children can see the toll the affair is having on you, even if they do not know the cause of your distress. They will be afraid and may want to help you. Resist the temptation to rely on them for support. Seek support elsewhere from your friends, a therapist or your pastor.

3) Children need to bond with both parents. Resist the urge to bad-mouth your cheating spouse. Do not express your rage to them about what you are suffering. Avoid having your children take sides.

4) Lost and confused, your children need to have some understanding of the turmoil they are experiencing in the home. It is best that you and your spouse explain together in broad terms the struggles you are having and trying to resolve. Be honest but do not overwhelm them with details. You have a right to privacy as much as they have a need to understand. Let your partner explain about the affair in his or her own way.

5) The children may side with you, because they sympathize with your pain. The older children may ask you about the affair directly. Sooner or later, children tell you what they want to know. Answer the direct questions as clearly and simply as you can, again, without going into details. Be truthful. Your children have had enough lies.

6) Do not cast blame around. If your children blame themselves, assure them it is not their fault. Do not blame the unfaithful parent for the current problems. Take responsibility for yourself and your actions.

7) If your children come to you expressing their anger and hurt, listen with an open mind and heart. Encourage them to express their feelings without pressuring them to do so. If they need to

be quiet and work it out for themselves, respect their need for solitude.

8) If your children appear overwhelmed by the turmoil in the family, seek professional help. You can just take the younger children to a therapist but you cannot force the older ones. However, you can invite and encourage them to see a counselor.

Suffering the trauma of betrayal, your greatest challenge will be overcoming the tendency to become lost in the helpless victim role. You can escape that trap by taking charge of your own recovery and healing yourself through the power of forgiveness. That forgiving heart will open in compassion to all your relationships, embracing especially your parents who betrayed you as a child. As you model forgiveness, your children will open their hearts to you and their offending parent.

PATH OF HEALING: BEING STRONG

1) **Calm the emotional storm.**
2) **Understand yourself and your partner.**
3) **Avoid clinging to your children.**
4) **Make a wise decision, maintaining boundaries.**
5) **Forgive yourself and your partner.**

EXERCISE: A MEDITATION

Spiritual practices offer both comfort and challenge. In distress, the practices console us, but once we are calmed they engage us to look more deeply and act more lovingly. A traditional spiritual practice for Christians, as mentioned previously, is a heartfelt meditation on a scriptural passage. The Bible expresses the wisdom of God for believers. Even nonbelievers can benefit from the human wisdom contained in the Bible. For you who are struggling to forgive your unfaithful partner, I recommend a passage from the gospel of John (8:3–11).

Retreat to your quiet place where there are no distractions and you can become attuned to the stirrings of your heart. Sit comfortably and relax. Focus on your breathing or the beating of your heart. Gently release the jumble of thoughts running around in your head. Pay attention to your body slowly releasing its tension. Once calm, read the next passage slowly. In fact, read it twice—once for the mind and once for the heart.

> The scribes and Pharisees brought a woman along who had been caught committing adultery; and making her stand there in full view of everybody, they said to Jesus, "Master, this woman was caught in the very act of committing adultery, and Moses has ordered us in the Law to condemn women like this to death by stoning. What have you to say?" They asked him this as a test, looking for something to use against him. But Jesus bent down and started writing on the ground with his finger. As they persisted with their questions, he looked up and said, "If there is one of you who has not sinned, let him be the first to throw a stone at her." Then he bent down and wrote on the ground again. When they heard this they went away one by one, beginning with the eldest, until Jesus was left alone with the woman, who remained standing there. He looked up and said, "Woman, where are they? Has no one condemned you?" "No one, sir," she replied. "Neither do I condemn you," said Jesus, "Go away, and do not sin anymore."[17]

Imagine yourself in that crowd, waiting for Jesus' answer. You know the law. Adultery is a sin that deserves punishment. (As an aside, when I read this passage, I wonder what happened to the man involved. Why was he not brought for judgment?) Look around at the faces in the crowd: their anticipation, their disgust at the woman and their desire for revenge. Sense their hatred and agitation. Observe the shame and fear in the woman, her downcast eyes and sloping shoulders. She awaits execution. Then notice Jesus and the difference in his demeanor. He remains calm and unperturbed by their testing of him. He knows the truth in his heart and the conniving falsehood in theirs. Sense his love and compassion as he looks upon the sad, scared woman before him. With whom do you identify most in this scene?

Now imagine your unfaithful partner standing before Jesus and the crowd. Undoubtedly, you are so angry and hurt that you desire revenge, like the crowd members do. Feel your rage and the deep pain. Do not ignore it. As Jesus invited the crowd to look inward at their own lives, acknowledge your own faults and your anger at yourself. Realize that in your mind you may also see yourself as that condemned woman. Feel the pain of self-condemnation. Let Jesus' words penetrate your heart: "Neither do I condemn you." Out of the magnanimity of his heart, he offers forgiveness. Jesus does not pretend what she did was acceptable. He instructs her not to sin again. His forgiveness frees her to live more lovingly.

Only forgiveness will bring you serenity. That forgiveness opens your heart and has no bounds. It embraces your unfaithful partner, yourself and your parents.

Chapter 15

What to Tell the Children

The principal from the high school her daughter attended called Sally one day, "Mrs. Nelson, I need you to come to the school. There's been a problem with your daughter, Ashley," he said.

"Is she okay?" Sally asked in a panic.

"She's fine. She just got herself into some trouble," he responded.

Sally rushed to the high school with anxious thoughts racing through her mind. "What did she do now?" she wondered. Her oldest, Ashley, was a sixteen-year-old whirlwind. She could never sit still as a child, at home or at school. In elementary school, the teachers constantly complained that Ashley disrupted the class with her talking and squirming. She could not pay attention and her grades suffered. Finally, Sally took her to a doctor who diagnosed her with Attention Deficit Disorder and prescribed medication. The medication helped but Ashley was still her energetic, accident-prone self, struggling just to pass her classes. As she neared the high school, Sally became more agitated about what kind of trouble Ashley had gotten herself into this time. In the past year, Ashley had begun sneaking out at night to be with her friends. Arguing and grounding her did not stop her. She had grown stubborn, defiant and hostile. "I'll do whatever I want and you can't stop me," she'd proclaimed smugly. Sally and her husband Brian became more concerned when Ashley came home drunk on several occasions and once they found a condom in her purse. Even her friends were becoming concerned about her drinking and her reputation for being loose.

Arriving at the high school, Sally went immediately to the office. Ashley was sitting next to a security guard. She looked defiant and would not even acknowledge her mother's presence. The principal immediately greeted Sally and escorted her into his office. He proceeded to explain: "Ashley was caught smoking marijuana on school property. The police have been called and she will be suspended from school." Sally sat deflated and defeated, wondering what she could do to help her wayward daughter.

Sally and her husband Brian had three children: Ashley, fourteen-year-old Kaitlyn and ten-year-old Trevor. Kaitlyn had just begun ninth grade and seemed Ashley's polar opposite. She was calm, quiet and studious. She never caused any problems and always offered to help around the house. Even as a young child, Kaitlyn was "mommy's little helper" and became her mother's constant companion. When Trevor was born, Kaitlyn loved to watch over him and was anxious to learn more about childcare. She became Trevor's "second mommy." Kaitlyn excelled in school and was a regular on the honor roll. Everybody loved Kaitlyn. Her sweetness and gentleness attracted young and old to her. Sally spent much time with Kaitlyn, shopping and talking about their activities. In the past year, Sally noticed that Kaitlyn seemed to cling to her more. She seemed anxious and distracted, less focused on her studies. Kaitlyn watched Sally closely, always wanting to know where she was going. Sally had the sense that Kaitlyn was mothering her.

Trevor was the son that both Sally and Brian had always wanted. They admitted that they spoiled him. He was quiet and carefree as a child. Growing up with two older sisters who pampered him, he expected everyone to baby him. Always wanting to please others, he did well in school and often became the teacher's pet. Like Kaitlyn, he never caused any problems. He seemed a happy child who loved to play with his friends. He enjoyed baseball in the summer, football in the fall and basketball during the winter months. He was a popular child with many friends in the neighborhood and at school. But Sally had noticed a change in Trevor during the past year. The fun seemed to disappear from his life. He refused more and more to go out with his friends, preferring to stay alone in his room playing video games. He lost interest in sports and outside activities.

Sally wondered what was happening to her children and if she could somehow be the cause of the changes she observed. Those thoughts quickly passed through her mind, because Sally was preoccupied with her own problems. During the past year, she was shocked to discover that Brian had been having an affair with someone at work. She further learned that he had had several affairs which had been hidden for many years. Sally was numb with disbelief. Her depression was punctuated by outrage and loud arguing with Brian. Their future together was uncertain and Sally did not know if she could trust Brian's promises that the affair had ended. A thought streaked through her mind. Perhaps her children mirrored her inner turmoil.

Realizing with the wake-up call about Ashley how her children were being harmed, Sally's resolve was strengthened to work through her problems with Brian. The first step would be to insist that his affair end or she would leave with the children.

IMPACT ON THE CHILDREN: COLLATERAL DAMAGE

When you marry, a physical and emotional bond is created through the commitment. The birth of children expresses most clearly both the physical and emotional nature of that bond. A couple then becomes a family with their children. They are set apart, united and bonded for the rest of their lives. Your children always remain your children, no matter the age, through a biological and emotional connection that can never be completely broken. The bond may be denied, strained or ignored, but it remains like a shadow that you can never run away from.

If you are unfaithful to your spouse, you betray that marriage bond, straining it to the breaking point. Your partner suffers a trauma—a deep wound that cuts to the core of his or her personal and marital identity. Your children are not just passive observers of the betrayal. As members of an emotionally bonded family, they too suffer the wound. Their identity as a united family is shattered, leaving them adrift in an emotional storm. Their security is replaced with confusion and uncertainty. They absorb all the pain and confusion that you feel without the cognitive and emotional maturity to manage it.

Experiencing the trauma of their parents' infidelity, seeds of heartbreak are planted in your children which bear fruit as they grow into adulthood, pursue intimate relationships and become parents themselves. These seeds, though tiny, can be identified if you pay close attention to the behavior of your children. Often, children cannot adequately put into words the pain, sorrow and confusion they experience but their behaviors express it. Actions speak louder than words, whatever the age. Their behavior reveals patterns of relating to themselves and others that will become more evident with passing years. I have observed three general patterns in the children of unfaithful parents. They become defiant, compliant or invisible.

1) CHILDREN DISPLAY ANGER.

Those children who by temperament become defiant act out the anger that has been unleashed in the family. Because they have witnessed the disregard of rules in the breaking of the marital bond between their parents, they feel justified in ignoring your authority. Unfaithful parents lose their credibility in the eyes of their children. Their lying and covering up further erodes their trustworthiness. Your children watch what you do closely and imitate you. They express their anger and mistrust of authority in many ways. They will argue more with you and with others. They may get involved in fights with other children. Their grades may suffer, especially if they know you value achievement in school. They may even become delinquent, breaking laws, using drugs, stealing or damaging property. They may begin to act out sexually. As parents you may feel that you are engaged in an intractable power struggle with your child. This pattern of defiance will likely continue into adulthood and express itself in more adult ways unless it is worked through. These children often grow up to follow in the footsteps of their betraying parent and are likely to become unfaithful themselves. When they become parents, their behavior toward their children is strict, unbending and domineering.

2) CHILDREN SWALLOW ANGER.

Those children who by temperament become compliant tend to internalize their anger. They become submissive to rules and to others and sacrifice themselves in the service of others. They turn the aggression against themselves into self-renunciation and often depression. Unfaithful parents damage themselves by their behavior and the children observe it and come to imitate it. They lose respect for both the offending parent for being so hurtful and for the offended parent for being so weak. Your child's compliant behavior hides the deep hurt and rage that he or she feels. You may not notice the emotional price this child is paying because you enjoy the relief of having a child who does not cause any trouble. That child may want to help you and care for you in your pain. You may welcome the attention and even be tempted to confide in this caring child. You praise the compliant child for being so good and helpful, which reinforces this behavior. You appreciate his agreeableness. As the compliant child grows into adulthood and gains the rewards of being accommodating, the pattern of self-sacrifice continues, becomes ingrained and is then expressed in adult ways. They become caretakers who are attracted to needy, demanding partners. So they set themselves up to be victimized in their relationships unless they learn to break the pattern and focus on their own needs. As parents, they value emotional closeness with their children but have trouble enforcing rules and maintaining boundaries.

3) CHILDREN HIDE ANGER.

Those children who by temperament become invisible project their anger outward onto the whole world of relationships. They distance themselves from their own anger and do not even recognize that they are angry. Because getting close to others is perceived as unsafe, they withdraw within themselves. They do not trust others or even themselves to manage the conflict of being involved with others. They learn from observing the intense conflicts in their parents' relationship that intimacy is dangerous and should be prevented at all costs. They avoid conflicts and confrontations. They learn well that children are to be seen and not heard and they take it one step further by not allowing themselves even to be seen by many others.

If you are caught up in the pain and turmoil of your marital problems you may not even notice your invisible child, especially the pain he is hiding. You appreciate that this child is not making any demands on you when you feel stretched to your limits already. You may notice that he spends more and more time alone in his room, playing video games, listening to music or pursuing his hobbies. Your withdrawn child may have few friends and may not be interested in making any new ones. You may vaguely sense his emotional absence when gathered at the dinner table, not really knowing what he thinks or feels about anything. As these invisible children grow into adulthood, the pattern of withdrawing into their own worlds and pursuing their own interests continues. They may choose to avoid making a commitment to a relationship, or if they do marry, remain emotionally disengaged partners. If they do choose to have children—many do not—they remain uninvolved in their children's lives.

Ask yourself: What are some of the signs that your children are silent sufferers in the wake of your infidelity?

QUESTIONING CHILDREN'S SUFFERING

- Is there a change in my child's school performance?
- Does my child seem sad or depressed?
- Does my child seem more nervous or anxious?
- Is my child more distracted or having more difficulty concentrating?
- Is my child isolating more or spending less time with his friends?
- Does my child always want to be away from home or always stays home?
- Does my child seem irritable and angry and have temper outbursts?
- Is my child getting into trouble at school or with the law?
- Are there signs that my child is drinking or using drugs?
- Does my child daydream more and seem to be in his or her own world?
- Is my child clinging to me more?
- Is my child more moody, sullen and argumentative?
- Am I catching my child in more lies?
- Does my child have sleep problems or nightmares?
- Does my child worry too much about school or the family?
- Is my child having more health problems?
- Is my child beginning to act out sexually?
- Does my child refuse to go to school or skip classes?
- Is my child getting involved in fights?
- Is my child beginning to steal or damage property?

TELLING THE CHILDREN

An affair is always a family tragedy. As parents involved in the drama of betrayal, you are just trying to keep your heads above water. It may take enormous energy for you to survive. You may feel like you are treading water. However, your children may be drowning also, with no life preservers in sight. The first step in helping your children is being aware of their suffering. Do not entertain the illusion that your problems have no effect on them. Children know more about what is going on than you imagine, although they may not fully understand what they perceive.

As broken as you feel you and your family are, do not give in to another illusion. Do not see all as hopeless. You can recover and help your children heal.

If you are the parent who has been unfaithful, you are the one who has spun the web of deceit in the family. The deception undermines trust with your spouse and children more than the affair itself. Both your partner and your children do not trust you, for good reason. You have not been trustworthy. They are also angry with you for the betrayal and for throwing their lives into turmoil and confusion. But they feel anxious and guilty about their anger, because deep down they need to be connected to you. To begin the process of healing in the family, you must tell the truth. If you want to continue the affair, give up the marriage. If you want to stay married, end the affair for good. Stop the hiding. Make your actions conform to your words. Be honest with yourself first of all, then with your partner and finally with your children at the appropriate time and in the appropriate way. You will need to rebuild trust with your children, as much as with your spouse, by becoming trustworthy.

If you are the parent who has been deceived, you need to be strong, or rather, to allow your inner strength to shine forth. Obviously, you have been deeply wounded, perhaps traumatized. You may feel that you can barely cope with your emotional storm, confusion and uncertainty about the future. Certainly, you need to care for yourself. Get the help you need. But do not forget the children by becoming preoccupied with your problem. In fact, expending energy to care for them may help you in your own recovery, enabling you to avoid obsessing about the betrayal. You can easily become lost in self-pity and being the victim. One way to escape the victim role is to exercise your power by taking care of your responsibilities. Loving others heals you and gives you strength. In caring for your children, despite your personal pain, you inspire them with your strength. Your children may see you as weak for not being aware of, allowing or tolerating the affair. You can show your strength by not letting the betrayal defeat you and doing what you need to do to recover.

Working through your trauma, you will need support from others. It is too much to suffer alone. Avoid the temptation to rely on your children for emotional support. Resist the urge to allow them to parent you, even if they are adults. The compliant, caretaking child may easily fall into the role of helping you through the crisis. Leaning on your children for emotional support will place an unfair burden on them that will interfere with their growth. Furthermore, avoid complaining to your children about their betraying father or mother. It will only create an impossible dilemma for them if they feel they have to take sides in your dispute. Their loyalties will be divided if you portray yourself as the innocent victim and your partner as the guilty persecutor. Remember that your children need to have a relationship with both their parents for their own emotional well-being. For the good of your children, do not complain or lean on them. Find others to support you, such as friends, a therapist, your minister or a support group.

Both parents need to be good role models, even in the midst of crisis. For better or worse, your children learn about intimate relationships from you. They also learn what it means to be a parent. They observe you closely and their image of marriage and parenting is formed from watching you. They see you as their future and they make decisions against the background of their experience growing up with you. As role models, your actions speak so loudly that your children can barely hear your words.

SOME RECOMMENDATIONS

I have several recommendations. Some I expressed previously, but I will repeat them to emphasize their importance. First, as much as possible, avoid arguing in the presence of the children. Seek privacy to resolve your differences and have respect for the sensitivity of your children. Research indicates that whether you divorce or remain together matters less than what happens as you resolve the conflict. The intensity of the fighting affects the children more negatively than the actual divorce. It provokes great anxiety in them.

Second, whatever you decide, make the boundaries clear. An affair is an intrusion in the secure domain of marriage. Adults and children both need the safety and security of a home with clear boundaries. After an affair, both the couple and the children are thrown into confusion about what is predictable and secure. The meaning of sex is changed. Is it an expression of love in a committed relationship or is it only for the pursuit of pleasure? You may decide to end the affair and rebuild the marriage or you may opt to divorce. Those decisions reaffirm clear boundaries. The children will adjust to whatever you decide, as long as you consistently, lovingly care for them. Children exhibit a remarkable resilience, even in the most difficult circumstances, if they have your ongoing support.

You may decide to continue living together and tolerate the ongoing affair. I strongly advise against it, for the sake of the children and yourselves. What is that teaching your children about committed relationships and sex? Your children will grow up confused and resentful if you do not come to some clear resolution.

Third, reassure your children. Children, because they imagine themselves as the center of the universe, may think they are somehow responsible for the problems in your marriage. They may want to fix it, but will feel powerless to do anything to help. Let them know that they are not the cause of your problem. It is entirely yours and you are working on it. Assure them also that they can remain children and do not have to take care of you. Do not burden them with too much responsibility around the house when you are so preoccupied with your problem. Finally, assure them that you love them and will take care of them no matter what happens, whether you stay together or divorce.

Despite all your personal problems in working through the infidelity, you are and will always be the parents of your children. It is easy to forget the importance of that role in the midst of your personal crisis. The children will still need to have their physical needs met—fed, cleaned, clothed and taken to school. They will still need your guidance and support and will need you to be parents who exert authority and keep a sense of order in the home. You may feel guilty for the harm you are causing them and be tempted to spoil them or be manipulated by them. Your children will feel deeply the insecurity you feel. They will need your emotional support and encouragement more than ever. You cannot give what you do not have. It is paramount that you take care of yourself so that you will be able to care for your children properly. Get the help you need. Your children will also be beneficiaries.

Many parents ask me what they should tell the children about the affair and their problems. I have expressed elements of a response in previous chapters. I invite parents to trust that they know best what their children need. I only caution them to avoid extremes: the silence of avoiding the elephant in the room or overburdening them with too much information. You have a right to privacy, even with your children. Your children are limited in what they can tolerate about their parents' problems, even as adults. Do not give them too much information. One woman who was betrayed by her husband invited her adult children to ask her whatever they wanted about the divorce. One said, "I don't want to know anything." Another responded, "I already know." The third asked a few general questions.

For example, in speaking with your ten-year-old son, you may say something like: "Your daddy and I have not been getting along for a while. We fight sometimes and have disagreements, like all friends. Your daddy and I disagree about a friendship he has with another woman. We are working it out. It is not your problem and you do not have to worry about it. Just know how much we love you and will always take care of you." Pay close attention to your child's reaction. Ask how he feels about all this and if he has any questions. Do not pressure your child to talk if he is not ready. Just keep the door open. Do not burden your child with details or more information than he can handle. Your child will let you know how much information he needs. Let him know that you are available at any time to talk with him. Create an atmosphere of openness to overcome all the hiding and deceit.

How to Help Your Children

1) **Take proper care of yourself.**
2) **Avoid arguing in their presence.**
3) **Make a clear decision about your marriage.**
4) **Reassure your children.**
5) **Create an atmosphere of openness.**
6) **Always be their parents.**

As you recover from the trauma of infidelity, you can help your children in their recovery. Your attention to their needs and compassion for their suffering can lessen the painful impact of the betrayal. As they grow older they will learn to grieve the losses of their childhood and come to forgive you for not being the perfect parents that all children wish for. Hopefully, they will begin to look inward in their own lives and give up blaming you so they do not repeat your mistakes. Then they can embrace the freedom to be themselves in any relationship they choose.

EXERCISE: LETTER OF FORGIVENESS

The wounds of betrayal by your own unfaithful parents are deep. The scars may remain for the rest of your life. Nevertheless, the wounds will heal to the extent that you forgive them. As impatient as you may become with yourself, you cannot rush forgiveness. You cannot force it by an act of will. Many will tell you, "Just forgive your parents." That is easier said than done. In fact, there is the danger, in rushing to forgiveness, that it is not genuine, from the heart and used to cover up painful feelings. If the pain and hurt are buried under a veil of forgiveness, those feelings will fester and grow in intensity. The poison will seep out and, sooner or later, the boil will burst. Instead, you need to be patient with yourself, work through your feelings and try to understand yourself and your parents. As the wound heals, you will discover, over time, that you are no longer angry with your parents and that you have learned to forgive them.

As an aid in the healing process, I recommend that you write a letter of forgiveness to your parents. Write this letter only when you are ready, when you feel that the emotional storm has quieted enough that you can reflect deeply on your childhood and its impact on your life. Letter writing is a powerful way of getting in touch with and expressing your feelings.

In writing the letter, it is important that you acknowledge the pain you have suffered because of your parents' infidelity. Allow memories of your childhood to emerge. Allow yourself to feel the hurt and confusion. As best you can, try to be honest with yourself, without minimizing or exaggerating what you experienced. You are entitled to all your feelings about what happened. After the honest, heartfelt reflection, write to your parents what you experienced and felt and its impact on you today. Do not hold back. The honesty will set you free.

Now, reflect as the adult you are and try to understand what your parents did and the reasons for their actions. As a child you could not possibly understand what your parents were going through. But as an adult, you have a more mature perspective. You can put together the pieces of the puzzle and fill in many of the blanks. What kind of people were your parents when you were a child? What was their marriage like? What influenced your parent to pursue an affair? What unhappiness drove them? Allow yourself to see them as the frail human beings they were at the time. Understanding them can open your heart to compassion and eventually to forgiveness. Write down how you have come to understand the tragedy of your parents' infidelity, fully aware that there is still much you cannot comprehend.

Finally, write from your heart expressing your desire to forgive them. Write specifically about the hurts you discovered that need forgiving. You may be angry at the deception, the neglect and the pressure you felt to take sides. Your parent may have asked you to keep the secret and become a partner in his betrayal. You may be enraged by the weakness of your betrayed parent, the selfishness of your unfaithful parent and the poor role modeling of both parents. When writing about what you forgive, feel the anger drain from your heart. Release the anger that has held you hostage for years.

Read over what you have written carefully and decide what you want to do with the letter. What would benefit you most? You may decide to keep the letter for yourself, as a sort of personal diary you can refer to as needed. You may decide to burn the letter as a symbol of giving up your anger. You may decide to share the letter with your siblings to encourage open communication about your shared past. The letter may become an invitation for them to look inward and begin their own healing. Finally, you may decide to share the letter with your parents if you believe it would also be beneficial for them.

Whatever you decide, the truth expressed in your letter has already set you free.

Grieving the Losses of Childhood

When Steven Spielberg, the legendary director/producer, was interviewed on *60 Minutes* along with his elderly parents, Spielberg related that he had been battling anxiety since childhood. He was a shy, sensitive child who suffered relentless teasing because of his Jewish heritage. He felt like an outsider. His parents unexpectedly divorced when he was nineteen years old and Spielberg blamed his father for many years afterward. His father worked long hours and was absent from the home. Spielberg was close to his mother, whom he called "a big sister" and placed on a pedestal. She encouraged him to cultivate his imagination and artistic interests, which enabled him to survive the hardships of his childhood. Despite learning that his mother fell in love with a family friend and divorced his father, Spielberg confessed that he held a grudge against his father for fifteen years. Aware of the emotional price he was paying for his anger, his wife urged him to reconcile with his father. Spielberg admitted how much he was held hostage by his hostility, then came to forgive his father and has now enjoyed twenty-five years of the closeness he desperately missed.

Spielberg revealed that all his films have been autobiographical, expressing his struggles as an outsider who was alienated from his father. His early films portrayed distant, uninvolved fathers. His later films, after the reconciliation with his father, presented strong, responsible, emotionally-connected fathers. He had great admiration for Abraham Lincoln and, in 2012, released a film recounting a significant period in his life. He saw Lincoln as a strong father of our nation, fighting valiantly against those who sought dissolution of the union and continued slavery. Lincoln was also a father transformed through the adversity of his own and his wife's depression. Spielberg's pain became a fertile ground for his creative work. Through embracing that suffering, he came to forgive his father and free his own spirit.

As you grew older and became more capable of understanding the meaning of betrayal, you may not have wanted to think of your parents as capable of such shameful behavior. All children need to admire and idealize their parents, who become their role models in life. Children put their parents on a pedestal and imagine them as the best. This imagined strength of their parents gives them a sense of security in a dangerous world. The illusions of powerful, noble parents are not easily given up for a child. The process naturally begins in adolescence when the teenager separates emotionally from his parents to establish his independence. The angelic parents become devils for a time in the service of emotional autonomy.

When an affair occurs, the children also feel a profound sense of betrayal and may be traumatized. The illusion of perfect parents is prematurely shattered, perhaps at a time when the child is most vulnerable and in need of powerful parental figures. Children need to see their parents as strong, loving, wise people whom they can trust and rely on. Their own sense of security depends on it. Furthermore, when infidelity happens, children absorb the shame of the parents. They feel somehow responsible and blame themselves. "If I only would have been a better kid..." they think to themselves in their own childish, self-centered way.

As you, the betrayed child, grew older, you may have mercifully forgotten the painful discovery of your parents' betrayal and fall from grace. In order to maintain your emotional stability, you forget what was too painful to endure. Or if you did learn about the infidelity, you just did not think about it or let it bother you. "That was a long time ago and it didn't affect me," you may rationalize to yourself, yet the illusion of the ideal parent is difficult to let go of at any age.

If your parents were unfaithful, your home was a place of pain, sorrow and confusion. There were happy times and perhaps most of your memories were happy ones. But you ignore the pain at your own peril. An emotional infection will develop that can fester and ruin your physical, emotional and spiritual health. The pain will steal your happiness and influence your behavior in indirect, unconscious ways as you try to escape it.

The wound will never heal unless you recognize and acknowledge the pain. For healing to occur, it is necessary that you ask yourself some difficult yet liberating questions.

"What did I miss growing up?" If there was an affair, your parents were undoubtedly preoccupied with cleaning up the rubble of their ruined relationship. The affair was a symptom of some disconnection in their marriage that became a full-blown break. A bomb exploded in your home that shattered the security, routine and predictability of your family life. Needing to repair the damage, your parents were likely distracted from paying full attention to you. They may have been absent while just trying to nurse their own wounds. They may have been intrusive and anxiously focused on you to compensate for a sense of powerlessness in their marriage. Or, more likely, they were inconsistent in attending to you, tossed about on the sea of their own emotional storms. Allow yourself to explore what you lost as a child because of your parents' absence or inconsistent presence: the innocence, happiness and sense of security.

"How did it all affect me?" In many ways you were left on your own to cope with the tragedy of your parents' infidelity. You had to find security in an emotionally chaotic home environment on your own. Traumatized by the betrayal, your parents failed to provide healthy role models and guidance for negotiating the normal trials and tribulations of life. You experienced extraordinary disruption and challenge to your sense of well-being in the wake of the betrayal. Pay attention to the ingenious and resourceful ways you adjusted to the insecurity and turmoil of your childhood. Notice how you created zones of safety for yourself. Perhaps you became the good, compliant child who was dependent on your parents and authority figures. You may have become defiant and acted out the anger of your home life to find a sense of identity. Or you may have withdrawn into your own world, detached and devoting yourself to your own interests.

"How is it affecting me now?" Take a close look at your current relationships and how you parent. Notice how patterns of coping from childhood have evolved and influence how you interact with others.

Your parents provided an enduring, unshakable model of marriage and parenting for you.

Biology is not destiny. You can choose, but only within the confines of your conditioning and personality. Be aware of your tendencies that have evolved from childhood through the influence of your upbringing. Notice your compulsion to repeat what you grew up with: whether to stray from commitment, attach to a cheater or disengage in some way.

You may want to ignore the pain, sorrow and confusion of your childhood that has reverberated into your adult life and affects how you relate to others. You may prefer not to dwell on the losses of childhood that have created deficits in your adulthood. "Always think positively," you lecture yourself. You may fantasize that by not thinking about your past traumas caused by your parents' infidelity and its effect on you, that it will go away as if it never happened. Instead, I have invited you throughout this book to see things clearly as they are and embrace the pain of loss. Do not turn away from the wound. Otherwise, you will miss an opportunity to heal and grow in unexpected ways.

The place of pain is also the place of healing, liberation and enlightenment.

You heal as you mourn the losses of your childhood and come to forgive your parents. Forgiveness does not come all at once but is a journey. You cannot simply will yourself to forgive and forget as many religions seem to suggest. Instead, an authentic forgiveness from the heart encompasses the whole person: the will, the mind, the emotions and the spirit. It is a journey marked by stages of grief that move toward a wholehearted acceptance of the losses and forgiveness of those who harmed you.

Grief has its own seasons. Passing through these changing psychological weather patterns, you move beyond the storm. At some point, often unexpectedly, you will realize that you are no longer angry with your parents or yourself. Forgiveness happens as the wound heals.

1) WINTER COLD

The seasons of grief usually begin with winter cold. After the trauma of the betrayal you suffered through your parents' infidelity, you may be numb to the pain and its impact on your life. You may not want to know what happened to your parents and might not believe it if you were told. The emotional numbness and mental denial serve a purpose: to protect you from a reality that is too painful for you. You need the respite of ignorance. As we've explored, your parents' shame and guilt causes them to withdraw into secrecy. They may feel immense relief that you seem to ignore what they have done. Your denial also serves their need to keep it all in the dark.

However, the buried pain never disappears. You often feel the pangs in quiet moments. Those brief heartthrobs are nagging invitations to search for its meaning, come to understand it and eventually surrender. The winter cold and numbness may last many years, until you are ready to enter the darkness.

2) SPRING THAW

Some event often initiates the spring thaw. Perhaps you experience trouble in your relationship and the distress, which you can no longer ignore, propels you to explore the cause. You feel pain in a current relationship that awakens you from your slumber. The pain, as unwelcome and uncomfortable as it is, indicates that you are alive. It grabs your attention, shakes you from your complacency and motivates you to turn inward. You begin to explore. Because the pain is so intense and confusing, you may want someone to accompany you.

Your exploration may eventually lead you to look backward to your childhood for understanding. It may begin to dawn on you that the conflicts you experience in your current relationship seem vaguely familiar and similar to what you witnessed growing up. Realizing the connection of your present struggles with your childhood, you feel a sense of loss. Sadness floods you. The sadness may deepen to depression and self-blame. Embracing the sadness and trying to understand it, you learn the truth that all is changing. Holding onto your images of perfection about your past and current life only brings more disappointment.

3) SUMMER HEAT

Another name for depression is anger turned inward. When the anger is eventually directed outward, your parents may become the targets. You enter the summer heat of anger. You think about your parents' marriage and remember their turmoil. Feelings of rage at your betraying parent and at your weak, victimized parent emerge. You ruminate about what your parents did and did not do for you and how they were preoccupied with themselves and their problems. Feeling the pain of their neglect inflames your anger. You may notice that you blame them for your struggles with intimacy, because you lacked healthy role models. The anger covers over the deep sadness you feel at the loss of security, tranquility and happiness you suffered as a child. Entering deeply into the anger and underlying sadness and making the effort to learn its wisdom will teach you how much you see yourself as a helpless victim. You entertain the illusion that others cause your misery. Giving up that illusion, you reclaim your power to create your own life.

4) AUTUMN CHILL

Eventually, you pass through the autumn of self-doubt and self-questioning. You wonder what your life would have been like if you had had a normal childhood. "If only my parents were different, my life would have been simpler," you tell yourself. You may even begin questioning the truth of what you experienced as a child or the stories you heard about your past. "Perhaps it wasn't as bad as I think," you speculate. Furthermore, you wonder if you are condemned to repeat the struggles of your parents' marriage, or if you can find a way to transcend their difficulties. You hope and pray you can be different, despite the struggles of your current relationship. Wracked with uncertainty, anxiety overtakes you. Embracing the anxiety and learning from it, you realize how attached you are to illusions of what you think your life should be, rather than accepting it as it is. You may pass through the different seasons for a long time.

5) HEALING ACCEPTANCE

If you embrace the pain with the desire to accept and transcend it, you will eventually escape the changing seasons of mourning. Through the acceptance of the reality of your childhood, you will come to forgive your parents. In fact, as surprising as it sounds, you can even become grateful for all that has been and all that has made you the person you are today. You can begin to see the benefits of your suffering and how your virtues could only have been forged in the fires of adversity.

As you grieve the losses of your childhood and all your subsequent life losses, you are transformed. You arrive at a place of surrender and acceptance of all that has been and is yet to come. In that open attitude, you become wise and see your life more clearly—as it is, not as you wish it to be. You become liberated from the tyranny of all your expectations of imagined perfection. You realize that your life is perfect—complete—just as it is. As you accept the suffering of your broken heart, you discover a spaciousness and graciousness you never imagined. Your heart has become compassionate and open to the suffering of the world and to new ways of loving.

SEASONS OF GRIEF

1) **Winter cold and numbness**
2) **Spring thaw of sadness**
3) **Summer heat of anger**
4) **Autumn of self-doubt and self-questioning**
5) **Acceptance and forgiveness beyond the changing seasons**

As you grieve the losses of your childhood, you will notice an evolving relationship with your feelings. At first, you were overwhelmed by the negative feelings. After the numbness, you were flooded with feelings of sadness, rage and anxiety and were fearful you would drown in the churning sea of emotions. Adrift without the life raft of understanding, you were gripped by confusion and a sense of powerlessness. You floundered on the rocks of negativity. And when you felt desperate enough, you sought relief by trying to escape the emotional storm through self-analysis. You embarked on a quest to transform those negative emotions into positive ones. With great effort you tried to get rid of the feelings you did not want and replace them with feelings of peace, happiness and courage. Finally, exhausted by all the work, you reached the distant shore of acceptance.

You could not win the battle against yourself, so you surrendered to the full reality of who you were: a person with both positive and negative qualities, bright and dark emotions. You arrived at self-acceptance, embracing yourself as you were, not as you wished

you would be. You gave up your images of perfection regarding yourself and your parents. In the process, your feelings flowed more freely
through you, without you being stuck on them.

You have learned that all the effort in the world could not make
you forgive, let go of the anger and the hurt. Rather, forgiveness
comes as a gift to a heart that is open. All your inner work—your self-
analysis, counseling and spiritual practices—have helped open your
mind and heart to the gifts of healing and forgiveness. The forgiving
heart releases you from the prison of your hatred and opens you to
love. The benefits of patience, acceptance and forgiveness are incalcu-
lable, as *The Way of the Bodhisattva*, a classic book of wisdom, affirms:

Those tormented by the pain of anger
Will never know tranquility of mind—
Strangers they will be to every pleasure;
Sleep departs them, they can never rest. (6:3)
For patience in samsara brings such things
As beauty, health, and good renown.
Its fruit is great longevity,
The vast contentment of a universal king. (6:134)[18]

ACKNOWLEDGMENTS

While fully accepting responsibility for the opinions expressed in this book, I acknowledge my indebtedness to many who shared their personal stories, insights, and suggestions. Above all, I thank my patients, who entrusted me with their lives and stories of sorrow and hope. The book is a testimony to their courage, resilience and the power of forgiveness. I am also grateful to my wife, Fran, who accompanied me every step of the way through the writing process, offering encouragement and perceptive insights. My cousin, Ed Benz, a retired English teacher, offered professional, constructive criticism, tightening up my thinking and writing.

Finally, I am grateful to the staff of New Horizon Press who expertly guided the publication process: Dr. Joan Dunphy, JoAnne Thomas, Caroline Russomanno, and Charley Nasta.

ENDNOTES

1. Shirley Glass, *Not Just Friends* (New York: Free Press, 2003) and Emily Brown, *Patterns of Infidelity and Their Treatment*, 2nd ed. (Minnesota: Fairview, 2007).

2. Don Richard Riso and Russ Hudson, *Understanding the Enneagram*, revised edition (Boston: Houghton Mifflin Company, 2000).

3. Sharon Salzburg, *Loving-Kindness* (Boston: Shambhala, 2002).

4. Yoichi Chida, MD, PhD, and Andrew Steptoe, DPhil. "The Association of Anger and Hostility with Future Coronary Heart Disease," *Journal of the American College of Cardiology*, 2009; 53(11): 936–946.

5. *The Way of the Bodhisattva*, Chapter 5, verse 48 from Shantideva, trans. Padmakara Translation Group (Boston: Shambhala, 1997), 69.

6. *Alcoholics Anonymous: The Big Book*, 3rd ed. (New York: World Services, 1976).

7. Reinhold Niebuhr, from a 1943 sermon, adopted by Alcoholics Anonymous.

8. Trayleg Kyabgon, *The Practice of Lojong* (Boston: Shambhala, 2007), 96–99.

9. *The Way of the Bodhisattva*, Chapter 8, verse 40 from Shantideva, trans. Padmakara Translation Group (Boston: Shambhala, 1997), 130.

10. Evelyn Waugh, *A Handful of Dust* (USA: Little, Brown, and Company, 1934).

11. Pema Chodron, *The Places That Scare You* (Boston: Shambhala, 2001), 55–60.

12. Matthew 18:1–5, *The Jerusalem Bible* (Garden City, New York: Doubleday and Company, 1966).

13. Worldwide Marriage Encounter: W.E.D.S.—Guidelines for Dialogue, http://www.wwme.org/content/weds-guidelines-dialogue.

14. John 8:32, *The Jerusalem Bible* (Garden City, New York: Doubleday and Company, 1966).

15. Emily Brown, *Patterns of Infidelity and Their Treatment*, 2nd ed. (Minnesota: Fairview, 2007), 29-49.

16. A. Mehrabian, *Silent Messages: Implicit Communications of Emotions and Attitudes* (Belmont, CA: Wordsworth, 1981).

17. John 8:3–11, *The Jerusalem Bible* (Garden City, New York: Doubleday and Company, 1966).

18. *The Way of the Bodhisattva*, Chapter 6, Verse 3, and Verse 134 from Shantideva, trans. Padmakara Translation Group (Boston: Shambhala, 1997), 78, 97.

NOTES